CAMBRIDGE International Examinations

Advanced Level Mathematics
Statistics 1
Steve Dobbs and Jane Miller

CAMBRIDGE UNIVERSITY PRESS

PUBLISHED BY THE PRESS SYNDICATE OF THE UNIVERSITY OF CAMBRIDGE
The Pitt Building, Trumpington Street, Cambridge, United Kingdom

CAMBRIDGE UNIVERSITY PRESS
The Edinburgh Building, Cambridge CB2 2RU, UK
40 West 20th Street, New York, NY 10011-4211, USA
477 Williamstown Road, Port Melbourne, VIC 3207, Australia
Ruiz de Alarcón 13, 28014 Madrid, Spain
Dock House, The Waterfront, Cape Town 8001, South Africa

http://www.cambridge.org

First published 2002
Reprinted 2003

Printed in the United Kingdom at the University Press, Cambridge

Typefaces Times, Helvetica   *Systems* Microsoft® Word, MathType™

A catalogue record for this book is available from the British Library

ISBN 0 521 53013 X   paperback

Cover image: © Tony Stone Images / Art Wolfe

Introduction

Cambridge International Examinations (CIE) Advanced Level Mathematics has been written especially for the CIE international examinations. There is one book corresponding to each syllabus unit, except that units P2 and P3 are contained in a single book. This book is the first Probability and Statistics unit, S1.

The syllabus content is arranged by chapters which are ordered so as to provide a viable teaching course. A few sections include important results that are difficult to prove or outside the syllabus. These sections are marked with an asterisk (*) in the section heading, and there is usually a sentence early on explaining precisely what it is that the student needs to know.

Some paragraphs within the text appear in *this type style*. These paragraphs are usually outside the main stream of the mathematical argument, but may help to give insight, or suggest extra work or different approaches.

Graphic calculators are not permitted in the examination, but they can be useful aids in learning mathematics. In the book the authors have noted where access to graphic calculators would be especially helpful but have not assumed that they are available to all students.

The authors have assumed that students have access to calculators with built-in statistical functions.

Numerical work is presented in a form intended to discourage premature approximation. In ongoing calculations inexact numbers appear in decimal form like $3.456\ldots$, signifying that the number is held in a calculator to more places than are given. Numbers are not rounded at this stage; the full display could be either $3.456\,123$ or $3.456\,789$. Final answers are then stated with some indication that they are approximate, for example '1.23 correct to 3 significant figures'.

Most chapters contain Practical activities. These can be used either as an introduction to a topic, or, later on, to reinforce the theory. There are also plenty of exercises, and each chapter ends with a Miscellaneous exercise which includes some questions of examination standard. There is a Revision exercise, and two Practice examination papers.

In some exercises a few of the later questions may go beyond the likely requirements of the examination, either in difficulty or in length or both. Some questions are marked with an asterisk, which indicates that they require knowledge of results outside the syllabus.

Cambridge University Press would like to thank OCR (Oxford, Cambridge and RSA Examinations), part of the University of Cambridge Local Examinations Syndicate (UCLES) group, for permission to use past examination questions set in the United Kingdom.

The authors thank OCR and Cambridge University Press for their help in producing this book. However, the responsibility for the text, and for any errors, remains with the authors.

1 Representation of data

This chapter looks at ways of displaying numerical data using diagrams. When you have completed it, you should

- know the difference between quantitative and qualitative data
- be able to make comparisons between sets of data by using diagrams
- be able to construct a stem-and-leaf diagram from raw data
- be able to draw a histogram from a grouped frequency table, and know that the area of each block is proportional to the frequency in that class
- be able to construct a cumulative frequency diagram from a frequency distribution table.

1.1 Introduction

The collection, organisation and analysis of numerical information are all part of the subject called **statistics**. Pieces of numerical and other information are called **data**. A more helpful definition of 'data' is 'a series of facts from which conclusions may be drawn'.

In order to collect data you need to observe or to measure some property. This property is called a **variable**. The data which follow were taken from the internet, which has many sites containing data sources. In this example a variety of measurements was taken on packets of breakfast cereal in the United States. Each column of Table 1.1 (pages 2 and 3) represents a variable. So, for example, 'type', 'sodium' and 'shelf' are all variables. (The amounts for variables 3, 4, 5 and 6 are per serving.)

Datafile name Cereals

Description Data which refer to various brands of breakfast cereal in a particular store. A value of −1 for nutrients indicates a missing observation.

Number of cases 77

Variable names
1. name: name of cereal
2. type: cold(C) or hot(H)
3. fat: grams of fat
4. sodium: milligrams of sodium
5. carbo: grams of complex carbohydrates
6. sugar: grams of sugars
7. shelf: display shelf (1, 2 or 3, counting from the floor)
8. mass: mass in grams of one serving
9. rating: a measure of the nutritional value of the cereal

name	type	fat	sodium	carbo	sugar	shelf	mass	rating
100%_Bran	C	1	130	5	6	3	30	68
100%_Natural_Bran	C	5	15	8	8	3	30	34
All-Bran	C	1	260	7	5	3	30	59
All-Bran_with_Extra_Fiber	C	0	140	8	0	3	30	94
Almond_Delight	C	2	200	14	8	3	30	34
Apple_Cinnamon_Cheerios	C	2	180	10.5	10	1	30	30
Apple_Jacks	C	0	125	11	14	2	30	33
Basic_4	C	2	210	18	8	3	40	37
Bran_Chex	C	1	200	15	6	1	30	49
Bran_Flakes	C	0	210	13	5	3	30	53
Cap'n'Crunch	C	2	220	12	12	2	30	18
Cheerios	C	2	290	17	1	1	30	51
Cinnamon_Toast_Crunch	C	3	210	13	9	2	30	20
Clusters	C	2	140	13	7	3	30	40
Cocoa_Puffs	C	1	180	12	13	2	30	23
Corn_Chex	C	0	280	22	3	1	30	41
Corn_Flakes	C	0	290	21	2	1	30	46
Corn_Pops	C	0	90	13	12	2	30	36
Count_Chocula	C	1	180	12	13	2	30	22
Cracklin'_Oat_Bran	C	3	140	10	7	3	30	40
Cream_of_Wheat_(Quick)	H	0	80	21	0	2	30	65
Crispix	C	0	220	21	3	3	30	47
Crispy_Wheat_&_Raisins	C	1	140	11	10	3	30	36
Double_Chex	C	0	190	18	5	3	30	44
Froot_Loops	C	1	125	11	13	2	30	32
Frosted_Flakes	C	0	200	14	11	1	30	31
Frosted_Mini-Wheats	C	0	0	14	7	2	30	58
Fruit_&_Fibre_Dates,_Walnuts,_and_Oats	C	2	160	12	10	3	40	41
Fruitful_Bran	C	0	240	14	12	3	40	41
Fruity_Pebbles	C	1	135	13	12	2	30	28
Golden_Crisp	C	0	45	11	15	1	30	35
Golden_Grahams	C	1	280	15	9	2	30	24
Grape_Nuts_Flakes	C	1	140	15	5	3	30	52
Grape-Nuts	C	0	170	17	3	3	30	53
Great_Grains_Pecan	C	3	75	13	4	3	30	46
Honey_Graham_Ohs	C	2	220	12	11	2	30	22
Honey_Nut_Cheerios	C	1	250	11.5	10	1	30	31
Honey-comb	C	0	180	14	11	1	30	29
Just_Right_Crunchy_Nuggets	C	1	170	17	6	3	30	37
Just_Right_Fruit_&_Nut	C	1	170	20	9	3	40	36
Kix	C	1	260	21	3	2	30	39
Life	C	2	150	12	6	2	30	45
Lucky_Charms	C	1	180	12	12	2	30	27

name	type	fat	sodium	carbo	sugar	shelf	mass	rating
Maypo	H	1	0	16	3	2	30	55
Muesli_Raisins,_Dates,_&_Almonds	C	3	95	16	11	3	30	37
Muesli_Raisins,_Peaches,_&_Pecans	C	3	150	16	11	3	30	34
Mueslix_Crispy_Blend	C	2	150	17	13	3	45	30
Multi-Grain_Cheerios	C	1	220	15	6	1	30	40
Nut_&_Honey_Crunch	C	1	190	15	9	2	30	30
Nutri-Grain_Almond-Raisin	C	2	220	21	7	3	40	41
Nutri-Grain_Wheat	C	0	170	18	2	3	30	60
Oatmeal_Raisin_Crisp	C	2	170	13.5	10	3	40	30
Post_Nat._Raisin_Bran	C	1	200	11	14	3	40	38
Product_19	C	0	320	20	3	3	30	42
Puffed_Rice	C	0	0	13	0	3	15	61
Puffed_Wheat	C	0	0	10	0	3	15	63
Quaker_Oat_Squares	C	1	135	14	6	3	30	50
Quaker_Oatmeal	H	2	0	−1	−1	1	30	51
Raisin_Bran	C	1	210	14	12	2	40	39
Raisin_Nut_Bran	C	2	140	10.5	8	3	30	40
Raisin_Squares	C	0	0	15	6	3	30	55
Rice_Chex	C	0	240	23	2	1	30	42
Rice_Krispies	C	0	290	22	3	1	30	41
Shredded_Wheat	C	0	0	16	0	1	25	68
Shredded_Wheat'n'Bran	C	0	0	19	0	1	30	74
Shredded_Wheat_spoon_size	C	0	0	20	0	1	30	73
Smacks	C	1	70	9	15	2	30	31
Special_K	C	0	230	16	3	1	30	53
Strawberry_Fruit_Wheats	C	0	15	15	5	2	30	59
Total_Corn_Flakes	C	1	200	21	3	3	30	39
Total_Raisin_Bran	C	1	190	15	14	3	45	29
Total_Whole_Grain	C	1	200	16	3	3	30	47
Triples	C	1	250	21	3	3	30	39
Trix	C	1	140	13	12	2	30	28
Wheat_Chex	C	1	230	17	3	1	30	50
Wheaties	C	1	200	17	3	1	30	52
Wheaties_Honey_Gold	C	1	200	16	8	1	30	36

Table 1.1. Datafile 'Cereals'.

The variable 'type' has two different letter codes, H and C.

The variable 'sodium' takes values such as 130, 15, 260 and 140.

The variable 'shelf' takes values 1, 2 or 3.

You can see that there are different types of variable. The variable 'type' is non-numerical: such variables are usually called **qualitative**. The other two variables are called **quantitative**, because the values they take are numerical.

Quantitative data can be subdivided into two categories. For example, 'sodium', the mass of sodium in milligrams, which can take any value in a particular range, is called a **continuous** variable. 'Display shelf', on the other hand, is a **discrete** variable: it can only take the integer values 1, 2 or 3, and there are clear steps between its possible values. It would not be sensible, for example, to refer to display shelf number 2.43.

In summary:

A variable is **qualitative** if it is not possible for it to take a numerical value.

A variable is **quantitative** if it can take a numerical value.

A quantitative variable which can take any value in a given range is **continuous**.

A quantitative variable which has clear steps between its possible values is **discrete**.

1.2 Stem-and-leaf diagrams

The datafile on cereals has one column which gives a rating of the cereals on a scale of 0−100. The ratings are given below.

68	34	59	94	34	30	33	37	49	53
18	51	20	40	23	41	46	36	22	40
65	47	36	44	32	31	58	41	41	28
35	24	52	53	46	22	31	29	37	36
39	45	27	55	37	34	30	40	30	41
60	30	38	42	61	63	50	51	39	40
55	42	41	68	74	73	31	53	59	39
29	47	39	28	50	52	36			

These values are what statisticians call **raw data**. Raw data are the values collected in a survey or experiment before they are categorised or arranged in any way. Usually raw data appear in the form of a list. It is very difficult to draw any conclusions from these raw data just by looking at the numbers. One way of arranging the values that gives some information about the patterns within the data is a **stem-and-leaf diagram**.

In this case the 'stems' are the tens digits and the 'leaves' are the units digits. You write the stems to the left of a vertical line and the leaves to the right of the line. So, for example, you would write the first value, 68, as 6|8. The leaves belonging to one stem are then written in the same row.

The stem-and-leaf diagram for the ratings data is shown in Fig. 1.2. The **key** shows what the stems and leaves mean.

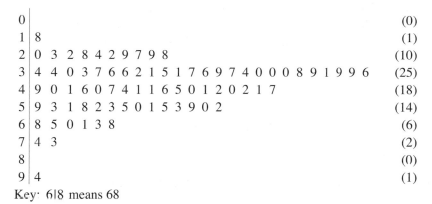

```
0 |                                                          (0)
1 | 8                                                        (1)
2 | 0 3 2 8 4 2 9 7 9 8                                      (10)
3 | 4 4 0 3 7 6 6 2 1 5 1 7 6 9 7 4 0 0 0 8 9 1 9 9 6        (25)
4 | 9 0 1 6 0 7 4 1 1 6 5 0 1 2 0 2 1 7                      (18)
5 | 9 3 1 8 2 3 5 0 1 5 3 9 0 2                              (14)
6 | 8 5 0 1 3 8                                              (6)
7 | 4 3                                                      (2)
8 |                                                          (0)
9 | 4                                                        (1)
```
Key: 6|8 means 68

Fig. 1.2. Stem-and-leaf diagram of cereal ratings.

The numbers in the brackets tell you how many leaves belong to each stem. The digits in each stem form a horizontal 'block', similar to a bar on a bar chart, which gives a visual impression of the distribution. In fact, if you rotate a stem-and-leaf diagram anticlockwise through 90°, it looks like a bar chart. It is also common to rewrite the leaves in numerical order; the stem-and-leaf diagram formed in this way is called an **ordered stem-and-leaf diagram**. The ordered stem-and-leaf diagram for the cereal ratings is shown in Fig. 1.3.

```
0 |                                                          (0)
1 | 8                                                        (1)
2 | 0 2 2 3 4 7 8 8 9 9                                      (10)
3 | 0 0 0 0 1 1 1 2 3 4 4 4 5 6 6 6 6 7 7 7 8 9 9 9 9        (25)
4 | 0 0 0 0 1 1 1 1 1 2 2 4 5 6 6 7 7 9                      (18)
5 | 0 0 1 1 2 2 2 3 3 3 5 5 8 9 9                            (14)
6 | 0 1 3 5 8 8                                              (6)
7 | 3 4                                                      (2)
8 |                                                          (0)
9 | 4                                                        (1)
```
Key: 6|8 means 68

Fig. 1.3. Ordered stem-and-leaf diagram of cereal ratings.

So far the stem-and-leaf diagrams discussed have consisted of data values which are integers between 0 and 100. With suitable adjustments, you can use stem-and-leaf diagrams for other data values.

For example, the data 6.2, 3.1, 4.8, 9.1, 8.3, 6.2, 1.4, 9.6, 0.3, 0.3, 8.4, 6.1, 8.2, 4.3 could be illustrated in the stem-and-leaf diagram in Fig. 1.4.

```
0 | 3 3                (2)
1 | 4                  (1)
2 |                    (0)
3 | 1                  (1)
4 | 8 3                (2)
5 |                    (0)
6 | 2 2 1              (3)
7 |                    (0)
8 | 3 4 2              (3)
9 | 1 6                (2)
```
Key: 0|3 means 0.3

Fig. 1.4. Stem-and-leaf diagram.

Table 1.5 is a datafile about brain sizes which will be used in several examples.

Datafile name Brain size
(Data from *Intelligence*, Vol. 15, Willerman et al., 'In vivo brain size …', 1991)

Description A team of researchers used a sample of 40 students at a university. The subjects took four subtests from the 'Wechsler (1981) Adult Intelligence Scale – Revised' test. Magnetic Resonance Imaging (MRI) was then used to measure the brain sizes of the subjects. The subjects' genders, heights and body masses are also included. The researchers withheld the masses of two subjects and the height of one subject for reasons of confidentiality.

Number of cases 40

Variable names
1   gender: male or female
2   FSIQ: full scale IQ scores based on the four Wechsler (1981) subtests
3   VIQ: verbal IQ scores based on the four Wechsler (1981) subtests
4   PIQ: performance IQ scores based on the four Wechsler (1981) subtests
5   mass: body mass in kg
6   height: height in cm
7   MRI_Count: total pixel count from 18 MRI brain scans

gender	FSIQ	VIQ	PIQ	mass	height	MRI_Count
Female	133	132	124	54	164	816 932
Male	140	150	124		184	1 001 121
Male	139	123	150	65	186	1 038 437
Male	133	129	128	78	175	965 353
Female	137	132	134	67	165	951 545
Female	99	90	110	66	175	928 799
Female	138	136	131	63	164	991 305
Female	92	90	98	79	168	854 258
Male	89	93	84	61	168	904 858
Male	133	114	147	78	175	955 466
Female	132	129	124	54	164	833 868
Male	141	150	128	69	178	1 079 549
Male	135	129	124	70	175	924 059
Female	140	120	147	70	179	856 472
Female	96	100	90	66	168	878 897
Female	83	71	96	61	173	865 363
Female	132	132	120	58	174	852 244
Male	100	96	102	81	187	945 088
Female	101	112	84	62	168	808 020
Male	80	77	86	82	178	889 083
Male	83	83	86	–	–	892 420
Male	97	107	84	84	194	905 940
Female	135	129	134	55	157	790 619
Male	139	145	128	60	173	955 003
Female	91	86	102	52	160	831 772
Male	141	145	131	78	183	935 494
Female	85	90	84	64	173	798 612
Male	103	96	110	85	196	1 062 462
Female	77	83	72	48	160	793 549
Female	130	126	124	72	169	866 662
Female	133	126	132	58	159	857 782
Male	144	145	137	87	170	949 589
Male	103	96	110	87	192	997 925
Male	90	96	86	82	175	879 987
Female	83	90	81	65	169	834 344
Female	133	129	128	69	169	948 066
Male	140	150	124	65	179	949 395
Female	88	86	94	63	164	893 983
Male	81	90	74	67	188	930 016
Male	89	91	89	81	192	935 863

Table 1.5. Datafile 'Brain size'.

The stems of a stem-and-leaf diagram may consist of more than one digit. So, for example, consider the following data, which are the heights of 39 people in cm (correct to the nearest cm), taken from the datafile 'Brain size'.

    164   184   186   175   165   175   164   168   168   175   164   178   175
    179   168   173   174   187   168   178   194   157   173   160   183   173
    196   160   169   159   170   192   175   169   169   179   164   188   192

You can represent these data with the stem-and-leaf diagram shown in Fig. 1.6, which uses stems from 15 to 19.

```
15 | 7 9                                    (2)
16 | 0 0 4 4 4 4 5 8 8 8 8 9 9 9            (14)
17 | 0 3 3 3 4 5 5 5 5 5 8 8 9 9            (14)
18 | 3 4 6 7 8                              (5)
19 | 2 2 4 6                                (4)
```
Key: 17|3 means 173 cm

Fig. 1.6. Stem-and-leaf diagram of heights of a sample of 39 people.

Exercise 1A

In this exercise if you are asked to construct a stem-and-leaf diagram you should give an ordered one.

1   The following stem-and-leaf diagram illustrates the lengths, in cm, of a sample of 15 leaves fallen from a tree. The values are given correct to 1 decimal place.

```
4 | 3                                       (1)
5 | 4 0 7 3 9                               (5)
6 | 3 1 2 4                                 (4)
7 | 6 1 6                                   (3)
8 |                                         (0)
9 | 3 2                                     (2)
```
    Key: 7|6 means 7.6 cm

    (a) Write the data in full, and in increasing order of size.

    (b) State whether the variable is (i) qualitative or quantitative, (ii) discrete or continuous.

2   Construct stem-and-leaf diagrams for the following data sets.

    (a) The speeds, in kilometres per hour, of 20 cars, measured on a city street.

        41 15 4 27 21 32 43 37 18 25 29 34 28 30 25 52 12 36 6 25

    (b) The times taken, in hours (to the nearest tenth), to carry out repairs to 17 pieces of machinery.

        0.9 1.0 2.1 4.2 0.7 1.1 0.9 1.8 0.9 1.2 2.3 1.6 2.1 0.3 0.8 2.7 0.4

3   Construct a stem-and-leaf diagram for the following ages (in completed years) of famous people with birthdays on June 14 and June 15, as reported in a national newspaper.

        75 48 63 79 57 74 50 34 62 67 60 58 30 81 51 58 91 71 67 56 74
        50 99 36 54 59 54 69 68 74 93 86 77 70 52 64 48 53 68 76 75 56

4 The tensile strength of 60 samples of rubber was measured and the results, in suitable units, were as follows.

```
174  160  141  153  161  159  163  186  179  167  154  145  156  159  171
156  142  169  160  171  188  151  162  164  172  181  152  178  151  177
180  186  168  169  171  168  157  166  181  171  183  176  155  161  182
160  182  173  189  181  175  165  177  184  161  170  167  180  137  143
```

Construct a stem-and-leaf diagram using two rows for each stem so that, for example, with a stem of 15 the first leaf may have digits 0 to 4 and the second leaf may have digits 5 to 9.

5 A selection of 25 of A. A. Michelson's measurements of the speed of light, carried out in 1882, is given below. The figures are in thousands of kilometres per second and are given correct to 5 significant figures.

```
299.84  299.96  299.87  300.00  299.93  299.65  299.88  299.98  299.74
299.94  299.81  299.76  300.07  299.79  299.93  299.80  299.75  299.91
299.72  299.90  299.83  299.62  299.88  299.97  299.85
```

Construct a suitable stem-and-leaf diagram for the data.

6 The contents of 30 medium-size packets of soap powder were weighed and the results, in kilograms correct to 4 significant figures, were as follows.

```
1.347  1.351  1.344  1.362  1.338  1.341  1.342  1.356  1.339  1.351
1.354  1.336  1.345  1.350  1.353  1.347  1.342  1.353  1.329  1.346
1.332  1.348  1.342  1.353  1.341  1.322  1.354  1.347  1.349  1.370
```

(a) Construct a stem-and-leaf diagram for the data.

(b) Why would there be no point in drawing a stem-and-leaf diagram for the data rounded to 3 significant figures?

1.3 Histograms

Sometimes, for example if the data set is large, a stem-and-leaf diagram is not the best method of displaying data, and you need to use other methods. For large sets of data you may wish to divide the data into groups, called **classes**.

In the data on cereals, the amounts of sodium may be grouped into classes as in Table 1.7.

Amount of sodium (mg)	Tally	Frequency
0–49	ǂǂǂ ǂǂǂ ‖	12
50–99	ǂǂǂ	5
100–149	ǂǂǂ ǂǂǂ ‖	12
150–199	ǂǂǂ ǂǂǂ ǂǂǂ ‖	17
200–249	ǂǂǂ ǂǂǂ ǂǂǂ ǂǂǂ		21
250–299	ǂǂǂ ‖‖‖	9
300–349			1

Table 1.7. Data on cereals grouped into classes.

Table 1.7 shows a **grouped frequency distribution**. It shows how many values of the variable lie in each class. The pattern of a grouped frequency distribution is decided to some extent by the choice of classes. There would have been a different appearance to the distribution if the classes 0−99, 100−199, 200−299 and 300−399 had been chosen. There is no clear rule about how many classes should be chosen or what size they should be, but it is usual to have from 5 to 10 classes.

Grouping the data into classes inevitably means losing some information. Someone looking at the table would not know the exact values of the observations in the 0−49 category. All he or she would know for certain is that there were 12 such observations.

Consider the class 50−99. This refers to cereals which contained from 50 to 99 mg of sodium per serving. The amount of sodium is a continuous variable and the amounts appear to have been rounded to the nearest mg. If this is true then the class labelled as 50−99 would actually contain values from 49.5 up to (but not including) 99.5. These real endpoints, 49.5 and 99.5, are referred to as the **class boundaries**. The class boundaries are generally used in most numerical and graphical summaries of data. In this example you were not actually told that the data were recorded to the nearest milligram: you merely assumed that this was the case. In most examples you will know how the data were recorded.

Example 1.3.1
For each case below give the class boundaries of the first class.

(a) The heights of 100 students were recorded to the nearest centimetre.

Height, h (cm)	160−164	165−169	170−174	...
Frequency	7	9	13	...

Table 1.8. Heights of 100 students.

(b) The masses in kilograms of 40 patients entering a doctor's surgery on one day were recorded to the nearest kilogram.

Mass, m (kg)	55−	60−	65−	...
Frequency	9	15	12	...

Table 1.9. Masses of 40 patients.

(c) A group of 40 motorists was asked to state the ages at which they passed their driving tests.

Age, a (years)	17−	20−	23−	...
Frequency	6	11	7	...

Table 1.10. Ages at which 40 motorists passed their driving tests.

(a) The minimum and maximum heights for someone in the first class are 159.5 cm and 164.5 cm. The class boundaries are given by $159.5 \leqslant h < 164.5$.

(b) The first class appears to go from 55 kg up to but not including 60 kg, but as the measurement has been made to the nearest kg the lower and upper class boundaries are 54.5 kg and 59.5 kg. The class boundaries are given by $54.5 \leqslant m < 59.5$.

(c) Age is recorded to the number of completed years, so the class 17– contains those who passed their tests from the day of their 17th birthday up to, but not including, the day of their 20th birthday. The class boundaries are given by $17 \leqslant a < 20$.

Sometimes discrete data are grouped into classes. For example, the test scores of 40 students might appear as in Table 1.11.

Score	0–9	10–19	20–29	30–39	40–59
Frequency	14	9	9	3	5

Table 1.11. Test scores of 40 students.

What are the class boundaries? There is no universally accepted answer, but a common convention is to use, for example, 9.5 and 19.5 as the class boundaries of the second class. Although it may appear strange, the class boundaries for the first class would then be −0.5 and 9.5.

When a grouped frequency distribution contains continuous data, one of the most common forms of graphical display is the **histogram**. A histogram looks similar to a bar chart, but there are two important conditions.

> A bar chart which represents continuous data is a histogram if
>
> - the bars have no spaces between them (though there may be bars of height zero, which look like spaces), and
>
> - the *area* of each bar is proportional to the frequency.

If all the bars of a histogram have the same width, the height is proportional to the frequency.

Consider Table 1.12, which gives the heights in centimetres of 30 plants.

Height, h (cm)	Frequency
$0 \leqslant h < 5$	3
$5 \leqslant h < 10$	5
$10 \leqslant h < 15$	11
$15 \leqslant h < 20$	6
$20 \leqslant h < 25$	3
$25 \leqslant h < 30$	2

Table 1.12. Heights of 30 plants.

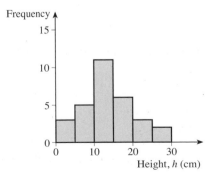

Fig. 1.13. Histogram of the data in Table 1.12.

The histogram to represent the set of data in Table 1.12 is shown in Fig. 1.13.

Another person recorded the same results by combining the last two rows as in Table 1.14, and then drew the diagram shown in Fig. 1.15.

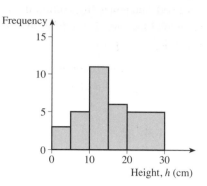

Height, h (cm)	Frequency
$0 \leqslant h < 5$	3
$5 \leqslant h < 10$	5
$10 \leqslant h < 15$	11
$15 \leqslant h < 20$	6
$20 \leqslant h < 30$	5

Table 1.14. Heights of 30 plants.

Fig. 1.15. Incorrect diagram for the data in Table 1.14.

Can you see why this diagram is misleading?

Fig. 1.15 makes it appear, incorrectly, that there are more plants whose heights are in the interval $20 \leqslant h < 30$ than in the interval $5 \leqslant h < 10$. It would be a more accurate representation if the bar for the class $20 \leqslant h < 30$ had a height of 2.5, as in Fig. 1.16.

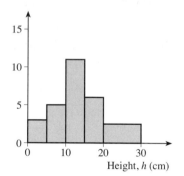

For the histogram in Fig 1.16 the areas of the five blocks are 15, 25, 55, 30 and 25. These are in the same ratio as the frequencies, which are 3, 5, 11, 6 and 5 respectively. This example demonstrates that when a grouped frequency distribution has unequal class widths, it is the area of the block in a histogram, and not its height, which should be proportional to the frequency in the corresponding interval.

Fig. 1.16. Histogram of the data in Table 1.14.

The simplest way of making the area of a block proportional to the frequency is to make the area equal to the frequency. This means that

width of class $\times$ height = frequency .

This is the same as

$$\text{height} = \frac{\text{frequency}}{\text{width of class}} .$$

These heights are then known as **frequency densities**.

Example 1.3.2

The grouped frequency distribution in Table 1.17 represents the masses in kilograms of a sample of 38 of the people from the datafile 'Brain size' (see Table 1.5). Represent these data in a histogram.

Mass (kg)	Frequency
47–54	4
55–62	7
63–66	8
67–74	7
75–82	8
83–90	4

Table 1.17. Masses of people from the datafile 'Brain size'.

Find the frequency densities by dividing the frequency of each class by the width of the class, as shown in Table 1.18.

Mass, m (kg)	Class boundaries	Class width	Frequency	Frequency density
47–54	$46.5 \leqslant m < 54.5$	8	4	0.5
55–62	$54.5 \leqslant m < 62.5$	8	7	0.875
63–66	$62.5 \leqslant m < 66.5$	4	8	2
67–74	$66.5 \leqslant m < 74.5$	8	7	0.875
75–82	$74.5 \leqslant m < 82.5$	8	8	1
83–90	$82.5 \leqslant m < 90.5$	8	4	0.5

Table 1.18. Calculation of frequency density for the data in Table 1.17.

The histogram is shown in Fig. 1.19.

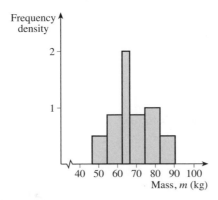

Fig. 1.19. Histogram of the data in Table 1.17.

Example 1.3.3

The grouped frequency distribution in Table 1.20 summarises the masses in grams (g), measured to the nearest gram, of a sample of 20 pebbles. Represent the data in a histogram.

Mass (g)	Frequency
101–110	1
111–120	4
121–130	2
131–140	7
141–150	2
over 150	4

Table 1.20. Masses of a sample of 20 pebbles.

The problem with this frequency distribution is that the last class is open-ended, so you cannot deduce the correct class boundaries unless you know the individual data values. In this case the individual values are not given. A reasonable procedure for this type of situation is to take the width of the last interval to be twice that of the previous one. Table 1.21 and the histogram in Fig. 1.22 are constructed using this assumption.

Mass, m (g)	Class boundaries	Class width	Frequency	Frequency density
101–110	$100.5 \leqslant m < 110.5$	10	1	0.1
111–120	$110.5 \leqslant m < 120.5$	10	4	0.4
121–130	$120.5 \leqslant m < 130.5$	10	2	0.2
131–140	$130.5 \leqslant m < 140.5$	10	7	0.7
141–150	$140.5 \leqslant m < 150.5$	10	2	0.2
over 150	$150.5 \leqslant m < 170.5$	20	4	0.2

Table 1.21. Calculation of frequency density for the data in Table 1.20.

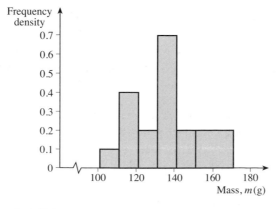

Fig. 1.22. Histogram of the data in Table 1.20.

All the previous examples of histograms have involved continuous data. You can also represent grouped discrete data in a histogram. Table 1.23 gives the class boundaries for the data in Table 1.11, which were the test scores of 40 students. Recall that the convention used is to take the class with limits 10 and 19 as having class boundaries 9.5 and 19.5. Using this convention you can find the frequency densities.

Score	Class boundaries	Class width	Frequency	Frequency density
0–9	−0.5–9.5	10	14	1.4
10–19	9.5–19.5	10	9	0.9
20–29	19.5–29.5	10	9	0.9
30–39	29.5–39.5	10	3	0.3
40–59	39.5 59.5	20	5	0.25

Table 1.23. Class boundaries for the data in Table 1.11.

Fig. 1.24 shows the histogram for the data. Notice that the left bar extends slightly to the left of the vertical axis, to the point −0.5. This accounts for the apparent thickness of the vertical axis.

In order to draw a histogram for a discrete variable it is necessary that each value is represented by a bar extending half a unit on each side of that value so that the bars touch. For example, the value 1 is represented by a bar extending from 0.5 to 1.5, and the group of values 0–9 by a bar extending from −0.5 to 9.5.

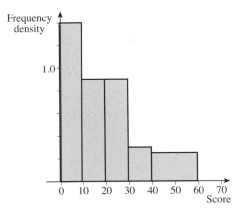

Fig 1.24. Histogram of the data in Table 1.23.

Exercise 1B

In Question 1 below, the upper class boundary of one class is identical to the lower class boundary of the next class. If you were measuring speeds to the nearest kilometre per hour (k.p.h.), then you might record a result of 60 k.p.h., and you would not know which class to put it in. This is not a problem in Question 1. You may come across data like these in examination questions, but it will be made clear what to do with them.

1   The speeds, in k.p.h., of 200 vehicles travelling on a motorway were measured by a radar device. The results are summarised in the following table.

Speed	45–60	60–75	75–90	90–105	105–120	over 120
Frequency	12	32	56	72	20	8

Draw a histogram to illustrate the data.

2 The mass of each of 60 pebbles collected from a beach was measured. The results, correct to the nearest gram, are summarised in the following table.

Mass	5–9	10–14	15–19	20–24	25–29	30–34	35–44
Frequency	2	5	8	14	17	11	3

Draw a histogram of the data.

3 For the data in Exercise 1A Question 4, form a grouped frequency table using six equal classes, starting 130–139. Assume that the data values are correct to the nearest integer. Draw a histogram of the data.

4 Thirty calls made by a telephone saleswoman were monitored. The lengths in minutes, to the nearest minute, are summarised in the following table.

Length of call	0–2	3–5	6–8	9–11	12–15
Number of calls	17	6	4	2	1

(a) State the boundaries of the first two classes.

(b) Illustrate the data with a histogram.

5 The following grouped frequency table shows the score received by 275 students who sat a statistics examination.

Score	0–9	10–19	20–29	30–34	35–39	40–49	50–59
Frequency	6	21	51	36	48	82	31

Taking the class boundaries for 0–9 as -0.5 and 9.5, represent the data in a histogram.

6 The haemoglobin levels in the blood of 45 hospital patients were measured. The results, correct to 1 decimal place, and ordered for convenience, are as follows.

9.1 10.1 10.7 10.7 10.9 11.3 11.3 11 4 11.4 11.4 11.6 11.8 12.0 12.1 12.3
12.4 12.7 12.9 13.1 13.2 13.4 13.5 13.5 13.6 13.7 13.8 13.8 14.0 14.2 14.2
14.2 14.6 14.6 14.8 14.8 15.0 15.0 15.0 15.1 15.4 15.6 15.7 16.2 16.3 16.9

(a) Form a grouped frequency table with eight classes.

(b) Draw a histogram of the data.

7 Each of the 34 children in a class of 7-year-olds was given a task to perform. The times taken in minutes, correct to the nearest quarter of a minute, were as follows.

4	$3\frac{3}{4}$	5	$6\frac{1}{4}$	7	3	7	$5\frac{1}{4}$	$7\frac{1}{2}$	$8\frac{3}{4}$	$7\frac{1}{2}$	$4\frac{1}{2}$
$6\frac{1}{2}$	$4\frac{1}{4}$	8	$7\frac{1}{4}$	$6\frac{3}{4}$	$5\frac{3}{4}$	$4\frac{3}{4}$	$8\frac{1}{4}$	7	$3\frac{1}{2}$	$5\frac{1}{2}$	$7\frac{3}{4}$
$8\frac{1}{2}$	$6\frac{1}{2}$	5	$7\frac{1}{4}$	$6\frac{3}{4}$	$7\frac{3}{4}$	$5\frac{3}{4}$	6	$7\frac{3}{4}$	$6\frac{1}{2}$		

(a) Form a grouped frequency table with six equal classes beginning with 3–$3\frac{3}{4}$.

(b) What are the boundaries of the first class?

(c) Draw a histogram of the data.

8 The table shows the age distribution of the 200 members of a chess club.

Age	16–19	20–29	30–39	40–49	50–59	over 59
Number of members	12	40	44	47	32	25

(a) Form a table showing the class boundaries and frequency densities.

(b) Draw a histogram of the data.

1.4 Cumulative frequency graphs

An alternative method of representing continuous data is a **cumulative frequency graph**. The cumulative frequencies are plotted against the upper class boundaries of the corresponding class. Consider the data from Example 1.3.2, reproduced in Table 1.25.

Mass (kg)	47–54	55–62	63–66	67–74	75–82	83–90
Frequency	4	7	8	7	8	4

Table 1.25. Masses of people from the datafile 'Brain size'.

There are 0 observations less than 46.5.

There are 4 observations less than 54.5.

There are $4 + 7$, or 11, observations less than 62.5.

There are $4 + 7 + 8$, or 19, observations less than 66.5.

    ⋮   ⋮   ⋮

There are 38 observations less than 90.5.

These cumulative frequencies are summarised in Table 1.26

Mass, m (kg)	< 46.5	< 54.5	< 62.5	< 66.5	< 74.5	< 82.5	< 90.5
Cumulative frequency	0	4	11	19	26	34	38

Table 1.26. Masses of people from the datafile 'Brain size'.

The points $(46.5, 0)$, $(54.5, 4)$, … , $(90.5, 38)$ are then plotted. The points are joined with straight lines, as shown in Fig. 1.27.

You may also see cumulative frequency graphs in which the points have been joined with a smooth curve. If you join the points with a straight line, then you are making the assumption that the observations in each class are evenly spread throughout the range of values in that class. This is usually the most sensible procedure unless you know

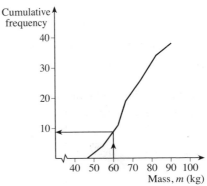

Fig. 1.27. Cumulative frequency graph for the data in Table 1.26.

something extra about the distribution of the data which would suggest that a curve was more appropriate. You should not be surprised, however, if you encounter cumulative frequency graphs in which the points are joined by a curve.

You can also use the graph to read off other information. For example, you can estimate the proportion of the sample whose masses are under 60 kg. Read off the cumulative frequency corresponding to a mass of 60 in Fig. 1.27. This is approximately 8.8. Therefore an estimate of the proportion of the sample whose masses were under 60 kg would be $\frac{8.8}{38} \approx 0.23$, or 23%.

Exercise 1C

1 Draw a cumulative frequency graph for the data in Exercise 1B Question 1.

With the help of the graph estimate

(a) the percentage of cars that were travelling at more than 100 k.p.h.,

(b) the speed below which 25% of the cars were travelling.

2 Draw a cumulative frequency graph for the examination marks in Exercise 1B Question 5.

(a) Candidates with at least 44 marks received Grade A. Find the percentage of the candidates that received Grade A.

(b) It is known that 81.8% of the candidates gained Grade E or better. Find the lowest Grade E mark for these students.

3 Estimates of the age distribution of a country for the year 2010 are given in the following table.

Age	under 16	16–39	40–64	65–79	80 and over
Percentage	14.3	33.1	35.3	11.9	5.4

(a) Draw a percentage cumulative frequency graph.

(b) It is expected that people who have reached the age of 60 will be drawing a state pension in 2010. If the projected population of the country is 42.5 million, estimate the number who will then be drawing this pension.

4 The records of the sales in a small grocery store for the 360 days that it opened during the year 2002 are summarised in the following table.

Sales, x (in \$100s)	$x<2$	$2\leqslant x<3$	$3\leqslant x<4$	$4\leqslant x<5$
Number of days	15	27	64	72

Sales, x (in \$100s)	$5\leqslant x<6$	$6\leqslant x<7$	$7\leqslant x<8$	$x\geqslant 8$
Number of days	86	70	16	10

Days for which sales fall below \$325 are classified as 'poor' and those for which the sales exceed \$775 are classified as 'good'. With the help of a cumulative frequency graph estimate the number of poor days and the number of good days in 2002.

5   A company has 132 employees who work in its city branch. The distances, x kilometres, that employees travel to work are summarised in the following grouped frequency table.

x	<5	5–9	10–14	15–19	20–24	>24
Frequency	12	29	63	13	12	3

Draw a cumulative frequency graph. Use it to find the number of kilometres below which

(a) one-quarter,   (b) three-quarters

of the employees travel to work.

6   The lengths of 250 electronic components were measured very accurately. The results are summarised in the following table.

Length (cm)	< 7.00	7.00–7.05	7.05–7.10	7.10–7.15	7.15–7.20	> 7.20
Frequency	10	63	77	65	30	5

Given that 10% of the components are scrapped because they are too short and 8% are scrapped because they are too long, use a cumulative frequency graph to estimate limits for the length of an acceptable component.

7   As part of a health study the blood glucose levels of 150 students were measured. The results, in mmol l^{-1} correct to 1 decimal place, are summarised in the following table.

Glucose level	< 3.0	3.0–3.9	4.0–4.9	5.0–5.9	6.0–6.9	⩾ 7.0
Frequency	7	55	72	10	4	2

Draw a cumulative frequency graph and use it to find the percentage of students with blood glucose level greater than 5.2.

The number of students with blood glucose level greater than 5.2 is equal to the number with blood glucose level less than a. Find a.

1.5 Practical activities

1 One-sidedness   Investigate whether reaction times are different when a person uses only information from one 'side' of their body.

(a) Choose a subject and instruct them to close their left eye. Against a wall hold a ruler pointing vertically downwards with the 0 cm mark at the bottom and ask the subject to place the index finger of their right hand aligned with this 0 cm mark. Explain that you will let go of the ruler without warning, and that the subject must try to pin it against the wall using the index finger of their right hand. Measure and record the distance dropped.

(b) Repeat this for, say, 30 subjects.

(c) Take a further 30 subjects and carry out the experiment again for each of these subjects, but for this second set of 30 make them close their right eye and use their left hand.

(d) Draw a stem-and-leaf diagram for both sets of data and compare the distributions.

(e) Draw two histograms and use these to compare the distributions.

(f) Do subjects seem to react more quickly using their right side than they do using their left side? Are subjects more erratic when using their left side? How does the fact that some people are naturally left-handed affect the results? Would it be more appropriate to investigate 'dominant' side versus 'non-dominant' side rather than left versus right?

2 High jump   Find how high people can jump.
(a) Pick a subject and ask them to stand against a wall and stretch their arm as far up the wall as possible. Make a mark at this point. Then ask the subject, keeping thier arm raised, to jump as high as they can. Make a second mark at this highest point. Measure the distance between the two marks. This is a measure of how high they jumped.
(b) Take two samples of students of different ages, say 11 years old and 16 years old, and plot a histogram of the results for each group.
(c) Do the older students jump higher than the younger students?

3 Memory
(a) Place twenty different small objects on a tray, for example a coin, a pebble and so on. Show the tray to a sample of students for one minute and then cover the tray. Give the students five minutes to write down as many objects as they can remember.
(b) Type a list of the same objects on a sheet of paper. Allow each of a different sample of students to study the sheet of paper for one minute and then remove the sheet. Give the students five minutes to write down as many objects as they can remember.

Draw a diagram which enables you to compare the distribution of the number of objects remembered in each of the two situations. Is it easier to remember objects for one situation rather than the other? Does one situation lead to a greater variation in the numbers of objects remembered?

Miscellaneous exercise 1

1   The following gives the scores of a cricketer in 40 consecutive innings.

6	18	27	19	57	12	28	38	45	66
72	85	25	84	43	31	63	0	26	17
14	75	86	37	20	42	8	42	0	33
21	11	36	11	29	34	55	62	16	82

Illustrate the data on a stem-and-leaf diagram. State an advantage that the diagram has over the raw data. What information is given by the data that does not appear in the diagram?

2   The service time, t seconds, was recorded for 120 shoppers at the cash register in a shop. The results are summarised in the following grouped frequency table.

t	< 30	30–60	60–120	120–180	180–240	240–300	300–360	> 360
Frequency	2	3	8	16	42	25	18	6

Draw a histogram of the data. Find the greatest service time exceeded by 30 shoppers.

3 At the start of a new school year, the heights of the 100 new pupils entering the school are measured. The results are summarised in the following table. The 10 pupils in the class written '110−' have heights not less than 110 cm but less than 120 cm .

Height (cm)	100−	110−	120−	130−	140−	150−	160−
Number of pupils	2	10	22	29	22	12	3

Use a graph to estimate the height of the tallest pupil of the 18 shortest pupils.

4 The following ordered set of numbers represents the salinity of 30 specimens of water taken from a stretch of sea, near the mouth of a river.

4.2   4.5   5.8   6.3   7.2   7.9   8.2   8.5   9.3   9.7   10.2   10.3   10.4   10.7   11.1

11.6   11.6   11.7   11.8   11.8   11.9   12.4   12.4   12.5   12.6   12.9   12.9   13.1   13.5   14.3

(a) Form a grouped frequency table for the data using six equal classes.

(b) Draw a cumulative frequency graph . Estimate the 12th highest salinity level. Calculate the percentage error in this estimate.

5 The following are ignition times in seconds, correct to the nearest 0.1 s, of samples of 80 flammable materials. They are arranged in numerical order by rows.

1.2   1.4   1.4   1.5   1.5   1.6   1.7   1.8   1.8   1.9   2.1   2.2   2.3   2.5   2.5   2.5

2.5   2.6   2.7   2.8   3.1   3.2   3.5   3.6   3.7   3.8   3.8   3.9   3.9   4.0   4.1   4.2

4.3   4.5   4.5   4.6   4.7   4.7   4.8   4.9   5.1   5.1   5.1   5.2   5.2   5.3   5.4   5.5

5.6   5.8   5.9   5.9   6.0   6.3   6.4   6.4   6.4   6.4   6.7   6.8   6.8   6.9   7.3   7.4

7.4   7.6   7.9   8.0   8.6   8.8   8.8   9.2   9.4   9.6   9.7   9.8   10.6   11.2   11.8   12.8

Group the data into eight equal classes, starting with 1.0−2.4 and 2.5−3.9, and form a grouped frequency table. Draw a histogram. State what it indicates about the ignition times.

6 A company employs 2410 people whose annual salaries are summarised as follows.

Salary (in $1000s)	<10	10−20	20−30	30−40	40−50	50−60	60−80	80−100	>100
Number of staff	16	31	502	642	875	283	45	12	4

(a) Draw a cumulative frequency graph for the grouped data.

(b) Estimate the percentage of staff with salaries between $26 000 and $52 000.

(c) If you were asked to draw a histogram of the data, what problem would arise and how would you overcome it?

7 Construct a grouped frequency table for the following data.

19.12	21.43	20.57	16.97	14.82	19.61	19.35
20.02	12.76	20.40	21.38	20.27	20.21	16.53
21.04	17.71	20.69	15.61	19.41	21.25	19.72
21.13	20.34	20.52	17.30			

(a) Draw a histogram of the data.

(b) Draw a cumulative frequency graph.

(c) Draw a stem-and-leaf diagram using leaves in hundredths, separated by commas.

8 Certain insects can cause small growths, called 'galls', on the leaves of trees. The numbers of galls found on 60 leaves of a tree are given below.

5	19	21	4	17	10	0	61	3	31	15	39	16	27	48
51	69	32	1	25	51	22	28	29	73	14	23	9	2	0
1	37	31	95	10	24	7	89	1	2	50	33	22	0	75
7	23	9	18	39	44	10	33	9	11	51	8	36	44	10

(a) Put the data into a grouped frequency table with classes 0–9 , 10–19 , ... , 70–99 .

(b) Draw a histogram of the data.

(c) Use a cumulative frequency graph to estimate the number of leaves with fewer than 34 galls.

(d) State an assumption required for your estimate in part (c), and briefly discuss its justification in this case.

9 The traffic noise levels on two city streets were measured one weekday, between 5.30 a.m. and 8.30 p.m. There were 92 measurements on each street, made at equal time intervals, and the results are summarised in the following grouped frequency table.

Noise level (dB)	< 65	65–67	67–69	69–71	71–73	73–75	75–77	77–79	> 79
Street 1 frequency	4	11	18	23	16	9	5	4	2
Street 2 frequency	2	3	7	12	27	16	10	8	7

(a) On the same axes, draw cumulative frequency graphs for the two streets.

(b) Use them to estimate the highest noise levels exceeded on 50 occasions in each street.

(c) Write a brief comparison of the noise levels in the two streets.

10 The time intervals (in seconds) between telephone calls received at an office were monitored on a particular day. The first 51 calls after 9.00 a.m. gave the following 50 intervals.

34	25	119	16	12	72	5	41	12	66
118	2	22	40	25	39	19	67	4	13
23	104	35	118	85	67	14	16	50	16
24	10	48	24	76	6	3	61	5	58
56	2	24	44	12	20	8	11	29	82

Illustrate the data with a stem-and-leaf diagram, and with a histogram, using six equal classes.

11 (For this question use the definition of frequency density on page 12.)

A histogram is drawn to represent a set of data.

(a) The first two classes have boundaries 2.0 and 2.2, and 2.2 and 2.5, with frequencies 5 and 12. The height of the first bar drawn is 2.5 cm . What is the height of the second bar?

(b) The class boundaries of the third bar are 2.5 and 2.7. What is the corresponding frequency if the bar drawn has height 3.5 cm ?

(c) The fourth bar has a height of 3 cm and the corresponding frequency is 9. The lower class boundary for this bar is 2.7 cm . Find the upper class boundary.

2 Measures of location

This chapter describes three different measures of location and their method of calculation. When you have completed it, you should

- know what the median is, and be able to calculate it
- know what the mean is, and be able to calculate it efficiently
- know what the mode and the modal class are, and be able to find them
- be able to choose which is the appropriate measure to use in a given situation.

2.1 Introduction

Suppose that you wanted to know the typical playing time for a compact disc (CD). You could start by taking a few CDs and finding out the playing time for each one. You might obtain a list of values such as

49, 56, 55, 68, 61, 57, 61, 52, 63

where the values have been given in minutes, to the nearest whole minute. You can see that the values are located roughly in the region of 1 hour (rather than, say, 2 hours or 10 minutes). It would be useful to have a single value which gave some idea of this location. A single value would condense the information contained in the data set into a 'typical' value, and would allow you to compare this data set with another one. Such a value is called a **measure of location**, or a **measure of central tendency**, or, in everyday language, an **average**.

2.2 The median

You can get a clearer picture of the location of the playing times by arranging them in ascending order of size:

49, 52, 55, 56, 57, 61, 61, 63, 68.

A simple measure of location is the 'middle' value, the value that has equal numbers of values above and below it. In this case there are nine values and the middle one is 57. This value is called the **median**.

If there are an even number of values, then there is no single 'middle' value. In the case of the six values

47, 49, 59, 62, 65, 68,

which are the playing times of another six CDs (in order), the median is taken to be halfway between the third and fourth values, which is $\frac{1}{2}(59 + 62)$, or 60.5. Again, there are equal numbers of values below and above this value: in this case, three.

To find the **median** of a data set of n values, arrange the values in order of increasing size.

If n is odd, the median is the $\frac{1}{2}(n+1)$th value. If n is even, the median is halfway between the $\frac{1}{2}n$th value and the following value.

A convenient way of sorting the values into order of increasing size is to draw an ordered stem-and-leaf diagram. Fig. 2.1 is a stem-and-leaf diagram of the heights of the female students from the 'Brain size' datafile in Table 1.5.

```
15 7 9                              (2)
16 0 0 4 4 4 4 5 8 8 8 9 9 9       (13)
17 3 3 4 5 9                        (5)
Key: 17 | 3 = 173 cm
```
Fig. 2.1. Stem-and-leaf diagram of the heights of female students.

There are 20 students and so the median is calculated from the 10th and 11th values. These two values are shown in bold type in Fig. 2.1. The median is $\frac{1}{2}(168+168)$, or 168 cm.

2.3 Finding the median from a frequency table

Data sets are often much larger than the ones in the previous section and the values will often have been organised in some way, maybe in a frequency table. As an example, Table 2.2 gives the number of brothers and sisters of the children at a school.

Number of brothers and sisters	Frequency	Cumulative frequency
0	36	36
1	94	130
2	48	178
3	15	193
4	7	200
5	3	203
6	1	204
Total: 204		

Table 2.2. Frequency distribution of the number of brothers and sisters of the children at a school.

To find the median using the method in the previous section you would write out a list of all the individual values, starting with 36 '0's, then 94 '1's and so on, and find the $\frac{1}{2}(204)$th, or 102nd, value and the 103rd value. A much easier method is to add a column of cumulative frequencies, as in Table 2.2. From this column you can see that when you have come to the end of the '0's you have not yet reached the 102nd value but, by the end of the '1's, you have reached the 130th value. This means that the 102nd and 103rd values are both 1, so the median is also 1.

In the above example the data have not been grouped, so it is possible to count to the median. Large data sets for continuous variables, however, are nearly always grouped, and the individual values are lost. This means that you cannot find the median exactly and you have to estimate it. Table 2.3 gives the grouped frequency distribution for the playing time of a large selection of CDs.

Playing time, x (min)	Class boundaries	Frequency	Cumulative frequency
40±44	$39.5 \leqslant x < 44.5$	1	1
45–49	$44.5 \leqslant x < 49.5$	7	8
50–54	$49.5 \leqslant x < 54.5$	12	20
55–59	$54.5 \leqslant x < 59.5$	24	44
60–64	$59.5 \leqslant x < 64.5$	29	73
65–69	$64.5 \leqslant x < 69.5$	14	87
70–74	$69.5 \leqslant x < 74.5$	5	92
75–79	$74.5 \leqslant x < 79.5$	3	95
		Total: 95	

Table 2.3. Playing times of 95 CDs.

A column for cumulative frequency has been added to the table, and Fig. 2.4 shows a cumulative frequency graph for the data.

Reminder: cumulative frequency is plotted against the upper class boundary of each class.

The cumulative frequency graph allows you to find the number of CDs with a playing time less than a given value. To obtain the median playing time from the cumulative frequency graph, you read off the value corresponding to a cumulative frequency equal to half the total frequency, in this case $\frac{1}{2} \times 95$, or 47.5. This gives a playing time of 60 minutes. This value is

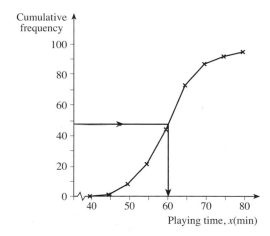

Fig. 2.4. Cumulative frequency graph for data in Table 2.3.

taken as an estimate of the median, because roughly half the playing times will be below it and consequently about half will be above it.

> To find the median value for grouped data from a cumulative
> frequency graph, read off the value of the variable corresponding
> to a cumulative frequency equal to half the total frequency.

Some books suggest reading off the value from the cumulative frequency graph which corresponds to a cumulative frequency of $\frac{1}{2}(n+1)$ rather than $\frac{1}{2}n$, where n is the total frequency. This will give a slightly different value but the difference is not important.

Sometimes discrete data are grouped into classes so that, once again, you cannot list the individual values. An example was given in Table 1.11. To estimate the median for such data, treat the variable as though it were continuous and find the median from the cumulative frequency graph.

Exercise 2A

1   Find the median mass of 6.6 kg, 3.2 kg, 4.8 kg, 7.6 kg, 5.4 kg, 7.1 kg, 2.0 kg, 6.3 kg and 4.3 kg.

  A mass of 6.0 kg is added to the set. What is the median of the 10 masses?

2   With the help of the stem-and-leaf diagram in Fig. 1.3, obtain the median cereal rating.

3   Using your stem-and-leaf diagrams from Exercise 1A Question 2, obtain the medians of the two data sets.

4   Obtain the median of the haemoglobin levels in Exercise 1B Question 6.

5   Using your cumulative frequency graph from Exercise 1C Question 4, obtain an estimate of the median value of the sales.

6   From the grouped frequency table you obtained in Miscellaneous exercise 1 Question 5, draw a cumulative frequency graph and use it to estimate the median ignition time.

  Find the exact median from the data set, and account for any difference between your two answers.

7   The number of rejected CDs produced each day by a machine was monitored for 100 days. The results are summarised in the following table.

Number of rejects	0−9	10−19	20−29	30−39	40−49	50−59
Number of days	5	8	19	37	22	9

  Estimate the median number of rejects.

8   For the 'Brain size' datafile of Table 1.5, find the median mass of
  (a) the men,   (b) the women,
  and compare them.

2.4 The mean

The median does not use the actual values of the observations in a data set, apart from the middle value(s) when the data are arranged in order of increasing size. A measure of location which does make use of the actual values of all the observations is the **mean**. This is the quantity which most people are referring to when they talk about the 'average'. The mean is found by adding all the values and dividing by the number of values. For the nine CDs in Section 2.1,

$$\text{mean} = \frac{49 + 56 + 55 + 68 + 61 + 57 + 61 + 52 + 63}{9} = \frac{522}{9} = 58 \text{ minutes}.$$

> The **mean** of a data set is equal to the sum of the values in the data set divided by the number of values.

2.5 Summation notation

It is possible to express the definition of the mean as a mathematical formula by introducing some new mathematical notation. Suppose you have n data values. The symbol x_i denotes the ith value in the data set. For the playing times of the nine CDs in the previous section, $x_1 = 49$, $x_2 = 56$, $x_3 = 55$ and so on. The sum of the nine values is

$$x_1 + x_2 + x_3 + x_4 + x_5 + x_6 + x_7 + x_8 + x_9.$$

The abbreviation for this sum is $\sum_{i=1}^{9} x_i$. The symbol $\sum$ (which is read as 'sigma') is a Greek capital S, standing for 'sum'. The '$i=1$' at the bottom and the '9' at the top of the $\sum$ tell you that the sum starts at x_1 and finishes at x_9. It is usually obvious which values should be summed and so the sum may be written more simply as $\sum x_i$, $\sum_i x_i$ or $\sum x$. This notation for a sum is called **Σ-notation**. A symbol is also needed for the sample mean. This is $\bar{x}$ (which is read as 'x bar').

> The mean, $\bar{x}$, of a data set of n values is given by
>
> $$\bar{x} = \frac{x_1 + x_2 + \ldots + x_n}{n} = \frac{\sum x_i}{n}. \qquad (2.1)$$

The following example illustrates some uses of Σ-notation which you will meet in this book.

Example 2.5.1

If $x_1 = 1$, $x_2 = 3$, $x_3 = 4$, $x_4 = 5$, evaluate

(a) $\displaystyle\sum_{i=1}^{4} x_i$,   (b) $\displaystyle\sum_{i=1}^{4} x_i^2$,   (c) $\bar{x}$,   (d) $\displaystyle\sum_{i=1}^{4} (x_i - \bar{x})$,   (e) $\displaystyle\sum_{i=1}^{4} (x_i - \bar{x})^2$.

(a) $\displaystyle\sum_{i=1}^{4} x_i = x_1 + x_2 + x_3 + x_4 = 1 + 3 + 4 + 5 = 13$.

(b) $\displaystyle\sum_{i=1}^{4} x_i^2 = x_1^2 + x_2^2 + x_3^2 + x_4^2 = 1^2 + 3^2 + 4^2 + 5^2 = 51$.

(c) $\displaystyle \bar{x} = \frac{\sum x}{n} = \frac{13}{4} = 3.25$.

(d) $\displaystyle\sum_{i=1}^{4} (x_i - \bar{x}) = (x_1 - \bar{x}) + (x_2 - \bar{x}) + (x_3 - \bar{x}) + (x_4 - \bar{x})$

$$= (1 - 3.25) + (3 - 3.25) + (4 - 3.25) + (5 - 3.25)$$
$$= -2.25 - 0.25 + 0.75 + 1.75 = 0.$$

The sum $\displaystyle\sum_{i=1}^{n} (x_i - \bar{x})$ is always equal to 0. Try to prove this result in the general case.

(e) $\displaystyle\sum_{i=1}^{4} (x_i - \bar{x})^2 = (x_1 - \bar{x})^2 + (x_2 - \bar{x})^2 + (x_3 - \bar{x})^2 + (x_4 - \bar{x})^2$

$$= (1 - 3.25)^2 + (3 - 3.25)^2 + (4 - 3.25)^2 + (5 - 3.25)^2$$
$$= (-2.25)^2 + (-0.25)^2 + 0.75^2 + 1.75^2 = 8.75.$$

2.6 Calculating the mean from a frequency table

Table 2.5 contains a copy of the data in Table 2.2, which was the frequency distribution of the number of brothers and sisters of the children at a school. Of the 204 values, 36 are '0's, 94 are '1's, 48 are '2's and so on. Their sum will be

$$(0 \times 36) + (1 \times 94) + (2 \times 48) + (3 \times 15) + (4 \times 7) + (5 \times 3) + (6 \times 1) = 284.$$

You can include this calculation in the table by adding a third column in which each value of the variable, x_i, is multiplied by its frequency, f_i.

Number of brothers and sisters, x_i	Frequency, f_i	$x_i f_i$
0	36	0
1	94	94
2	48	96
3	15	45
4	7	28
5	3	15
6	1	6
Totals:	$\sum f_i = 204$	$\sum x_i f_i = 284$

Table 2.5. Calculation of the mean for the data in Table 2.2.

The mean is equal to $\dfrac{284}{204} = 1.39$, correct to 3 significant figures.

Although the number of brothers and sisters of each child must be a whole number, the mean of the data values need not be a whole number.

In this example the answer is a recurring decimal, and so the answer has been rounded to 3 significant figures. This degree of accuracy is suitable for the answers to most statistical calculations. However, it is important to keep more significant figures when values are carried forward for use in further calculations.

The calculation of the mean can be expressed in Σ-notation as follows:

> The mean, $\bar{x}$, of a data set in which the variable takes the value x_1 with frequency f_1, x_2 with frequency f_2 and so on is given by
>
> $$\bar{x} = \frac{x_1 f_1 + x_2 f_2 + \ldots + x_n f_n}{f_1 + f_2 + \ldots + f_n} = \frac{\sum x_i f_i}{\sum f_i}. \qquad (2.2)$$

If the data in a frequency table are grouped, you need a single value to represent each class before you can calculate the mean using Equation 2.2. A reasonable choice is to take the value halfway between the class boundaries. This is called the **mid-class value**. Table 2.6 contains a copy of the data in Table 2.3 for the playing times of 95 CDs. Two other columns have been included, one giving the mid-class value for each class and the other the product of this mid-class value and the frequency.

Playing time, x (min)	Class boundaries	Frequency, f_i	Mid-class value, x_i	$x_i f_i$
40–44	$39.5 \leqslant x < 44.5$	1	42	42
45–49	$44.5 \leqslant x < 49.5$	7	47	329
50–54	$49.5 \leqslant x < 54.5$	12	52	624
55–59	$54.5 \leqslant x < 59.5$	24	57	1368
60–64	$59.5 \leqslant x < 64.5$	29	62	1798
65–69	$64.5 \leqslant x < 69.5$	14	67	938
70–74	$69.5 \leqslant x < 74.5$	5	72	360
75–79	$74.5 \leqslant x < 79.5$	3	77	231
	Totals: $\sum f_i = 95$			$\sum x_i f_i = 5690$

Table 2.6. Calculation of the mean playing time for 95 CDs.

Thus the estimate of the mean is $\dfrac{\sum x_i f_i}{\sum f_i} = \dfrac{5690}{95} = 59.9$ minutes, correct to 3 significant figures.

This value is only an estimate of the mean playing time for the discs, because individual values have been replaced by mid-class values: some information has been lost by grouping the data.

2.7 Making the calculation of the mean easier

Some calculators will calculate $\bar{x}$ for you if you key in the values of x and f. You should check that you get the same answers to the calculations in the previous section when you use your calculator in this way.

You can see that the calculation of the mean involves quite large numbers. Even with a calculator the calculation can become tedious because of the amount of data entry involved. There are ways in which you can simplify the calculation. Suppose you had to find the mean of the numbers 907, 908, 898, 902 and 897. The direct method of calculation would be to add the numbers and divide by 5. You can check that this gives 902.4. Alternatively you could first make these numbers smaller by subtracting 900 from each of them, giving 7, 8, -2, 2 and -3. You can add these numbers in your head to obtain 12. Their mean is $\frac{12}{5}$, or 2.4. To find the mean of the original values you add 900 to obtain 902.4, as before.

Example 2.7.1

The heights, x cm, of a sample of 80 female students are summarised by the equation $\sum(x-160) = 240$. Find the mean height of a female student.

$$\bar{x} = \frac{\sum(x-160)}{80} + 160 = \frac{240}{80} + 160 = 163.$$

The mean height of a female student is 163 cm.

The general result is

$$\bar{x} = \frac{\sum(x-a)}{n} + a, \text{ where } a \text{ is a constant.}$$

Exercise 2B

1   The test marks of 8 students were $18, 2, 5, 0, 17, 15, 16$ and 11. Find the mean test mark.

2   For the data set in Table 1.5, find the mean male height. The mean height of adult males is about 175 cm. Comment on your answer in the light of this information.

3   (a) Find $\bar{x}$ given that $\sum_{i=1}^{20} x_i = 226$.   (b) Find $\bar{y}$ given that $\sum_{i=1}^{12}(y_i - 100) = 66$.

4   The number of misprints on each page of the draft of a book containing 182 pages is summarised in the following table.

Number of misprints	0	1	2	3	4
Number of pages	144	24	10	2	2

Find the mean number of misprints on a page.

5 The following table gives the frequency distribution for the lengths of rallies (measured by the number of shots) in a tennis match.

Length of rally	1	2	3	4	5	6	7	8
Frequency	2	20	15	12	10	5	3	1

Find the mean length of a rally.

6 The table below gives the number of shoots produced by 50 plants in a botanical research laboratory.

No. of shoots	0–4	5–9	10–14	15–19	20–24	25–29	30–34	35–39	40–44
Frequency	1	1	1	6	17	16	4	2	2

Calculate the mean number of shoots per plant.

7 The speeds, in kilometres per hour, of 200 vehicles travelling on a motorway were measured using a radar device. The results are summarised in the following grouped frequency table.

Speed (k.p.h.)	45–60	60–75	75–90	90–105	105–120	over 120
Frequency	12	32	56	72	20	8

Estimate the mean speed.

8 Calls made by a telephone saleswoman were monitored. The lengths (in minutes, to the nearest minute) of 30 calls are summarised in the following table.

Length of call	0–2	3–5	6–8	9–11	12–15
Number of calls	17	6	4	2	1

(a) Write down the class boundaries.

(b) Estimate the mean length of the calls.

9 The price of a CD is denoted by $\$x$. For 60 CDs bought in different stores it is found that $\sum(x-12) = 53.40$. Calculate the mean price of these CDs. The mean price of a further 40 CDs is found to be $11.64. Find the mean price of the 100 CDs.

10 The volumes of the contents of 48 half-litre bottles of orangeade were measured, correct to the nearest millilitre. The results are summarised in the following table.

Volume (ml)	480–489	490–499	500–509	510–519	520–529	530–539
Frequency	8	11	15	8	4	2

Estimate the mean volume of the contents of the 48 bottles.

2.8   The mode and the modal class

A third measure of location is the **mode**, sometimes called the **modal value**. This is defined
to be the most frequently occurring value. You can pick it out from a frequency table (if the
data have not been grouped) by looking for the value with the highest frequency. If you look
back to Table 2.2, you will see that the mode for the number of brothers and sisters is 1.

If the data have been grouped, then it only possible to estimate the mode. Alternatively,
you can give the **modal class**, which is the class with the highest frequency density. For
example, the modal class for the playing times in Table 2.3 is 60–64 minutes.

If you are given a small data set, then you can find the mode just by looking at the data.
For the first nine CDs in Section 2.2, with playing times

$$49, 52, 55, 56, 57, 61, 61, 63, 68,$$

the mode is 61.

It is not uncommon for all the values to occur only once, so that there is no mode. For
example, the next six CDs had playing times

$$47, 49, 59, 62, 65, 68,$$

and there is no modal value. Combining the two data sets gives

$$47, 49, 49, 52, 55, 56, 57, 59, 61, 61, 62, 63, 65, 68, 68.$$

Now there are three values which have a frequency of 2, giving three modes: 49, 61 and
68. One of these values is low, one is high and the other is near the centre of the data set. In
this case, the mode fails to provide only one measure of location to represent the data set.
You can see that the mode is not a very useful measure of location for small data sets.

In contrast to the mean and median, the mode can be found for qualitative data. For example,
for the datafile 'Cereals' in Table 1.1 the mode for the variable 'type' is C (standing for
'cold'), since there are 74 cereals of type C and only 3 of type H ('hot').

> The **mode** of a data set is the value which occurs with the
> highest frequency. A data set can have more than one mode if
> two or more values have the same maximum frequency. A
> data set has no mode if all the values have the same frequency.
>
> The **modal class** for a grouped frequency distribution is the
> class with the highest frequency density.

2.9   Comparison of the mean, median and mode

The examples in this chapter show that the mean, median and mode of a data set can differ
from each other. For example, for the nine CDs in Section 2.1, the median was 57, the mean
58 and the mode 61. The question then arises as to why there are different ways of
calculating the average of a data set. The answer is that an average describes a large amount
of information with a single value, and there is no completely satisfactory way of doing this.

Each average conveys different information and each has its advantages and disadvantages. You can see this by comparing the mean, median and mode for the following data set, which gives the monthly salaries of the 13 employees in a small firm.

$1000 $1000 $1000 $1000 $1100 $1200 $1250
$1400 $1600 $1600 $1700 $2900 $4200

Median $= \frac{1}{2}(n+1)$th value $= \frac{1}{2}(13+1)$th value $= 7$th value $= \$1250$.

Mean $=$ sum of the values $\div n = \frac{20\,950}{13} = \$1612$, correct to the nearest dollar.

Mode $=$ value with the highest frequency $= \$1000$.

A new employee who had been told that the 'average' wage was $1612 (the mean) would probably be disappointed when he learnt his own salary, because 10 out of the 13 employees earn less than $1612. In this example the median would measure the centre of the distribution better because the median is not affected by the large distance of the last two salaries from the other salaries, whereas the mean is 'pulled up' by them. Normally the median is preferable to the mean as an average when there are values which are not typical. Such values are called **outliers**. The mode is not a very useful measure of the centre in this example, because it is $1000, the lowest salary: 9 of the 13 employees earn more than this.

You can see the same effect of a few high values on the mean for the data set in Table 2.5. The frequency distribution is illustrated in Fig. 2.8. The distribution is not symmetrical but is said to be **skewed**. The 'tail' of high values on the right of the distribution has the effect of making the mean (1.4) higher than the median (1).

A distribution which has a 'tail' of low values on the left will have a mean which is less than the median.

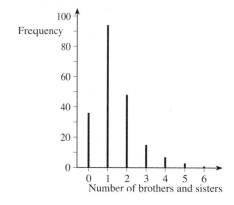

Fig. 2.8. Bar chart of the data in Table 2.5.

Distributions which are roughly symmetrical will have similar values for the mean and the median. The data for the CD playing times in Table 2.3 illustrate this. The histogram in Fig. 2.9, which illustrates this distribution, is approximately symmetrical; the estimates for the mean (59.9) and median (60) are nearly equal. For such a distribution the mean might be considered the 'best' average, because it uses all the information in the data set.

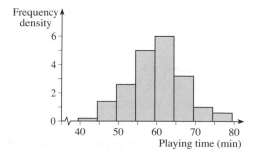

Fig. 2.9. Histogram of the data in Table 2.3.

From these examples it should be clear that the mean, median and mode often provide different information. When you are given an 'average' it is important to know whether it is the mean, the median or the mode. When you calculate an average, it is important to choose the average which is the most 'typical' value.

Example 2.9.1

A commuter who travels to work by car has a choice of two different routes, V and W.
He decides to compare his journey times for each route. So he records the journey times,
in minutes, for 10 consecutive working days, for each route. The results are:

Route V	53	52	48	51	49	47	42	48	57	53
Route W	43	41	39	108	52	42	38	45	39	51

Calculate the mean and median for route V, and the mean and median for route W. Which
average do you think is more suitable for comparing the time taken on each route?

For route V, $\bar{v} = \dfrac{\sum v_i}{n} = \dfrac{500}{10} = 50$.   For route W, $\bar{w} = \dfrac{\sum w_i}{n} = \dfrac{498}{10} = 49.8$.

Arranging the values in order of increasing size gives:

Route V	42	47	48	48	49	51	52	53	53	57
Route W	38	39	39	41	42	43	45	51	52	108

For route V, median $= \frac{1}{2}(5\text{th} + 6\text{th})$ values $= \frac{1}{2}(49 + 51) = 50$.

For route W, median $= \frac{1}{2}(5\text{th} + 6\text{th})$ values $= \frac{1}{2}(42 + 43) = 42.5$.

For route V, the mean and the median are equal. For route W, the mean is greater
than the median, because the single high value of 108 pulls up the mean. This
unusual value was probably due to bad weather or an accident and is not typical.
So it is better to use the median as the average journey time, because it is not
affected by such outliers. This suggests that route W, with a median of 42.5
minutes, is quicker than route V, with a median of 50 minutes.

2.10 Practical activities

1 One-sidedness   Calculate the mean and median for each set of data in Practical
activity 1 in Section 1.5. Which average is more appropriate for comparing the reaction
times? Give a reason for your choice.

2 High jump   Calculate the mean and median for each set of data in Practical
activity 2 in Section 1.5. Which average is more appropriate for comparing the heights
jumped? Give a reason for your choice.

3 Memory   Calculate the mean and median for each set of data in Practical activity 3
in Section 1.5. Which average is more appropriate for comparing the number of objects
remembered? Give a reason for your choice.

<hr>

Exercise 2C

1 For the following distributions state, where possible, the mode or the modal class.

(a)

x	0	1	2	3	4
f	7	4	2	5	1

(b)

x	70	75	80	85	90
f	5	5	5	5	5

(c)

x	2–3	4–5	6–7	8–9	10–11
f	7	4	4	4	1

(d)

Eye colour	Blue	Brown	Green
f	23	39	3

2 State, giving a reason, which of the mean, median or mode would be most useful in the following situations.

   (a) The manager of a shoe shop wishes to stock shoes of various sizes.

   (b) A city council wishes to plan for a school to serve a new housing development. In order to estimate the number of pupils, it studies family sizes on similar developments.

   (c) A person makes a particular car journey regularly and has kept a record of the times taken. She wishes to make an estimate of the time that her next journey will take.

3 A newspaper makes the following statement.

   'Over 60% of houses sold this month were sold for more than the average selling price.'

   Consider the possible truth of this statement, and what is meant by 'average'.

4 State whether you would expect the following variables to have distributions which are skewed, or which are roughly symmetrical.

   (a) The heights of female students in a university.

   (b) The running times of competitors in a marathon race.

   (c) The scores obtained by candidates in an easy examination.

   (d) The numbers of pages in the books in a library.

5 A mental arithmetic test of 8 questions was given to a class of 32 pupils. The results are summarised in the following table.

Number of correct answers	0	1	2	3	4	5	6	7	8
Number of pupils		1	2	1	4	4	6	7	4	3

   (a) Find the mean, median and mode of the number of correct answers. Interpret the median and mode in the context of this arithmetic test.

   (b) Describe the shape of the distribution.

Miscellaneous exercise 2

1 The costs, x, of all telephone calls costing over $0.40 made by a household over a period of three months are as follows.

    0.92   0.66   0.46   0.42   0.54   0.41   0.49   0.59   0.75   0.52   0.42

    0.40   0.49   0.52   0.64   0.48   0.57   0.46   0.49   0.42   0.65   0.73

    0.40   1.12   0.94   0.76   0.48   0.85   1.66   0.40   0.50

    $\sum x = 19.14$

   (a) State why it is advisable to omit 1.66 from a stem-and-leaf diagram of these data.

   (b) Draw an ordered stem-and-leaf diagram, with 1.66 omitted but noted as HI 1.66 next to the diagram. (HI is short for 'high'.)

   (c) For the data obtain the median, the mean and the mode.

   (d) Which of the median, mean and mode would be the best to use to give the average cost of a phone call costing over $0.40? Give a reason for your answer.

   (e) In the same period, the number of calls which cost $0.40 or under was 125, with mean cost $0.142. Find the mean cost of all the calls for the period.

2 The number of times each week that a factory machine broke down was noted over a period of 50 consecutive weeks. The results are given in the following table.

Number of breakdowns	0	1	2	3	4	5	6
Number of weeks	2	12	14	8	8	4	2

   (a) Find the mean number of breakdowns in this period. Is this value exact or an estimate?

   (b) Give the mode and median of the number of breakdowns.

3 The following table summarises the maximum daily temperatures in two holiday resorts in July and August 2002.

Temperature (°C)	18.0±19.9	20.0–21.9	22.0–23.9	24.0–25.9	26.0–27.9	28.0–29.9
Resort 1 frequency	9	13	18	10	7	5
Resort 2 frequency	6	21	23	8	3	1

   (a) State the modal classes for the two resorts.

   (b) A student analysed the data and came to the conclusion that, on average, Resort 1 was hotter than Resort 2 during July and August 2002. Is this conclusion supported by your answer to part (a)? If not, then obtain some evidence that does support the conclusion.

4 The following table shows data about the time taken (in seconds, to the nearest second) for each one of a series of 75 similar chemical experiments.

Time (s)	50–60	61–65	66–70	71–75	76–86
Number of experiments	4	13	26	22	10

(a) State the type of diagram appropriate for illustrating the data.

(b) A calculation using the data in the table gave an estimate of 69.64 seconds for the mean time of the experiments. Explain why this value is an estimate.

(c) Estimate the median of the times taken for completing the experiment.

(d) It was discovered later that the four experiments in the class 50–60 had actually taken 57, 59, 59 and 60 seconds. State, without more calculation, what effect (if any) there would be on the estimates of the median and mean if this information were taken into account.

(OCR, adapted)

5 The standardised marks received by 318 students who took a mechanics examination are summarised in the following grouped frequency table.

Mark	0–29	30–39	40–49	50–59	60–69	70–79	80–89	90–100
Frequency	12	7	13	25	46	78	105	32

(a) Draw a histogram of these data, and describe the skewness of the distribution.

(b) Estimate the mean mechanics mark.

(c) Estimate the median mechanics mark by drawing a cumulative frequency graph.

The same 318 students also took a statistics examination during the same session. The mean and median of those marks were 71.5 and 70.0 respectively. Write a brief comparison of the students' performances in the two examinations.

6 An ordinary dice was thrown 50 times and the resulting scores were summarised in a frequency table. The mean score was calculated to be 3.42. It was later found that the frequencies 12 and 9, of two consecutive scores, had been swapped. What is the correct value of the mean?

7 Three hundred pupils were asked to keep a record of the total time they spent watching television during the final week of their summer holiday. The times, to the nearest $\frac{1}{4}$ hour, are summarised in the following table.

Number of hours	$0\pm4\frac{3}{4}$	$5\pm9\frac{3}{4}$	$10\pm14\frac{3}{4}$	$15\pm19\frac{3}{4}$	$20\pm24\frac{3}{4}$	$25\pm29\frac{3}{4}$	$30\pm34\frac{3}{4}$	$35\pm39\frac{3}{4}$
Frequency	4	21	43	62	90	56	18	6

(a) Estimate the mean viewing time.

(b) State two sources of inaccuracy in your estimate of the mean.

(c) Find an estimate of the median viewing time.

(d) What do the values of the mean and median indicate about the skewness of the data?

8 It is sometimes said that for any set of quantitative data, the median (me), mode (mo) and mean ($\bar{x}$) are such that either $\bar{x} \leqslant$ me $\leqslant$ mo or mo $\leqslant$ me $\leqslant \bar{x}$. Check that this is true of the distribution in Question 2. Show that the statement is untrue for the following data.

x	1	2	3	4	5
f	2	1	11	9	7

9 The table gives the prices (in dollars) of shares in 10 firms on Monday and Tuesday of a particular week. The Monday price is m, the Tuesday price is t, and $d = t - m$.

Firm	A	B	C	D	E	F	G	H	I	J
m	151	162	200	233	287	302	303	571	936	1394
t	144	179	182	252	273	322	260	544	990	1483
d	–7	17	–18	19	–14	20	–43	–27	54	89

   (a) Calculate $\bar{m}$, $\bar{t}$ and $\bar{d}$. Does $\bar{d} = \bar{t} - \bar{m}$?

   (b) Calculate the medians of m, t and d. Is it true that $\text{me}_d = \text{me}_t - \text{me}_m$?

10 The height, correct to the nearest metre, was recorded for each of the 59 birch trees in an area of woodland. The heights are summarised in the following table.

Height (m)	5–9	10–12	13–15	16–18	19–28
Number of trees	14	18	15	4	8

   (a) A student was asked to draw a histogram to illustrate the data and produced the following diagram. Give two criticisms of this attempt at a histogram.

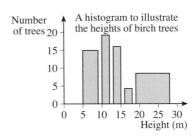

   (b) Using graph paper, draw a correct histogram to illustrate the above data.

   (c) Calculate an estimate of the mean height of the birch trees, giving your answer correct to 3 significant figures.

                                                             (OCR)

3 Measures of spread

This chapter describes three different measures of spread and their methods of calculation. When you have completed it, you should

- know what the range is, and be able to calculate it
- know what the quartiles are and how to find the interquartile range from them
- be able to construct a box-and-whisker plot from a set of data
- know what the variance and standard deviation are, and be able to calculate them
- be able to select an appropriate measure of spread to use in a given situation.

3.1 Introduction

You saw in Chapter 2 how a set of data could be summarised by choosing an appropriate typical value, or 'measure of location' as it is more correctly known. Three different measures of location, the mean, the median and the mode, were introduced.

Now consider the two sets of data A and B given below.

A: 48 52 60 60 60 68   72
B: 0 10 60 60 60 110 120

For both data sets A and B, mean = median = mode = 60. If you were given nothing but a measure of location for each set you might be tempted to think that the two sets of data were similar. Yet if you look in detail at the two sets of data you can see that they are quite different. The most striking difference between the two data sets is that set B is much more spread out than set A. Measures of location do not give any indication of these differences in spread, so it is necessary to devise some new measures to summarise the spread of data.

3.2 The range

The most obvious method of measuring spread is to calculate the difference between the lowest value and the highest value. This difference is called the **range**.

> The **range** of a set of data values is defined by the equation
>
> range = largest value ± smallest value.

The range of data set A is $72 - 48 = 24$, whereas the range of data set B is $120 - 0 = 120$. Calculating the ranges shows clearly that data set B is more spread out than data set A.

It is quite common for students to give the range as an interval. This would mean, for instance, that the range of data set A would be given as 72, or 48–72, or $48 \rightarrow 72$. In statistics it is usually much more helpful to give the range as a single value, so the definition above is used.

If you are going to use the range as a measure of spread it is helpful to realise its limitations. If you consider the two further data sets C and D shown below, you will see that they both have the same range, 8.

$$C: \quad 2 \quad 4 \quad 6 \quad 8 \quad 10$$
$$D: \quad 2 \quad 6 \quad 6 \quad 6 \quad 10$$

Although both data sets C and D have the same range, the patterns of their distributions are quite different from one another. Data set C is evenly spread within the interval 2 to 10 whereas data set D has more of its values 'bunched' centrally. Because the range is calculated from extreme values it ignores the pattern of spread for the rest of the values. This is a major criticism of the range as a measure of spread. Although the range is easy to calculate, it ignores the *pattern* of spread and considers only the extreme values.

3.3 The interquartile range

Since the range ignores the internal spread of the values in a data set, an alternative measure is needed. One possibility is to look at the spread between two values which are at some fixed, but interior, position. A sensible choice, which is associated naturally with the median, is to choose the values that are at the positions one-quarter and three-quarters of the way through the data when the values are arranged in order. These points are known as the **lower quartile** and the **upper quartile** respectively, and they are usually denoted by the symbols Q_1 and Q_3 respectively. The difference between these values is called the **interquartile range**.

> Interquartile range $=$ upper quartile $-$ lower quartile $= Q_3 - Q_1$.

The interquartile range is really just the range of the middle 50% of the distribution.

Notice that there is also a **middle quartile**, Q_2, which is the median.

To find the position of the quartiles for small data sets there are several possible methods that you might see in textbooks. The one suggested below is fairly easy to apply.

Finding the quartiles
- First arrange the data in ascending order.

Case 1 An even number of data values
- Split the data into their upper half and lower half.
- Then the median of the upper half is Q_3, and the median of the lower half is Q_1.

Case 2 An odd number of data values
- Find the median, Q_2, and delete it from the list.
- Split the remaining data into their upper half and lower half.
- Then the median of the upper half is Q_3, and the median of the lower half is Q_1.

Example 3.3.1

Find the quartiles and the interquartile range for each of the two sets of data below.

(a) 7 9 12 13 8 11

(b) 7 8 22 20 15 18 19 13 11

> (a) First, arrange the data in numerical order.
>
>   7 8 9 11 12 13
>
> The number of data values is even, so divide the data into its lower and upper halves:
>
>   Lower half: 7 8 9   Upper half: 11 12 13
>
> The lower quartile Q_1 is the median of the lower half, which is 8. The upper quartile Q_3 is the median of the upper half, which is 12. So
>
> $$\text{interquartile range} = Q_3 - Q_1 = 12 - 8 = 4.$$
>
> (b) Arrange the data in numerical order.
>
>   7 8 11 13 15 18 19 20 22
>
> Since the number of data values (9) is odd, find the median $Q_2 = 15$ and delete it.
>
>   7 8 11 13   18 19 20 22
>
> This automatically divides the data into lower and upper halves.
>
> The median of the lower half is the lower quartile, so $Q_1 = \frac{1}{2}(8 + 11) = 9.5$, and the median of the upper half is the upper quartile, so $Q_3 = \frac{1}{2}(19 + 20) = 19.5$.
>
> The interquartile range is $Q_3 - Q_1 = 19.5 - 9.5 = 10$.

In Chapter 2 you saw how the median of the heights of female students taken from the 'Brain size' datafile could be found with the aid of the stem-and-leaf diagram in Fig. 2.1. The diagram is reproduced in Fig. 3.1.

```
15 | 7 9                              (2)
16 | 0 0 4 4 4 5 8 8 8 9 9 9         (13)
17 | 3 3 4 5 9                        (5)
Key: 17 | 3 = 173 cm
```

Fig. 3.1. Stem-and-leaf diagram of the heights of female students.

Since there are 20 students, the upper and lower halves of the data set will contain 10 values each. The lower quartile is then at the position which is equivalent to the median of the lower half. This is half way between the 5th and 6th values (in ascending order). These are shown in bold type in Fig. 3.1.

Therefore $Q_1 = \frac{1}{2}(164 + 164) = 164$.

Similarly the upper quartile is at the position which is equivalent to the median of the upper half of the data set. This is halfway between the 15th and 16th values (in ascending order). These are also shown in bold type in Fig. 3.1.

Therefore $Q_3 = \frac{1}{2}(169 + 173) = 171$.

The interquartile range is therefore $Q_3 - Q_1 = 171 - 164 = 7$.

It is quite likely that the size of a data set will be much larger than the ones which you have met so far. Larger data sets are usually organised into frequency tables and it is then necessary to think carefully about how to find the position of the quartiles. In Chapter 2 you saw how to find the median of a set of data which referred to the numbers of brothers and sisters of children in a school. This data set was given in Table 2.2. Table 3.2 below reproduces Table 2.2.

Number of brothers and sisters	Frequency	Cumulative frequency
0	36	36
1	94	130
2	48	178
3	15	193
4	7	200
5	3	203
6	1	204
Total: 204		

Table 3.2. Frequency distribution of the number of brothers and sisters of the children at a school.

There are 204 observations. This means that each half will have 102 data values.

The position of the lower quartile, Q_1, will be halfway between the 51st and 52nd values (in ascending order). From the cumulative frequency column you can see that both values are 1, so $Q_1 = 1$. The position of the upper quartile, Q_3, will be halfway between the $(102 + 51)$th and $(102 + 52)$th values (in ascending order); that is, between the 153rd and 154th values. From the cumulative frequency column you can see that both values are 2, so $Q_3 = 2$.

For continuous variables large data sets are usually grouped and so the individual values are lost. The quartiles are estimated from a cumulative frequency graph using a method similar to that described in Chapter 2 to find the median.

Table 3.3 gives the frequency distribution for the playing times of the selection of CDs which you first met in Table 2.3.

Playing time, x (min)	Class boundaries	Frequency	Cumulative frequency
40±44	$39.5 \leqslant x < 44.5$	1	1
45–49	$44.5 \leqslant x < 49.5$	7	8
50–54	$49.5 \leqslant x < 54.5$	12	20
55–59	$54.5 \leqslant x < 59.5$	24	44
60–64	$59.5 \leqslant x < 64.5$	29	73
65–69	$64.5 \leqslant x < 69.5$	14	87
70–74	$69.5 \leqslant x < 74.5$	5	92
75–79	$74.5 \leqslant x < 79.5$	3	95
		Total: 95	

Table 3.3. Playing times of 95 CDs.

To obtain an estimate of the lower quartile of the playing times you read off the value corresponding to a cumulative frequency equal to one-quarter of the total frequency, which in this case is $\frac{1}{4} \times 95 = 23.75$. From the cumulative frequency graph in Fig. 3.4 you can see that $Q_1 \approx 55$ minutes. Similarly you find an estimate of the upper quartile by reading off the value corresponding to a cumulative frequency equal to three-quarters of the total frequency, which is $\frac{3}{4} \times 95 = 71.25$. From the cumulative frequency graph in Fig. 3.4 this method gives $Q_3 \approx 64$ minutes.

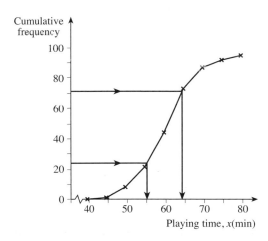

Fig. 3.4. Cumulative frequency graph for the data in Table 3.3.

Then the interquartile range is

$$Q_3 - Q_1 \approx 64 - 55 = 9,$$

so the interquartile range is approximately 9 minutes.

You may be wondering how to interpret the interquartile range for a set of data. For example, is the value of 9 in the example above large or small? The answer is that you cannot tell without more information. Normally you would be comparing the spreads of two or more data sets. You can then make a more sensible comment on whether a particular interquartile range is large or small by comparing its size with the other interquartile ranges. The following example illustrates this idea.

Example 3.3.2

Two people did separate traffic surveys at different locations. Each person noted down the speed of 50 cars which passed their observation point. The results are given in Table 3.5.

Speed, v ($\mathrm{km\,h^{-1}}$)	A frequency	B frequency
$0 \leqslant v < 20$	7	1
$20 \leqslant v < 40$	11	3
$40 \leqslant v < 60$	13	5
$60 \leqslant v < 80$	12	20
$80 \leqslant v < 100$	5	18
$100 \leqslant v < 120$	2	3
Totals: 50	50

Table 3.5. Speeds of 50 cars at each of two locations.

(a) Draw a cumulative frequency graph for each set of data and use it to estimate the median speed and the interquartile range of speeds at each observation point.

(b) Use your results to part (a) to comment on the locations.

(a)

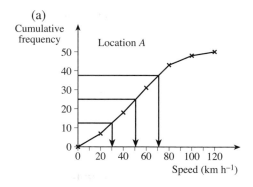

Fig. 3.6. Cumulative frequency graph for the distribution of speeds of 50 cars at location A.

Fig. 3.7. Cumulative frequency graph for the distribution of speeds of 50 cars at location B.

From Fig. 3.6, you can estimate the median and quartiles for the cars at location A. The median corresponds to a cumulative frequency of 25 and, from Fig. 3.6, it is approximately 51. The lower quartile corresponds to a cumulative frequency of 12.5, and it is approximately 30. The upper quartile corresponds to a cumulative frequency of 37.5, and it is approximately 71.

From Fig. 3.7, you can estimate the median and quartiles for the cars at location B. The values of the median and the quartiles are approximately 76, 64 and 89.

(b) You can now compare the medians and the interquartile ranges.

For A the median is 51 and the interquartile range is 41.

For B the median is 76 and the interquartile range is 25.

The median speed at A is lower than the median speed at B and the interquartile range at A is greater than the interquartile range at B. So at location A the cars go more slowly and there is a greater variation in their speeds. Perhaps B is on or near a motorway, and A may be in a town near some point of congestion. You cannot say for certain what types of location A and B are, but the summary values do give you an idea of the type of road at each position.

3.4 The five-number summary

One helpful way of summarising data is to give values which provide essential information about the data set. One such summary is called the **five-number summary**. This summary gives the median, Q_2, the lower quartile Q_1, the upper quartile Q_3, the minimum value and the maximum value.

Example 3.4.1

The data below give the number of fish caught each day over a period of 11 days by an angler. Give a five-number summary of the data.

    0   2   5   2   0   4   4   8   9   8   8

Rearranging the data in order gives:

    0   0   2   2   4   4   5   8   8   8   9

The median value is $Q_2 = 4$. As the number of data values is odd, deleting the middle one and finding the medians of the lower and upper halves gives

$$Q_1 = 2 \quad \text{and} \quad Q_3 = 8.$$

The five-number summary is then the minimum value, 0, the lower quartile, 2, the median, 4, the upper quartile, 8, and the maximum value, 9.

3.5 Box-and-whisker plots

You can convert a five-number summary into a useful diagram, called a **box-and-whisker plot** or a **boxplot**. To draw a box-and-whisker plot, first draw a scale, preferably using graph paper. You can draw the scale vertically or horizontally, but in this book, the scale and the diagram are always drawn horizontally. Above the scale draw a box (or rectangle) in which the left side is above the point corresponding to the lower quartile and the right side is above the point corresponding to the upper quartile.

Then mark a third line inside the box above the point which corresponds to the median value. After this you draw the two whiskers. The left whisker extends from the lower quartile to the minimum value and the right whisker extends from the upper quartile to the maximum. Fig. 3.8 shows the box-and-whisker plot for the data in Example 3.4.1.

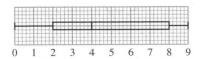

Fig. 3.8. Box-and-whisker plot for the distribution of the numbers of fish caught by an angler over 11 days.

In a box-and-whisker plot the box itself indicates the location of the middle 50% of the data. The whiskers then show how the data is spread overall.

Another important feature of a set of data is its shape when represented as a frequency diagram. The three pictures in Fig. 3.9 show three different shapes which commonly occur when you draw histograms or bar charts.

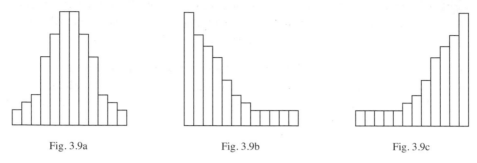

Fig. 3.9a   Fig. 3.9b   Fig. 3.9c

Fig 3.9. Possible shapes of frequency distributions.

The distribution in Fig. 3.9a is symmetrical. If a distribution is not symmetrical it is said to be **skewed**, or to have **skewness**. The distribution in Fig. 3.9a may therefore be said to have zero skewness. You were briefly introduced to the term 'skewed' in Section 2.9.

The distribution in Fig. 3.9b is certainly not symmetrical; there is a 'tail' which stretches towards the higher values. This distribution is said to have **positive skew**, or to be **skewed positively**.

The distribution in Fig. 3.9c is also not symmetrical; there is a 'tail' which stretches towards the lower values. This distribution is said to have **negative skew**, or to be **skewed negatively**.

Another method of assessing the skewness of a distribution is to use the quartiles Q_1, Q_2 and Q_3. Remember that Q_2 denotes the median, and that Q_1 and Q_3 denote the lower and upper quartiles.

If $Q_3 - Q_2 \approx Q_2 - Q_1$, then the distribution is said to be (almost) symmetrical, and a box-and-whisker plot of such data, as in Fig. 3.10, would show a box in which the line corresponding to the median is in the centre of the box.

Fig 3.10. Box-and-whisker plot for a set of data in which $Q_3 - Q_2 \approx Q_2 - Q_1$.

If $Q_3 - Q_2 > Q_2 - Q_1$, as in Fig. 3.11, then the distribution is said to have positive skew, and the line representing the median would be nearer to the left side of the box.

Fig 3.11. Box-and-whisker plot for a set of data in which $Q_3 - Q_2 > Q_2 - Q_1$.

If $Q_3 - Q_2 < Q_2 - Q_1$, as in Fig. 3.12, then the distribution would be said to have negative skew, and the line representing the median would be nearer to the right side of the box.

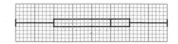

Fig 3.12. Box-and-whisker plot for a set of data in which $Q_3 - Q_2 < Q_2 - Q_1$.

For the data in Example 3.4.1, $Q_1 = 2$, $Q_2 = 4$ and $Q_3 = 8$, so $Q_3 - Q_2 = 8 - 4 = 4$ and $Q_2 - Q_1 = 4 - 2 = 2$. The set of data in Example 3.4.1 therefore has positive skew.

The length of the whiskers can also give some indication of skewness. If the left whisker is shorter than the right whisker, then that would tend to indicate positive skew; whereas if the right whisker is shorter than the left whisker, negative skew would be implied.

It is possible for the data to give different results for skewness depending on what measure you use. For example, it is perfectly possible for a box-and-whisker plot to have $Q_3 - Q_2 > Q_2 - Q_1$, indicating positive skew, but for the left whisker to be longer than the right whisker, which would tend to suggest negative skew. In such cases you must make a judgement about which method of assessing skewness you think is the more important. Fortunately data of this sort do not occur commonly.

3.6* Outliers

The quartiles of a data set can also be used to assess whether the data set has any outliers. Outliers are unusual or 'freak' values which differ greatly in magnitude from the majority of the data values. But just how large or small does a value have to be to be an outlier? There is no simple answer to this question, but one 'rule of thumb' developed by the statistician John Tukey is to use 'fences'.

The upper fence is at a value 1.5 times the interquartile range above the upper quartile:

$$\text{Upper fence} = Q_3 + 1.5(Q_3 - Q_1).$$

The lower fence is at a value 1.5 times the interquartile range below the lower quartile:

$$\text{Lower fence} = Q_1 - 1.5(Q_3 - Q_1).$$

John Tukey then said that any value which is bigger than the upper fence or smaller than the lower fence is considered to be an outlier.

For the data of Example 3.4.1, $Q_1 = 2$ and $Q_3 = 8$, so

$$\text{upper fence} = Q_3 + 1.5(Q_3 - Q_1) = 8 + 1.5 \times (8 - 2) = 17,$$

$$\text{lower fence} = Q_1 - 1.5(Q_3 - Q_1) = 2 - 1.5(8 - 2) = -7.$$

In this case there is no value above 17 or below −7, so this data set does not contain any values which could be said to be outliers.

Exercise 3A

1 Find the range and interquartile range of each of the following data sets.
   (a)   7   4   14   9   12   2   19   6   15
   (b)   7.6   4.8   1.2   6.9   4.8   7.2   8.1   10.3   4.8   6.7

2 Find the interquartile range of the leaf lengths displayed in Exercise 1A Question 1.

3   The number of times each week that a factory machine broke down was noted over a
    period of 50 consecutive weeks. The results are given in the following table.

Number of breakdowns	0	1	2	3	4	5	6
Number of weeks	2	12	14	8	8	4	2

    Find the interquartile range of the number of breakdowns in a week.

4   For the data in Miscellaneous exercise 1 Question 6, find the lower and upper quartiles of
    the annual salaries.

5   For the data in Miscellaneous exercise 1 Question 8, find the median and interquartile
    range for the traffic noise levels in the two streets. Use the statistics to compare the noise
    levels in the two streets.

6   The audience size in a theatre performing a long-running detective play was monitored
    over a period of one year. The sizes for Monday and Wednesday nights are summarised in
    the following table.

Audience size	50−99	100−199	200−299	300−399	400−499	500−599
Number of Mondays	12	20	12	5	3	0
Number of Wednesdays	2	3	20	18	5	4

    Compare the audience sizes on Mondays and Wednesdays.

7   The following stem-and-leaf diagrams refer to the datafile 'Cereals' in Chapter 1. They are
    the ratings of the cereals with fat content 0 and with fat content 1.

Fat content 0

```
2 | 9                          (1)
3 | 1 3 5 6                    (4)
4 | 1 1 1 2 2 4 6 7            (8)
5 | 3 3 3 5 8 9                (6)
6 | 0 1 3 5 8                  (5)
7 | 3 4                        (2)
8 |                            (0)
9 | 4                          (1)
```

Fat content 1

```
2 | 2 3 4 7 8 8 9                    (7)
3 | 0 1 1 2 6 6 6 7 8 9 9 9 9       (13)
4 | 0 7 9                            (3)
5 | 0 0 2 2 5 9                      (6)
6 | 8                                (1)
```

Key: 4|7 means 47

    Compare the two sets of ratings by finding the ranges, medians and quartiles.

8   Draw box-and-whisker plots for data which have the following five-number summaries,
    and in each case describe the shape of the data.

    (a)   6.0 kg   10.2 kg   12.7 kg   13.2 kg   15.7 kg
    (b)   ±12 °C   ±8 °C   ±6 °C   3 °C   11 °C
    (c)   37 m   48 m   60 m   72 m   82 m

9   State, giving reasons, whether box-and-whisker plots or histograms are better for
    comparing two distributions.

10 The following figures are the amounts spent on food by a family for 13 weeks.

$48.25 $43.70 $52.83 $49.24 $58.28 $55.47 $47.29
$51.82 $58.42 $38.73 $42.76 $50.42 $40.85

(a) Obtain a five-number summary of the data.

(b) Construct a box-and-whisker plot of the data.

(c) Describe any skewness of the data.

11* The lower and upper quartiles for a data set are 56 and 84. Decide which of the following data values would be classified as an outlier according to the criteria of Section 3.6.

(a) 140   (b) 10   (c) 100

12* For the data of Exercise 1A Question 3, construct a box-and-whisker plot.

(a) Calculate the inner and outer fences.

(b) State, giving a reason, whether there are any outliers.

(c) Comment on the shape of the distribution.

3.7 Variance and standard deviation

One of the reasons for using the interquartile range in preference to the range as a measure of spread is that it takes some account of how the interior values are spread rather than concentrating solely on the spread of the extreme values. The interquartile range, however, does not take account of the spread of all of the data values and so, in some sense, it is still an inadequate measure. An alternative measure of spread which does take into account the spread of all the values can be devised by finding how far each data value is from the mean. To do this you would calculate the quantities $x_i - \bar{x}$ for each x_i.

The example in Section 2.4 used the playing times, in minutes, of nine CDs.

49   56   55   68   61   57   61   52   63

The mean of these times was found to be 58 minutes. If the mean is subtracted from each of the original data values you get the following values.

−9   −2   −3   10   3   −1   3   −6   5

If you ignore the negative signs, then the resulting values give an idea of the distance of each of the original values from the mean. So these distances would be

9   2   3   10   3   1   3   6   5.

The mean of these distances would be a sensible measure of spread. It would represent the mean distance from the mean.

In this case the mean distance would be

$$\tfrac{1}{9}(9+2+3+10+3+1+3+6+5) = \tfrac{1}{9} \times 42 = 4.66\ldots.$$

To represent this method with a simple formula it is necessary to use the modulus symbol $|v|$, which denotes the magnitude, or numerical value, of v. It is now possible to write a precise formula for the mean distance:

$$\text{mean distance} = \frac{1}{n}\sum |x_i - \bar{x}|.$$

Unfortunately a formula involving the modulus sign is awkward to handle algebraically. The modulus sign can be avoided by squaring each of the quantities $x_i - \bar{x}$.

This leads to the expression $\dfrac{1}{n}\sum (x_i - \bar{x})^2$ as a measure of spread.

This quantity is called the **variance** of the data values. It is the mean of the squared distances from the mean. So, for the data on playing times of CDs,

$$\begin{aligned}
\text{variance} &= \frac{1}{n}\sum (x_i - \bar{x})^2 \\
&= \tfrac{1}{9}\left(9^2 + 2^2 + 3^2 + 10^2 + 3^2 + 1^2 + 3^2 + 6^2 + 5^2\right) \\
&= \tfrac{1}{9}(81 + 4 + 9 + 100 + 9 + 1 + 9 + 36 + 25) = \tfrac{274}{9} = 30.4\dots.
\end{aligned}$$

If the data values x_1, x_2, ... , x_n have units associated with them, then the variance will be measured in units^2. In the example the data values were measured in minutes and therefore the variance would be measured in minutes^2. This is something which can be avoided by taking the positive square root of the variance. The positive square root of the variance is known as the **standard deviation**, often shortened to 'SD', and it always has the same units as the original data values. The formula for standard deviation is

$$\sqrt{\frac{1}{n}\sum (x_i - \bar{x})^2}.$$

So the standard deviation of the playing times of the nine CDs is $\sqrt{30.4\dots} = 5.52$, correct to 3 significant figures.

The calculation of the variance can be quite tedious, particularly when the mean is not a whole number. Fortunately, there is an alternative formula which is easier to use:

$$\text{variance} = \frac{1}{n}\left(x_1^2 + x_2^2 + \dots + x_n^2\right) - \bar{x}^2.$$

This can be written in Σ-notation as

$$\text{variance} = \frac{1}{n}\sum x_i^2 - \bar{x}^2.$$

Using this alternative formula with the data on the playing times of CDs gives

$$\begin{aligned}
\text{variance} &= \frac{1}{n}\sum x_i^2 - \bar{x}^2 \\
&= \tfrac{1}{9}\left(49^2 + 56^2 + 55^2 + 68^2 + 61^2 + 57^2 + 61^2 + 52^2 + 63^2\right) - 58^2 \\
&= \tfrac{1}{9}(2401 + 3136 + 3025 + 4624 + 3721 + 3249 + 3721 + 2704 + 3969) - 3364 \\
&= \tfrac{1}{9} \times 30\,550 - 3364 = 3394.4\dots - 3364 = 30.4\dots.
\end{aligned}$$

This is the same value found by using the original formula. This does not, of course, prove that the two formulae are always equivalent to each other. A proof is given in Section 3.8.

The **variance** of a set of data values $x_1, x_2, \ldots, x_n$ whose mean is

$$\bar{x} = \frac{x_1 + x_2 + \ldots + x_n}{n} = \frac{1}{n} \sum x_i$$

is given by either of the two alternative formulae

$$\text{variance} = \frac{1}{n} \sum (x_i - \bar{x})^2 \quad \text{or} \quad \text{variance} = \frac{1}{n} \sum x_i^2 - \bar{x}^2. \qquad (3.1), (3.2)$$

The **standard deviation** is the square root of the variance.

Example 3.7.1

The 12 boys and 13 girls, in a class of 25 students, were given a test. The mean mark for the 12 boys was 31 and the standard deviation of the boys' marks was 6.2. The mean mark for the girls was 36 and the standard deviation of the girls' marks was 4.3. Find the mean mark and standard deviation of the marks of the whole class of 25 students.

Let $x_1, x_2, \ldots, x_{12}$ be the marks of the 12 boys in the test and let $y_1, y_2, \ldots, y_{13}$ be the marks of the 13 girls in the test.

Since the mean of the boys' marks is 31, $\dfrac{\sum x}{12} = 31$, so $\sum x = 12 \times 31 = 372$.

As the standard deviation of the boys' marks is 6.2, the variance is $6.2^2 = 38.44$.

Therefore, using Equation 3.2,

$$38.44 = \frac{\sum x^2}{12} - 31^2, \text{ which gives } \sum x^2 = 12 \times (38.44 + 31^2) = 11\,993.28.$$

Similarly,

$$\sum y = 13 \times 36 = 468, \text{ and}$$

$$\sum y^2 = 13 \times (4.3^2 + 36^2) = 17\,088.37.$$

The overall mean is $\dfrac{\sum x + \sum y}{25} = \dfrac{372 + 468}{25} = \dfrac{840}{25} = 33.6.$

The overall variance is $\dfrac{\sum x^2 + \sum y^2}{25} - 33.6^2 = \dfrac{11\,993.28 + 17\,088}{25} - 33.6^2$

$$= 34.306.$$

The overall standard deviation is $\sqrt{34.306} = 5.86$, correct to 3 significant figures.

Although the standard deviation makes use of all the data values, it suffers from the same disadvantage as the mean, namely that an outlier can have an undue influence. Either a very low value or a very high value will increase the standard deviation considerably. Consider the data below.

$$45 \quad 46 \quad 46 \quad 48 \quad 49 \quad 50 \quad 52$$

It is left as an exercise for you to check the following values for this data set.

Standard deviation = 2.33, correct to 3 significant figures.

Interquartile range = $50 \pm 46 = 4$.

Now consider what would happen if the lowest value were 25 instead of 45.

$$25 \quad 46 \quad 46 \quad 48 \quad 49 \quad 50 \quad 52$$

The interquartile range is unchanged, but you can check that the standard deviation is now 8.44, correct to 3 significant figures. This is several times larger than its previous value.

3.8* Proof of the equivalence of the variance formulae

You may omit this section if you wish.

First note that $\bar{x} = \dfrac{x_1 + x_2 + \ldots + x_n}{n}$, so $n\bar{x} = x_1 + x_2 + \ldots + x_n$.

Then variance $= \dfrac{1}{n} \sum (x_i - \bar{x})^2$

$$= \frac{1}{n}\left\{ (x_1 - \bar{x})^2 + (x_2 - \bar{x})^2 + \ldots + (x_n - \bar{x})^2 \right\}$$

$$= \frac{1}{n}\left\{ (x_1^2 - 2x_1\bar{x} + \bar{x}^2) + (x_2^2 - 2x_2\bar{x} + \bar{x}^2) + \ldots + (x_n^2 - 2x_n\bar{x} + \bar{x}^2) \right\}$$

$$= \frac{1}{n}\left\{ (x_1^2 + x_2^2 + \ldots + x_n^2) - 2\bar{x}(x_1 + x_2 + \ldots + x_n) + \overbrace{\left(\bar{x}^2 + \bar{x}^2 + \ldots + \bar{x}^2 \right)}^{n \text{ of these}} \right\}$$

$$= \frac{1}{n}\left\{ (x_1^2 + x_2^2 + \ldots + x_n^2) - 2\bar{x} \times n\bar{x} + n\bar{x}^2 \right\}$$

$$= \frac{1}{n}\left\{ (x_1^2 + x_2^2 + \ldots + x_n^2) - 2n\bar{x}^2 + n\bar{x}^2 \right\}$$

$$= \frac{1}{n}\left\{ (x_1^2 + x_2^2 + \ldots + x_n^2) - n\bar{x}^2 \right\}$$

$$= \frac{1}{n} \sum x_i^2 - \bar{x}^2.$$

This shows that the two formulae for variance are equivalent.

Exercise 3B

1   State or find the mean of
    (a) $1, 2, 3, 4, 5, 6, 7,$ (b) $4, 12, -2, 7, 0, 9.$

    Using the formula $\sqrt{\dfrac{1}{n}\sum(x-\bar{x})^2}$, find the standard deviation of each data set.

2   Find the standard deviation of the following data sets, using the formula $\sqrt{\dfrac{1}{n}\sum(x-\bar{x})^2}$.
    (a) $2, 1, 5.3, -4.2, 6.7, 3.1$ (b) $15.2, 12.3, 5.7, 4.3, 11.2, 2.5, 8.7$

3   The masses, x grams, of the contents of 25 tins of Brand A anchovies are summarised by
    $\sum x = 1268.2$ and $\sum x^2 = 64\,585.16$. Find the mean and variance of the masses. What is
    the unit of measurement of the variance?

4   The standard deviation of 10 values of a variable is 2.8. The sum of the squares of the 10
    values is 92.8. Find the mean of the 10 values.

5   The mean and standard deviation of the heights of 12 boys in a class are 148.8 cm and
    5.4 cm respectively. A boy of height 153.4 cm joins the class. Find the mean and standard
    deviation of the heights of the 13 boys.

6   The runs made by two batsmen, Anwar and Qasim, in 12 innings during the 1999 cricket
    season are shown in the following table.

Anwar	23	83	40	0	89	98	71	31	102	48	15	18
Qasim	43	32	61	75	68	92	17	15	25	43	86	12

    Giving your reasons, state which batsman you consider to be
    (a) better,   (b) more consistent.

7   The following stem-and-leaf diagrams are for the masses of 20 female students and 18
    male students from the datafile 'Brain size' in Chapter 1.

    Females   **Males**

```
4 | 8                         (1)      4 |
5 | 2 4 4 5 8 8               (6)      5 |
6 | 1 2 3 3 4 5 6 6 7 9       (10)     6 | 0 1 5 5 7 9          (6)
7 | 0 2 9                     (3)      7 | 0 8 8 8              (4)
8 |                                    8 | 1 1 2 2 4 5 7 7      (8)
```

    Key: 6|1 means 61 kg

    Summary: $\sum f = 1246,$ $\sum f^2 = 78\,704,$
                      $\sum m = 1360,$ $\sum m^2 = 104\,162,$

    where f and m represent the masses of female and male students respectively.

    Compare the masses of the females and males by drawing box-and-whisker plots and
    calculating the means and standard deviations of the masses.

3.9 Calculating variance from a frequency table

Table 3.13 reproduces Table 2.5, which gave the frequency distribution of the numbers of brothers and sisters of children in a school.

Number of brothers and sisters, x_i	Frequency, f_i	$x_i f_i$
0	36	0
1	94	94
2	48	96
3	15	45
4	7	28
5	3	15
6	1	6
Totals: $\sum f_i = 204$		$\sum x_i f_i = 284$

Table 3.13. Frequency distribution of the number of brothers and sisters of children in a school.

In order to calculate the variance you need first to find the mean. This was done in Section 2.6, and the mean was $\dfrac{284}{204} = 1.39\ldots$.

Since the 204 values consist of 36 '0's, 94 '1's, 48 '2's and so on,

$$x_1^2 + x_2^2 + \ldots + x_n^2 = \left(\overbrace{0^2 + 0^2 + \ldots + 0^2}^{36 \text{ of these}} \right) + \left(\overbrace{1^2 + 1^2 + \ldots + 1^2}^{94 \text{ of these}} \right) + \ldots$$

$$+ \left(\overbrace{4^2 + 4^2 + \ldots + 4^2}^{7 \text{ of these}} \right) + \left(\overbrace{5^2 + 5^2 + 5^2}^{3 \text{ of these}} \right) + 6^2$$

$$= \left(0^2 \times 36\right) + \left(1^2 \times 94\right) + \left(2^2 \times 48\right)$$

$$+ \left(3^2 \times 15\right) + \left(4^2 \times 7\right) + \left(5^2 \times 3\right) + \left(6^2 \times 1\right)$$

$$= 0 + 94 + 192 + 135 + 112 + 75 + 36 = 644.$$

You can include this calculation in the table by adding a fourth column for $x_i^2 \times f_i$.

Number of brothers and sisters, x_i	Frequency, f_i	$x_i f_i$	$x_i^2 f_i$
0	36	0	0
1	94	94	94
2	48	96	192
3	15	45	135
4	7	28	112
5	3	15	75
6	1	6	36
Totals: $\sum f_i = 204$		$\sum x_i f_i = 284$	$\sum x_i^2 f_i = 644$

Table 3.14. Calculation of the variance for the data in Table 3.13.

So the variance is $\frac{644}{204} - (1.39\ldots)^2 = 1.218\ldots = 1.22$, correct to 3 significant figures.

The standard deviation is then $\sqrt{1.218\ldots} = 1.10$, correct to 3 significant figures.

To summarise the method used to find the variance:

The variance of data given in a frequency table in which the variable takes the value x_1 with frequency f_1, the value x_2 with frequency f_2 and so on is given by the two formulae

$$\text{variance} = \frac{\sum (x_i - \bar{x})^2 f_i}{\sum f_i} \quad \text{or} \quad \text{variance} = \frac{\sum x_i^2 f_i}{\sum f_i} - \bar{x}^2. \qquad (3.3), (3.4)$$

The second formula is usually easier to use.

If the data are grouped, you need a single value to represent each class. In Section 2.6 you saw that the most reasonable choice was the mid-class value. After you have made this simplifying assumption, then the calculation proceeds in the same way as in Table 3.14.

Example 3.9.1
Calculate an estimate of the variance of the data given in Table 2.6.

Table 3.15 reproduces Table 2.6 with an extra column representing $x_i^2 f_i$.

Playing time, x (min)	Class boundaries	Frequency, f_i	Mid-class value, x_i	$x_i f_i$	$x_i^2 f_i$
40–44	$39.5 \leqslant x < 44.5$	1	42	42	1764
45–49	$44.5 \leqslant x < 49.5$	7	47	329	15 463
50–54	$49.5 \leqslant x < 54.5$	12	52	624	32 448
55–59	$54.5 \leqslant x < 59.5$	24	57	1368	77 976
60–64	$59.5 \leqslant x < 64.5$	29	62	1798	111 476
65–69	$64.5 \leqslant x < 69.5$	14	67	938	62 846
70–74	$69.5 \leqslant x < 74.5$	5	72	360	25 920
75–79	$74.5 \leqslant x < 79.5$	3	77	231	17 787
Totals:		$\sum f_i = 95$		$\sum x_i f_i = 5\,690$	$\sum x_i^2 f_i = 345\,680$

Table 3.15. Calculation of the variance of the playing times for 95 CDs.

Using the formula $\text{variance} = \frac{\sum x_i^2 f_i}{\sum f_i} - \bar{x}^2$,

$$\text{variance} = \frac{345\,680}{95} - \left(\frac{5690}{95}\right)^2 = 51.4, \text{ correct to 3 significant figures.}$$

The variance is therefore 51.4 minutes^2, correct to 3 significant figures.

You should remember that, just as with the calculation of the mean in Section 2.6, the value of the variance calculated from grouped data is only an estimate. This is because the individual values have been replaced by mid-class values.

3.10 Making the calculation of variance easier

You saw in Section 2.7 that you could simplify the calculation of the mean. To find the mean of 907, 908, 898, 902 and 897 you subtracted 900 from each of the numbers, giving 7, 8, -2, 2 and -3. You then found the mean of these numbers, which was 2.4. To recover the mean of the original five numbers 907, 908, 898, 902 and 897 you simply added 900 to 2.4 to give a mean for the original numbers of 902.4. You can also use this idea of simplifying the numbers when calculating variance, but the details are slightly different.

To find the variance of 907, 908, 898, 902 and 897, subtract 900 as before to obtain 7, 8, -2, 2 and -3. The spread of the two sets of numbers will be identical, so the variance of 907, 908, 898, 902 and 897 will be the same as the variance of 7, 8, -2, 2 and -3.

The variance of 7, 8, -2, 2 and -3 is given by

$$\tfrac{1}{5}\left(7^2 + 8^2 + (-2)^2 + 2^2 + (-3)^2\right) - 2.4^2 = 20.24.$$

This value will also represent the variance of the original numbers. Notice also that the standard deviation will be $\sqrt{20.24} = 4.498\ldots$ for both sets of data. After you found the mean of the new numbers it was necessary to add 900 to the new mean to recover the mean of the original set of numbers. You do *not* need to add anything to the variance of the new numbers to recover the variance of the original set of numbers. This is because the amount of spread is the same for both sets of data.

Example 3.10.1

The heights, x cm, of a sample of 80 female students are summarised by the equations

$$\sum(x-160) = 240 \qquad \text{and} \qquad \sum(x-160)^2 = 8720.$$

Find the standard deviation of the heights of the 80 female students.

Let $y = x - 160$ and then $\sum y = 240$ and $\sum y^2 = 8720$.

The variance of the y-values is given by

$$\text{variance} = \frac{\sum y^2}{n} - \bar{y}^2 = \frac{8720}{80} - \left(\frac{240}{80}\right)^2 = 109 - 3^2 = 100.$$

Therefore the standard deviation of the y-values is 10.

But the standard deviation of the x-values will be the same as the standard deviation of the y-values. Therefore the standard deviation of the female students' heights will also be 10.

Exercise 3C

1 The number of absences each day among employees in an office was recorded over a period of 96 days, with the following results.

Number of absences	0	1	2	3	4	5
Number of days	54	24	11	4	2	1

Calculate the mean and variance of the number of daily absences, setting out your work in a table similar to Table 3.14.

2 Plates of a certain design are painted by a particular factory employee. At the end of each day the plates are inspected and some are rejected. The table shows the number of plates rejected over a period of 30 days.

Number of rejects	0	1	2	3	4	5	6
Number of days	18	5	3	1	1	1	1

Show that the standard deviation of the daily number of rejects is approximately equal to one-quarter of the range.

3 The times taken in a 20 km race were noted for 80 people. The results are summarised in the following table.

Time (minutes)	60–80	80–100	100–120	120–140	140–160	160–180	180–200
No. of people	1	4	26	24	10	7	8

Estimate the variance of the times of the 80 people in the race.

4 The mass of coffee in each of 80 packets of a certain brand was measured correct to the nearest gram. The results are shown in the following table.

Mass (grams)	244–246	247–249	250–252	253–255	256–258
Number of packets	10	20	24	18	8

Estimate the mean and standard deviation of the masses, setting out your work in a table similar to Table 3.15.

State two ways in which the accuracy of these estimates could be improved.

5 Here are 10 values of a variable x. Find the variance using the formula $u = x - 20$.

18.9   20.7   19.3   20.1   21.3   19.6   20.5   20.9   18.8   20.8

6 The formula $u = x + 20$ is used to find the standard deviation of the values of x given in a frequency table. It is found that $\sum f_i = 40$, $\sum u_i f_i = 112$ and $\sum u_i^2 f_i = 10\,208$. Find the mean and variance of the values of x.

7   At the start of a new school year, the heights of the 100 new pupils entering the school are measured. The results are summarised in the following table. The 10 pupils in the 110– group have heights not less than 110 cm but less than 120 cm.

Height (h cm)	100–	110–	120–	130–	140–	150–	160–
Number of pupils	2	10	22	29	22	12	3

By using the formula $u = h - 135$, obtain estimates of the mean and variance of the heights of the 100 pupils.

8   The ages, in completed years, of the 104 workers in a company are summarised as follows.

Age (years)	16–20	21–25	26–30	31–35	36–40	41–50	51–60	61–70
Frequency	5	12	18	14	25	16	8	6

Estimate the mean and standard deviation of the workers' ages.

In another company, with a similar number of workers, the mean age is 28.4 years and the standard deviation is 9.9 years. Briefly compare the age distribution in the two companies.

3.11 Choosing how to represent data

In the first three chapters of this book you have met a variety of ways of representing data. The purpose of this section is to give an overview of these methods and to discuss the advantages and disadvantages of the different methods in more detail.

When you are faced with a set of raw data for a variable, it is helpful to split it into groups in some way. This will allow you to see how the values of the variable are distributed. A very effective way of doing this for a small data set is to construct a stem-and-leaf diagram. You can then see the shape of the distribution by rotating the diagram through 90° anticlockwise. You can compare two sets of data by drawing a 'back-to-back' stem-and-leaf diagram. Fig. 3.16 shows such a diagram for the data in Exercise 3B Question 7. From it you can see that the masses for women have a greater spread than those for men but that the mass of a woman is, on average, less than that of a man.

	Females			**Males**	
(1)	8	4			
(6)	8 8 5 4 4 2	5			
(10)	9 7 6 6 5 4 3 3 2 1	6	0 1 5 5 7 9		(6)
(3)	9 2 0	7	0 8 8 8		(4)
		8	1 1 2 2 4 5 7 7		(8)

Key: 6|1 means 61 kg

Fig. 3.16. Back-to-back stem-and-leaf diagram of the masses in kg of 20 female and 18 male students.

A stem-and-leaf diagram has the advantage that it contains all the original data values and so you can easily find the range, the median and the quartiles from it. You can also calculate the mean and standard deviation exactly from a stem-and-leaf diagram because information about all the values is there.

For larger data sets, however, a stem-and-leaf diagram would be very tedious to draw, and it can look confusing because it contains so much information. In these cases it may be better to make a frequency table and draw a histogram in order to show the shape of the distribution. Histograms have the advantage over stem-and-leaf diagrams that you can group the data into classes of any width you like and these classes need not have the same widths.

From the scale on the horizontal axis of a histogram you can easily see the range of values that the variable takes. This information is not so easily seen from a stem-and-leaf diagram: you have to use the 'key' to interpret the values.

Some of the information in the original data set is lost when the data are assembled into a grouped frequency table. This is the price which you pay for making it easier to see the distribution of the data. As a result, values for the median, quartiles, mean and standard deviation which are found from a frequency table (or a histogram) are estimates rather than exact values.

Cumulative frequency diagrams are usually drawn in order to estimate the median and quartiles of grouped data. They are also useful for estimating the number of data values that lie below or above a given value of the variable.

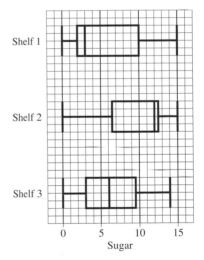

Box-and-whisker plots give a compact means of showing the shape of a distribution. They have the advantage over histograms and stem-and-leaf diagrams that they give the lowest and highest values, the median and the quartiles directly. They are particularly useful when you want to compare several sets of related data. Fig. 3.17 shows box-plots of 'sugar' for different shelf numbers for data taken from the datafile 'Cereals' in Chapter 1. At a glance you can see that the distribution for shelf 1 is positively skewed, that for shelf 2 is negatively skewed and that for shelf 3 is symmetrical. More importantly, the sugar content for cereals on shelf 2, which is at 'child height', is higher than for the other two shelves.

Fig. 3.17. Box-and-whisker plots for 'sugar' for different supermarket shelves.

Box-and-whisker plots have the disadvantage that, unlike histograms and stem-and-leaf diagrams, you cannot find the mean and standard deviation from them. Also, unlike histograms and stem-and-leaf diagrams, they give no indication of the size of the data set. For example, you cannot tell from Fig. 3.17 how many types of cereal there were on each of the shelves.

Once you have an idea of the distribution of a variable you are in a position to decide the most appropriate measures of location and spread for representing it. The location of a data set can be represented by the mean, the median or the mode. The mean has the advantage that it uses all the data values but has the disadvantage that outliers affect it unduly. The median makes less use of the actual values but has the advantage that outliers do not affect it at all. The mode has the advantage that it can be used for qualitative as well as quantitative variables.

The spread of a data set can be represented by the range, the standard deviation or the interquartile range. The range has the disadvantage that it depends only on the highest and lowest values and so it is very sensitive to the presence of outliers. The standard deviation, like the mean, has the advantage that it uses all the data values, but it too has the disadvantage that outliers affect it unduly. The interquartile range, like the median, makes less use of the actual values, but it has the advantage that outliers do not affect it at all.

3.12 Practical activities

Each of Practical activities 1 to 4 requires you to obtain data for two or more different groups. For Practical activity 5 you are provided with the data.

For Practical activities 1 to 4 analyse the data by

(a)   illustrating them in a way which allows you to compare the distributions of the groups;

(b)   choosing suitable measures of location and spread for representing the groups and finding their values;

(c)   comparing the results of (a) and (b) for the groups and commenting on them.

1 Wastepaper   Select a student and ask them to try to throw a ball of paper into a wastepaper bin about 4 metres away with their 'natural' or stronger throwing arm. Ask them to repeat this until they are successful, and record the total number of attempts needed. Repeat this experiment with about 30 students.

Repeat this whole procedure with a second group of students but ask them to use their 'weaker' arm.

2 Age distributions   From the internet or the library obtain data giving the age distribution of the population of your town or country for males and for females.

3 Newspapers   Does the length of the sentences in a newspaper vary from one paper to another?

Choose two or more newspapers, preferably with different styles of journalism, and for each newspaper count the number of words per sentence for at least 100 sentences. (You should ignore the headlines.)

(Alternatively you could compare the styles of different authors.)

4 Just a minute!   How well can people estimate time?

Ask at least 90 people to estimate a time interval of one minute. You will need to decide on a standard procedure for doing this. Record the value of the estimate to the nearest second. Have three distinct groups of at least 30 people, for example children of two different ages and adults.

5 Exam performance   The data set below refers to a group of students who started to study A-level mathematics at the same time. There are three variables. These are: 'Gender', where 'F' denotes female and 'M' denotes male; 'Grade' which gives the grade obtained by the student in the International GCSE mathematics exam and 'Mark' which is the percentage which the student obtained in a test taken at the end of the first term of A-level study.

By means of appropriate diagrams and calculations, investigate (a) possible differences in exam performance between genders, (b) a possible relationship between IGCSE grade and test mark.

Gender	Grade	Mark	Gender	Grade	Mark	Gender	Grade	Mark
M	B	86	M	B	88	M	A	48
F	B	41	F	A*	89	M	A	67
M	B	58	F	A	76	F	B	59
F	B	50	M	B	59	M	A	50
F	B	70	M	B	65	F	A*	52
M	A	62	F	B	82	M	A	52
M	B	56	M	A*	100	M	A*	55
M	A*	74	M	A*	59	F	A	93
M	A	43	F	A	74	M	A	71
F	B	48	M	A*	62	F	B	66
M	B	54	F	A	92	F	B	50
M	B	67	F	A*	67	F	A	71
M	A*	54	M	A	63	F	A	84
M	B	69	F	A	83	F	B	67
M	A	64	F	B	72	F	B	83
M	A	73	F	B	75	M	A*	87
M	A*	73	F	A	64	M	A*	82
F	A	51	F	A	65	M	A*	97
M	A	64	F	B	56	M	B	54
M	A	74	F	A	57	F	A	85
F	B	64	F	A*	91	M	A	82

Miscellaneous exercise 3

1   Seven mature robins (*Erithacus rubecula*) were caught and their wingspans were measured. The results, in centimetres, were as follows.

    23.1   22.7   22.1   24.2   23.9   20.9   25.2

Here are the corresponding figures for seven mature house sparrows (*Passer domesticos*).

    22.6   24.1   23.5   21.8   21.0   24.4   22.8

Find the mean and standard deviation of each species' wingspan, and use these statistics to compare the two sets of figures.

2   The depth of water in a lake was measured at 50 different points on the surface of the lake. The depths, x metres, are summarised by $\sum x = 934.5$ and $\sum x^2 = 19\,275.81$.

    (a)   Find the mean and variance of the depths.

    (b)   Some weeks later the water level in the lake rose by $0.23\,\text{m}$. What would be the mean and variance of the depths taken at the same points on the lake as before?

3   The following histograms are of two sets of 100 weights.

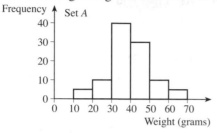 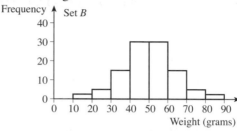

    (a)   Which set has the greater mean?   (b)   Which set has the greater variance?

    (c)   Estimate the mean and variance of Set A.   (d)   Why are your answers to (c) estimates?

4   The lengths of 120 nails of nominal length $3\,\text{cm}$ were measured, each correct to the nearest $0.05\,\text{cm}$. The results are summarised in the following table.

Length (cm)	2.85	2.90	2.95	3.00	3.05	3.10	3.15
Frequency	1	11	27	41	26	12	2

    (a)   Draw a box-and-whisker plot of these results, taking the extremes as $2.825\,\text{cm}$ and $3.175\,\text{cm}$.

    (b)   Estimate the standard deviation.

    (c)   It is claimed that for a roughly symmetrical distribution the statistic obtained by dividing the interquartile range by the standard deviation is approximately 1.3. Calculate the value of this statistic for these data, and comment.

5   Three statistics students, Ali, Les and Sam, spent the day fishing. They caught three different types of fish and recorded the type and mass (correct to the nearest $0.01\,\text{kg}$) of each fish caught. At 4 p.m. they summarised the results as follows.

	Number of fish by type			All fish caught	
	Perch	Tench	Roach	Mean mass (kg)	Standard deviation (kg)
Ali	2	3	7	1.07	0.42
Les	6	2	8	0.76	0.27
Sam	1	0	1	1.00	0

    (a)   State how you can deduce that the mass of each fish caught by Sam was $1.00\,\text{kg}$.

    (b)   The winner was the person who had caught the greatest total mass of fish by 4 p.m. Determine who was the winner, showing your working.

    (c)   Before leaving the waterside, Sam catches one more fish and weighs it. He then announces that if this extra fish is included with the other two fish he caught, the standard deviation is $1.00\,\text{kg}$. Find the mass of this extra fish.   (OCR)

6 The heights of 94 policemen based at a city police station were measured, and the results (in metres) are summarised in the following table.

Height (m)	1.65–1.69	1.70–1.74	1.75–1.79	1.80–1.84	1.85–1.89
Frequency	2	4	11	23	38

Height (m)	1.90–1.94	1.95–1.99	2.00–2.04	2.05–2.09
Frequency	9	4	2	1

(a) Draw a cumulative frequency diagram and estimate the median and quartiles.

(b) What do the values found in part (a) indicate about the shape of the distribution?

(c) Estimate the mean and standard deviation of the heights.

(d) A possible measure of skewness is $\dfrac{3(\bar{x} - Q_2)}{\text{standard deviation}}$ with the usual notation.

Calculate this number and state how it confirms your answer to part (b).

7 The diagram shows a cumulative frequency curve for the lengths of telephone calls from a house during the first six months of last year.

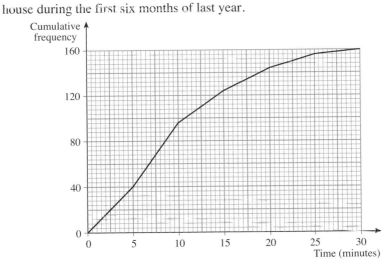

(a) Find the median and interquartile range.

(b) Construct a histogram with six equal intervals to illustrate the data.

(c) Use the frequency distribution associated with your histogram to estimate the mean length of call.

(d) State whether each of the following is true or false.

(i) The distribution of these call times is skewed.

(ii) The majority of the calls last longer than 6 minutes.

(iii) The majority of the calls last between 5 and 10 minutes.

(iv) The majority of the calls are shorter than the mean length.

8 The following table gives the ages in completed years of the 141 persons in a town involved in road accidents during a particular year.

Age (years)	12–15	16–20	21–25	26–30	31–40	41–50	51–70
Frequency	15	48	28	17	14	7	12

Working in years, and giving your answers to 1 decimal place, calculate estimates of

(a) the mean and standard deviation of the ages,

(b) the median age.

Which do you consider to be the better representative average of the distribution, the mean or the median? Give a reason for your answer.

4 Probability

This chapter is about calculating with probabilities. When you have completed it, you should

- know what a 'sample space' is
- know the difference between an 'outcome' and an 'event' and be able to calculate the probability of an event from the probabilities of the outcomes in the sample space
- be able to use the addition law for mutually exclusive events
- know the multiplication law of conditional probability, and be able to use tree diagrams
- know the multiplication law for independent events.

4.1 Assigning probability

In many situations you may be unsure of the outcome of some activity or experiment, although you know what the possible outcomes are. For example, you do not know what number you will get when you roll a dice, but you do know that you will get 1, 2, 3, 4, 5 or 6. You know that if you toss a coin twice, then the possible outcomes are (H,H), (H,T), (T,H) and (T,T). If you are testing a transistor to see if it is defective, then you know that the possible outcomes are 'defective' and 'not defective'.

The list of all the possible outcomes is called the **sample space** of the experiment. The list is usually written in curly brackets, $\{\ \}$.

Thus the sample space for rolling the dice is $\{1,2,3,4,5,6\}$, the sample space for tossing a coin twice is $\{(H,H),(H,T),(T,H),(T,T)\}$, and the sample space for testing a transistor is $\{\text{defective, not defective}\}$.

It is conventional when writing pairs of things like H,H to put them in brackets, like coordinates.

Each of the outcomes of an experiment has a probability assigned to it. Sometimes you can assign the probability using symmetry. For example, the sample space for throwing a dice is $\{1,2,3,4,5,6\}$, and you would assign each outcome the probability $\frac{1}{6}$, in the belief that the dice is fair, and that each outcome is equally likely. This is the usual method for calculations about games of chance.

Now suppose that the dice is not fair, so that you cannot use the method of symmetry for assigning probabilities. In this case you will have to carry out an experiment and throw the dice a large number of times. Suppose that you throw the dice 1000 times and the frequencies of the six possible outcomes in the sample space are as in Table 4.1.

Outcome	1	2	3	4	5	6
Frequency	100	216	182	135	170	197

Table 4.1. Frequencies for the outcomes when rolling a dice 1000 times.

You would then assign the probabilities $\frac{100}{1000}$, $\frac{216}{1000}$, $\frac{182}{1000}$, $\frac{135}{1000}$, $\frac{170}{1000}$ and $\frac{197}{1000}$ to the outcomes $1, 2, 3, 4, 5$ and 6 respectively. These are called the **relative frequencies** of the outcomes, and you can use them as estimates of the probabilities. You should realise that if you were to roll the dice another 1000 times, the results would probably not be exactly the same, but you would hope that they would not be too different. You could roll the dice more times and hope to improve the relative frequency as an approximation to the probability.

Sometimes you cannot assign a probability by using symmetry or by carrying out an experiment. For example, there is a probability that my house will be struck by lightning next year, and I could insure against this happening. The insurance company will have to have a probability in mind when it calculates the premium I have to pay, but it cannot calculate it by symmetry, or carry out an experiment for a few years. It will assign its probability using its experience of such matters and its records.

When **probabilities** are assigned to the outcomes in a sample space,

- each probability must lie between 0 and 1 inclusive, and
- the sum of all the probabilities assigned must be equal to 1.

Example 4.1.1

How would you assign probabilities to the following experiments or activities?

(a) Choosing a card from a standard pack of playing cards.

(b) The combined experiment of tossing a coin and rolling a dice.

(c) Tossing a drawing pin on to a table to see whether it lands point down or point up.

(d) Four international football teams, Argentina, Cameroon, Nigeria, Turkey (A, C, N and T), play a knockout tournament. Who will be the winner?

(a) The sample space would consist of the list of the 52 playing cards $\{AC, 2C, 3C, \dots, KS\}$ in some order. (Here A means ace, C means clubs, and so on.) Assuming that these cards are equally likely to be picked, the probability assigned to each of them is $\frac{1}{52}$.

(b) The sample space is $\begin{Bmatrix} (H,1),(H,2),(H,3),(H,4),(H,5),(H,6), \\ (T,1),\ (T,2),\ (T,3),\ (T,4),\ (T,5),\ (T,6) \end{Bmatrix}$, and each of the outcomes would be assigned a probability of $\frac{1}{12}$.

(c) The sample space is $\{\text{point down, point up}\}$. You would need to carry out an experiment to assign probabilities.

(d) The sample space is $\{A \text{ wins, } C \text{ wins, } N \text{ wins, } T \text{ wins}\}$. You have to assign probabilities subjectively, according to your knowledge of the teams and the game. The probabilities p_A, p_C, p_N and p_T must all be non-negative and satisfy $p_A + p_C + p_N + p_T = 1$.

4.2 Probabilities of events

Sometimes you may be interested, not in one particular outcome, but in two or three or more of them. For example, suppose you toss a coin twice. You might be interested in whether the result is the same both times. The list of outcomes in which you are interested is called an **event**, and is written in curly brackets. The event that both tosses of the coin give the same result is $\{(H,H),(T,T)\}$. Events are often denoted by capital letters. Thus if A denotes this event, then $A = \{(H,H),(T,T)\}$. An event can be just one outcome, or a list of outcomes or even no outcomes at all.

You can find the probability of an event by looking at the sample space and adding the probabilities of the outcomes which make up the event. For example, if you were tossing a coin twice, the sample space would be $\{(H,H),(H,T),(T,H),(T,T)\}$. There are four outcomes, each equally likely, so they each have probability $\frac{1}{4}$. The event A consists of the two outcomes (H,H) and (T,T), so the probability of A is $\frac{1}{4} + \frac{1}{4}$, or $\frac{1}{2}$.

This is an example of a general rule.

> The probability, $P(A)$, of an event A is the sum of the probabilities of the outcomes which make up A.

Often a list of outcomes can be constructed in such a way that all of them are equally likely. If all the outcomes are equally likely, then the probability of any event A can be found by finding the number of outcomes which make up event A and dividing by the total number of outcomes. When the outcomes are not equally likely, then the probability of any event has to be found by adding the individual probabilities of all the outcomes which make up event A.

Example 4.2.1
A fair 20-sided dice has eight faces coloured red, ten coloured blue and two coloured green. The dice is rolled.
(a) Find the probability that the bottom face is red.
(b) Let A be the event that the bottom face is not red. Find the probability of A.

(a) Each face has an equal probability of being the bottom face: as there are 20 faces, each of them has a probability of $\frac{1}{20}$. There are eight red faces, each with probability $\frac{1}{20}$, so $P(\text{red}) = \frac{8}{20} = \frac{2}{5}$.

(b) $P(A) = P(\text{blue or green}) = P(\text{blue}) + P(\text{green}) = \frac{10}{20} + \frac{2}{20} = \frac{12}{20} = \frac{3}{5}$.

Example 4.2.2
The numbers $1, 2, \dots, 9$ are written on separate cards. The cards are shuffled and the top one is turned over. Calculate the probability that the number on this card is prime.

The sample space for this activity is $\{1, 2, 3, 4, 5, 6, 7, 8, 9\}$. As each outcome is equally likely each has probability $\frac{1}{9}$.

Let B be the event that the card turned over is prime. Then $B = \{2, 3, 5, 7\}$.

$P(B) =$ sum of the probabilities of the outcomes in $B = \frac{4}{9}$.

Example 4.2.3

A circular wheel is divided into three equal sectors, numbered
1, 2 and 3, as shown in Fig. 4.2. The wheel is spun twice.
Each time, the score is the number to which the black arrow
points. Calculate the probabilities of the following events:

(a) both scores are the same as each other,

(b) neither score is a 2,

(c) at least one of the scores is a 3,

(d) neither score is a 2 and both scores are the same,

(e) neither score is a 2 or both scores are the same.

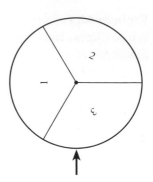

Fig. 4.2

Start by writing down the sample space.

$$\{(1,1),(1,2),(1,3),(2,1),(2,2),(2,3),(3,1),(3,2),(3,3)\}$$

Each outcome has probability $\frac{1}{9}$.

(a) Let A be the event that both scores are the same, so $A = \{(1,1),(2,2),(3,3)\}$.

 $P(A)$ = sum of the probabilities of the outcomes in $A = \frac{3}{9} = \frac{1}{3}$.

(b) Let B be the event that neither score is a 2, so $B = \{(1,1),(1,3),(3,1),(3,3)\}$.

 $P(B)$ = sum of the probabilities of the outcomes in $B = \frac{4}{9}$.

(c) Let C be the event that at least one of the scores is a 3, so
 $C = \{(1,3),(2,3),(3,1),(3,2),(3,3)\}$. Then $P(C) = \frac{5}{9}$.

(d) Let D be the event that neither score is a 2 *and* both scores are the same, so
 $D = \{(1,1),(3,3)\}$. Then $P(D) = \frac{2}{9}$.

(e) Let E be the event that neither score is a 2 *or* both scores are the same, so
 $E = \{(1,1),(1,3),(3,1),(3,3),(2,2)\}$. Then $P(E) = \frac{5}{9}$.

Example 4.2.4

Jafar has three playing cards, two queens and a king. Tandi selects one of the cards at
random, and returns it to Jafar, who shuffles the cards. Tandi then selects a second card.
Tandi wins if both cards selected are kings. Find the probability that Tandi wins.

Imagine that the queens are different, and call them Q_1 and Q_2, and call the king
K. Then the sample space is:

$$\{(Q_1,Q_1),(Q_1,Q_2),(Q_1,K),(Q_2,Q_1),(Q_2,Q_2),(Q_2,K),(K,Q_1),(K,Q_2),(K,K)\}.$$

Each outcome has probability $\frac{1}{9}$.

Let T be the event that Tandi wins. Then $T = \{(K,K)\}$ and

 $P(T)$ = sum of the probabilities of the outcomes in $T = \frac{1}{9}$.

The probability that Tandi wins a prize is $\frac{1}{9}$.

Although the event that Tandi wins is just a single outcome, it is still listed in curly brackets.

Example 4.2.5
A dice with six faces has been made from brass and aluminium, and is not fair. The probability of a 6 is $\frac{1}{4}$, the probabilities of 2, 3, 4, and 5 are each $\frac{1}{6}$, and the probability of 1 is $\frac{1}{12}$. The dice is rolled. Find the probability of rolling (a) 1 or 6, (b) an even number.

(a) $P(1 \text{ or } 6) = P(1) + P(6) = \frac{1}{12} + \frac{1}{4} = \frac{1}{3}$.

(b) $P(\text{an even number}) = P(2 \text{ or } 4 \text{ or } 6) = P(2) + P(4) + P(6) = \frac{1}{6} + \frac{1}{6} + \frac{1}{4} = \frac{7}{12}$.

Sometimes it is worth using a different approach to calculating the probability of an event.

Example 4.2.6
You draw two cards from an ordinary pack. Find the probability that they are not both kings.

The problem is that the sample space has a large number of outcomes. In fact there are 52 ways of picking the first card, and then 51 ways of picking the second, so there $52 \times 51 = 2652$ possibilities. The sample space therefore consists of 2652 outcomes, each of which is assigned a probability $\frac{1}{2652}$.

To avoid counting all the outcomes which are not both kings, it is easier to look at the number of outcomes which *are* both kings.

Writing the first card to be drawn as the first of the pair, these outcomes are (KC,KD), (KD,KC), (KC,KH), (KH,KC), (KC,KS), (KS,KC), (KD,KH), (KH,KD), (KD,KS), (KS,KD), (KH,KS) and (KS,KH).

There are thus 12 outcomes that are both kings. So the number which are not both kings is $2652 - 12 = 2640$. All 2640 of these outcomes have probability $\frac{1}{2652}$, so $P(\text{not both kings}) = \frac{2640}{2652} = \frac{220}{221}$.

It is always worth watching for this short cut, and it is also useful to have some language to describe it. If A is an event, the event 'not A' is the event consisting of those outcomes in the sample space which are not in A. Since the sum of the probabilities assigned to outcomes in the sample space is 1,

$$P(A) + P(\text{not } A) = 1.$$

The event 'not A' is called the **complement** of the event A. The symbol A' is used to denote the complement of A.

> If A is an event, then A' is the complement of A, and
>
> $$P(A) + P(A') = 1. \qquad (4.1)$$

4.3 Addition of probabilities

Consider a game in which a fair cubical dice with faces numbered 1 to 6 is rolled twice. A prize is won if the total score on the two rolls is 4 or if each individual score is over 4.

You can write the sample space of all possible outcomes as 36 equally likely pairs,

$$\left\{ \begin{array}{cccccc} (1,1) & (1,2) & (1,3) & (1,4) & (1,5) & (1,6) \\ (2,1) & (2,2) & & \cdots & & (2,6) \\ \vdots & \vdots & & & & \vdots \\ (6,1) & (6,2) & & \cdots & & (6,6) \end{array} \right\},$$

each having probability $\frac{1}{36}$.

Let A be the event that the total score is 4 and let B be the event that each roll of the dice gives a score over 4.

Then $A = \{(1,3),(2,2),(3,1)\}$, and $B = \{(5,5),(5,6),(6,5),(6,6)\}$, so

$$P(A) = \tfrac{3}{36} = \tfrac{1}{12} \quad \text{and} \quad P(B) = \tfrac{4}{36} = \tfrac{1}{9}.$$

A prize is won if A happens *or* if B happens, so $P(\text{a prize is won}) = P(A \text{ or } B)$.

This means that a prize will be won if any of the outcomes in $\{(1,3),(2,2),(3,1),(5,5),(5,6),(6,5),(6,6)\}$ occurs. Therefore

$$P(\text{a prize is won}) = P(A \text{ or } B) = \tfrac{7}{36}.$$

The key point is that $P(A \text{ or } B) = P(A) + P(B)$. The word 'or' is important. Whenever you see it, it should suggest to you the idea of adding probabilities. Notice, however, that A and B have no outcomes which are common to both events. Two events which have no outcomes common to both are called **mutually exclusive** events. So the result $P(A \text{ or } B) = P(A) + P(B)$ is known as the **addition law of mutually exclusive events**.

The addition law of mutually exclusive events can be extended to apply to more than two events if none of the events has any outcome in common with any of the other events.

If $A_1, A_2, \ldots, A_n$ are n mutually exclusive events, then

$$P(A_1 \text{ or } A_2 \text{ or } \ldots \text{ or } A_n) = P(A_1) + P(A_2) + \ldots + P(A_n). \qquad (4.2)$$

The addition law needs to be modified when the events are not mutually exclusive. Here is an example.

Example 4.3.1

Two fair dice are thrown. A prize is won if the total is 10 or if each individual score is over 4. Find the probability that a prize is won.

The sample space is the same set of 36 pairs listed at the top of this page.

Let C be the event that the total score is 10, so $C = \{(5,5),(4,6),(6,4)\}$.

Let B be the event that each roll of the dice results in a score over 4, as before, so $B = \{(5,5),(5,6),(6,5),(6,6)\}$.

Therefore $P(C) = \frac{3}{36} = \frac{1}{12}$ and $P(B) = \frac{4}{36} = \frac{1}{9}$.

A prize is won if B or C occurs, and the possible outcomes which make up this event are $\{(5,5),(4,6),(6,4),(5,6),(6,5),(6,6)\}$.

Therefore $P(B \text{ or } C) = \frac{6}{36} = \frac{1}{6}$. But $P(B) + P(C) = \frac{1}{12} + \frac{1}{9} = \frac{7}{36}$, so in this case $P(B \text{ or } C) \neq P(B) + P(C)$.

For events such as B and C, which are not mutually exclusive, the addition rule given by Equation (4.2) is not valid.

The rule can be modified so that it applies to any two events. This will be studied later in the course. Can you see how to modify the rule?

Exercise 4A

1   A fair dice is thrown once. Find the probabilities that the score is

(a) bigger than 3,   (b) bigger than or equal to 3,

(c) an odd number,   (d) a prime number,

(e) bigger than 3 and a prime number,   (f) bigger than 3 or a prime number or both,

(g) bigger than 3 or a prime number, but not both.

2   A card is chosen at random from an ordinary pack. Find the probability that it is

(a) red,   (b) a picture card (K, Q, J),

(c) an honour $(A, K, Q, J, 10)$,   (d) a red honour,

(e) red, or an honour, or both.

3   Two fair dice are thrown simultaneously. Find the probability that

(a) the total is 7,   (b) the total is at least 8,

(c) the total is a prime number,   (d) neither of the scores is a 6,

(e) at least one of the scores is a 6,   (f) exactly one of the scores is a 6,

(g) the two scores are the same,

(h) the difference between the scores is an odd number.

4   A fair dice is thrown twice. If the second score is the same as the first, the second throw does not count, and the dice is thrown again until a different score is obtained. The two different scores are added to give a total.

List the possible outcomes.

Find the probability that

(a) the total is 7,   (b) the total is at least 8,

(c) at least one of the two scores is a 6,   (d) the first score is higher than the last.

5 A bag contains ten counters, of which six are red and four are green. A counter is chosen at random; its colour is noted and it is replaced in the bag. A second counter is then chosen at random. Find the probabilities that

    (a) both counters are red,   (b) both counters are green,

    (c) just one counter is red,   (d) at least one counter is red,

    (e) the second counter is red.

6 Draw a bar chart to illustrate the probabilities of the various total scores when two fair dice are thrown simultaneously.

4.4 Conditional probability

Consider a class of 30 pupils, of whom 17 are girls and 13 are boys. Suppose further that five of the girls and six of the boys are left-handed, and all of the remaining pupils are right-handed. If a pupil is selected at random from the whole class, then the chance that he or she is left-handed is $\dfrac{6+5}{30} = \dfrac{11}{30}$. However, suppose now that a pupil is selected at random from the girls in the class. The chance that this girl will be left-handed is $\dfrac{5}{17}$. So being told that the selected pupil is a girl alters the chance that the pupil will be left-handed. This is an example of **conditional probability**. The probability has been calculated on the basis of an extra 'condition' which you have been given.

There is some notation which is used for conditional probability. Let L be the event that a left-handed person is chosen, and let G be the event that a girl is chosen. The symbol $P(L \mid G)$ stands for the probability that the pupil chosen is left-handed *given* that the pupil chosen is a girl. So in this case $P(L \mid G) = \frac{5}{17}$, although $P(L) = \frac{11}{30}$.

It is useful to find a connection between conditional probabilities (where some extra information is known) and probabilities where you have no extra information. Notice that the probability $P(L \mid G)$ can be written as

$$P(L \mid G) = \tfrac{5}{17} = \frac{5/30}{17/30}.$$

The fraction in the numerator is the probability of choosing a left-handed girl if you are selecting from the whole class, and the denominator is the probability of choosing a girl if you are selecting from the whole class. In symbols this could be written as

$$P(L \mid G) = \frac{P(L \text{ and } G)}{P(G)}.$$

This equation can be generalised to any two events A and B for which $P(A) > 0$.

If A and B are two events and $P(A) > 0$, then the **conditional probability** of B given A is

$$P(B \mid A) = \frac{P(A \text{ and } B)}{P(A)}. \qquad (4.3)$$

Rewriting this equation gives

$$P(A \text{ and } B) = P(A) \times P(B \mid A), \qquad (4.4)$$

which is known as the **multiplication law of probability**.

Suppose a jar contains seven red discs and four white discs. Two discs are selected without replacement. ('Without replacement' means that the first disc is not put back in the jar before the second disc is selected.) Let R_1 be the event {the first disc is red}, let R_2 be the event {the second disc is red}, let W_1 be the event {the first disc is white} and let W_2 be the event {the second disc is white}. To find the probability that both of the discs are red you want to find $P(R_1 \text{ and } R_2)$.

Using the multiplication law, Equation 4.4, to find this probability,

$$P(R_1 \text{ and } R_2) = P(R_1) \times P(R_2 \mid R_1).$$

Now $P(R_1) = \frac{7}{11}$, since there are 7 red discs in the jar and 11 discs altogether. The probability $P(R_2 \mid R_1)$ appears more complicated, but it represents the probability that the second disc selected is red *given* that the first disc was red. To find this just imagine that one red disc has already been removed from the jar. The jar now contains 6 red discs and 4 white discs. The probability *now* of getting a red disc is $P(R_2 \mid R_1) = \frac{6}{10}$.

Therefore, using the multiplication law,

$$P(R_1 \text{ and } R_2) = P(R_1) \times P(R_2 \mid R_1) = \frac{7}{11} \times \frac{6}{10}.$$

You can represent all the possible outcomes when two discs are selected from the jar in a **tree diagram**, as in Fig. 4.3.

Notice that probabilities on the first 'layer' of branches give the chances of getting a red disc or a white disc when the first disc is selected. The probabilities on the second 'layer' are the conditional probabilities. You can use the tree diagram to calculate the probability of any of the four possibilities, R_1 and R_2, R_1 and W_2, W_1 and R_2 and W_1 and W_2.

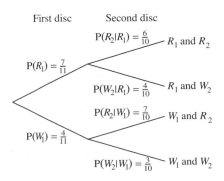

Fig. 4.3. Tree diagram to show the outcomes when two discs are drawn without replacement from a jar.

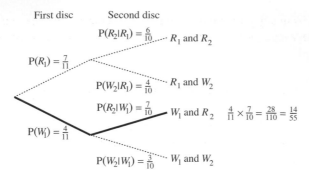

Fig. 4.4. Tree diagram to show the calculation of $P(W_1 \text{ and } R_2)$.

To do this you move along the appropriate route, multiplying the probabilities, as shown in Fig. 4.4. For example, to find the probability of getting a white disc followed by a red disc, $P(W_1 \text{ and } R_2)$, trace that route on the tree diagram and multiply the relevant probabilities.

You could also have found $P(W_1 \text{ and } R_2)$ by using the multiplication law.

$$P(W_1 \text{ and } R_2) = P(W_1) \times P(R_2 \mid W_1) = \tfrac{4}{11} \times \tfrac{7}{10} = \tfrac{14}{55}.$$

You can now use the addition and multiplication laws together to find the probability of more complex events. For example,

P(both discs are the same colour) $= P\big((R_1 \text{ and } R_2) \text{ or } (W_1 \text{ and } W_2)\big)$.

The event R_1 and R_2 is the event that both discs are red, and the event W_1 and W_2 is the event that both discs are white. These events cannot both be satisfied at the same time, so they must be mutually exclusive. Therefore you can use the addition law, giving

$$P\big((R_1 \text{ and } R_2) \text{ or } (W_1 \text{ and } W_2)\big) = P(R_1 \text{ and } R_2) + P(W_1 \text{ and } W_2)$$
$$= P(R_1) \times P(R_2 \mid R_1) + P(W_1) \times P(W_2 \mid W_1)$$
$$= \tfrac{7}{11} \times \tfrac{6}{10} + \tfrac{4}{11} \times \tfrac{3}{10} = \tfrac{42}{110} + \tfrac{12}{110} = \tfrac{54}{110} = \tfrac{27}{55}.$$

You can also use the tree diagram for this calculation. This time there is more than one route through the tree diagram which satisfies the event whose probability is to be found. As before, you follow the appropriate routes and multiply the probabilities. You then add all the resulting products, as in Fig. 4.5.

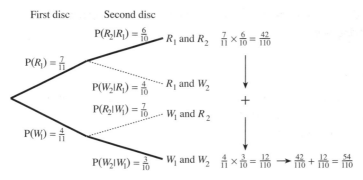

Fig. 4.5. Tree diagram to show the calculation of $P\big((R_1 \text{ and } R_2) \text{ or } (W_1 \text{ and } W_2)\big)$.

You can use tree diagrams in any problem in which there is a clear sequence to the outcomes, including problems which are not necessarily to do with selection of objects.

Example 4.4.1

Weather records indicate that the probability that a particular day is dry is $\frac{3}{10}$. Arid F.C. is a football team whose record of success is better on dry days than on wet days. The probability that Arid win on a dry day is $\frac{3}{8}$, whereas the probability that they win on a wet day is $\frac{3}{11}$. Arid are due to play their next match on Saturday.

(a) What is the probability that Arid will win?

(b) Three Saturdays ago Arid won their match. What is the probability that it was a dry day?

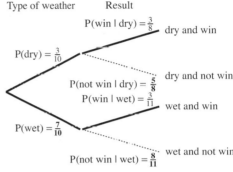

Here the sequence involves first the type of weather and then the result of the football match. The tree diagram in Fig. 4.6 illustrates the information.

Notice that the probabilities in bold type were not given in the statement of the question. They have been calculated by using equations like $P(\text{wet}) + P(\text{dry}) = 1$.

Fig. 4.6. Tree diagram for football results.

(a) $P(\text{win}) = P\big((\text{dry and win}) \text{ or } (\text{wet and win})\big)$

$\qquad = P(\text{dry and win}) + P(\text{wet and win})$

$\qquad = P(\text{dry}) \times P(\text{win} \mid \text{dry}) + P(\text{wet}) \times P(\text{win} \mid \text{wet})$

$\qquad = \frac{3}{10} \times \frac{3}{8} + \frac{7}{10} \times \frac{3}{11} = \frac{9}{80} + \frac{21}{110} = \frac{267}{880}.$

(b) In this case you have been asked to calculate a conditional probability. However, here the sequence of events has been reversed and you want to find $P(\text{dry} \mid \text{win})$.

$$P(\text{dry} \mid \text{win}) = \frac{P(\text{dry and win})}{P(\text{win})} = \frac{9/80}{267/880} = \frac{99}{267}.$$

You can think of $P(\text{dry} \mid \text{win})$ *as being the proportion of times that the weather is dry out of all the times that Arid win.*

4.5 Independent events

Consider again a jar containing seven red discs and four white discs. Two discs are selected, but this time with replacement. This means that the first disc is returned to the jar before the second disc is selected.

Let R_1 be the event that the first disc is red, R_2 be the event that the second disc is red, W_1 be the event that the first disc is white and W_2 be the event that the second disc is white. You can represent the selection of the two discs with Fig. 4.7, a tree diagram similar to Fig. 4.3 but with different probabilities on the second 'layer'.

The probability $P(R_2)$ that the second disc is red can also be found using the addition and multiplication laws.

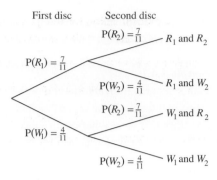

First disc   Second disc

Fig 4.7. Tree diagram to show the outcomes when two discs are drawn with replacement from a jar.

$$P(R_2) = P((R_1 \text{ and } R_2) \text{ or } P(W_1 \text{ and } R_2))$$
$$= P(R_1 \text{ and } R_2) + P(W_1 \text{ and } R_2) = \tfrac{7}{11} \times \tfrac{7}{11} + \tfrac{4}{11} \times \tfrac{7}{11} = \tfrac{7}{11}.$$

In this case $P(R_2) = P(R_2 \mid R_1)$, which means that the first disc's being red has no effect on the chance of the second disc being red. This is what you would expect, since the first disc was replaced before the second was removed. Two events A and B for which $P(B \mid A) = P(B)$ are called **independent**. Independent events have no effect upon one another.

Recall also that, from the definition of conditional probability, $P(B \mid A) = \dfrac{P(A \text{ and } B)}{P(A)}$.

So when you equate the two expressions for $P(B \mid A)$ for independent events, you get

$$\dfrac{P(A \text{ and } B)}{P(A)} = P(B), \quad \text{which when rearranged gives} \quad P(A \text{ and } B) = P(A) \times P(B).$$

> Independent events are events which have no effect on one another.
> For two independents events A and B,
>
> $$P(A \text{ and } B) = P(A) \times P(B). \tag{4.5}$$
>
> This result is called the **multiplication law for independent events.**

Example 4.5.1

In a carnival game, a contestant has to first spin a fair coin and then roll a fair cubical dice whose faces are numbered 1 to 6. The contestant wins a prize if the coin shows heads and the dice score is below 3. Find the probability that a contestant wins a prize.

$P(\text{prize won}) = P((\text{coin shows heads}) \text{ and } (\text{dice score is lower than 3})).$

The event that the coin shows heads and the event that the dice score is lower than 3 are independent, because the score on the dice can have no effect on the result of the spin of the coin. Therefore the multiplication law for independent events can be used.

$P(\text{prize won}) = P((\text{coin shows heads}) \text{ and } (\text{dice score is lower than 3}))$
$= P(\text{coin shows heads}) \times P(\text{dice score is lower than 3}) = \tfrac{1}{2} \times \tfrac{2}{6} = \tfrac{1}{6}.$

The law of multiplication for independent events can be extended to more than two events, provided they are all independent of one another.

> If $A_1, A_2, \ldots, A_n$ are n independent events, then
>
> $$P(A_1 \text{ and } A_2 \text{ and } \ldots \text{ and } A_n) = P(A_1) \times P(A_2) \times \ldots \times P(A_n). \qquad (4.6)$$

Example 4.5.2

A fair cubical dice with faces numbered 1 to 6 is thrown four times. Find the probability that three of the four throws result in a 6.

You can use the addition law of mutually exclusive events and the multiplication law of independent events to break the event {three of the four scores are 6} down into smaller sub-events whose probabilities you can easily determine:

$$P(\text{three of the scores are 6s}) = P\begin{pmatrix} (6_1 \text{ and } 6_2 \text{ and } 6_3 \text{ and } N_4) \text{ or} \\ (6_1 \text{ and } 6_2 \text{ and } N_3 \text{ and } 6_4) \text{ or} \\ (6_1 \text{ and } N_2 \text{ and } 6_3 \text{ and } 6_4) \text{ or} \\ (N_1 \text{ and } 6_2 \text{ and } 6_3 \text{ and } 6_4) \end{pmatrix},$$

where, for example, 6_1 means that the first score was a 6 and N_3 means that the third score was not a 6.

Using the addition and multiplication laws,

$$P(\text{three of the scores are 6s}) = P\begin{pmatrix} (6_1 \text{ and } 6_2 \text{ and } 6_3 \text{ and } N_4) \text{ or} \\ (6_1 \text{ and } 6_2 \text{ and } N_3 \text{ and } 6_4) \text{ or} \\ (6_1 \text{ and } N_2 \text{ and } 6_3 \text{ and } 6_4) \text{ or} \\ (N_1 \text{ and } 6_2 \text{ and } 6_3 \text{ and } 6_4) \end{pmatrix}$$

$$= P(6_1 \text{ and } 6_2 \text{ and } 6_3 \text{ and } N_4)$$
$$+ P(6_1 \text{ and } 6_2 \text{ and } N_3 \text{ and } 6_4)$$
$$+ P(6_1 \text{ and } N_2 \text{ and } 6_3 \text{ and } 6_4)$$
$$+ P(N_1 \text{ and } 6_2 \text{ and } 6_3 \text{ and } 6_4)$$

$$= P(6_1) \times P(6_2) \times P(6_3) \times P(N_4)$$
$$+ P(6_1) \times P(6_2) \times P(N_3) \times P(6_4)$$
$$+ P(6_1) \times P(N_2) \times P(6_3) \times P(6_4)$$
$$+ P(N_1) \times P(6_2) \times P(6_3) \times P(6_4)$$

$$= \left(\tfrac{1}{6} \times \tfrac{1}{6} \times \tfrac{1}{6} \times \tfrac{5}{6}\right) + \left(\tfrac{1}{6} \times \tfrac{1}{6} \times \tfrac{5}{6} \times \tfrac{1}{6}\right)$$
$$+ \left(\tfrac{1}{6} \times \tfrac{5}{6} \times \tfrac{1}{6} \times \tfrac{1}{6}\right) + \left(\tfrac{5}{6} \times \tfrac{1}{6} \times \tfrac{1}{6} \times \tfrac{1}{6}\right)$$

$$= 4 \times \left(\tfrac{1}{6}\right)^3 \times \tfrac{5}{6} = \tfrac{5}{324}.$$

4.6 Practical activities

1 Cylinder   When you throw a coin it is very unlikely to land on its edge (or curved surface). However, if you were to drop a soft-drinks can on the floor there is quite a good chance that it will land on its curved surface. Both the coin and the can are (nearly) cylindrical in shape.

(a) Find several cylinders for which the ratio of the height to the radius is different, and investigate how the ratio of height to radius affects the chance of a cylinder landing on its curved surface.

(b) Throw each cylinder 50 times and work out the experimental probability that the cylinder lands on its curved surface. Plot a graph of this experimental probability against the ratio of height to radius.

(c) For what ratio of height to radius would you estimate that the cylinder was equally likely to land on its curved surface as it is to land on one of its plane faces?

2 Buffon's needle   For this experiment you require a needle (or a similar object). On a sheet of paper rule parallel lines, separated by a distance equal to half the length of the needle. Place the sheet of paper on a table and throw the needle on to the paper 'at random'. Note whether the needle falls across a line. Repeat this 100 times in all. From your results find the experimental probability that the needle will fall across a line.

This experiment is named after the Comte de Buffon (1707–1788) who carried it out in order to obtain an estimate for π. It can be shown that the theoretical probability of the needle falling across a line is $\frac{2}{\pi}$. (For a proof see, for example, *Practical Statistics* by Mary Rouncefield and Peter Holmes, Macmillan, 1993). Use your results to obtain an estimate for π.

3 Cards

(a) Shuffle a pack of cards and pick a card at random. Record the identity of the card. Repeat this to give 50 selections in all, replacing the card and shuffling after every selection. From your data calculate the experimental probabilities of picking

(i) a red card,   (ii) an even score $\{2, 4, 6, 8, 10\}$,   (iii) a picture card $\{J, Q, K\}$.
Check whether the following statements are true for your experimental probabilities:

(b) P(even or picture) = P(even) + P(picture),

(c) P(even or red) = P(even) + P(red),   (d) P(even and red) = P(even) × P(red).
Compare with what you would expect theoretically.

Exercise 4B

1   A bag contains six red and four green counters. Two counters are drawn, without replacement. Use a carefully labelled tree diagram to find the probabilities that

(a) both counters are red,   (b) both counters are green,   (c)   just one counter is red,

(d) at least one counter is red,   (e) the second counter is red.

Compare your answers with those to Exercise 4A Question 5.

Does it make any difference to your answers to parts (a), (b), (c) and (d) if the two counters are drawn simultaneously rather than one after the other?

2 Two cards are drawn, without replacement, from an ordinary pack. Find the probabilities that

(a) both are picture cards (K, Q, J),

(b) neither is a picture card,

(c) at least one is a picture card,

(d) at least one is red.

3 Events A, B and C satisfy these conditions:

$$P(A) = 0.6, \quad P(B) = 0.8, \quad P(B \mid A) = 0.45, \quad P(B \text{ and } C) = 0.28.$$

Calculate

(a) $P(A \text{ and } B)$,

(b) $P(C \mid B)$,

(c) $P(A \mid B)$.

4 A class consists of seven boys and nine girls. Two different members of the class are chosen at random. A is the event {the first person is a girl}, and B is the event {the second person is a girl}. Find the probabilities of

(a) $B \mid A$,

(b) $B' \mid A$,

(c) $B \mid A'$

(d) $B' \mid A'$,

(e) B.

Is it true that

(f) $P(B \mid A) + P(B' \mid A) = 1$,

(g) $P(B \mid A) + P(B \mid A') = 1$?

5 A weather forecaster classifies all days as wet or dry. She estimates that the probability that 1 June next year is wet is 0.4. If any particular day in June is wet, the probability that the next day is wet is 0.6; otherwise the probability that the next day is wet is 0.3. Find the probability that, next year,

(a) the first two days of June are both wet,

(b) June 2nd is wet,

(c) at least one of the first three days of June is wet.

6 Two chess players, K1 and K2, are playing each other in a series of games. The probability that K1 wins the first game is 0.3. If K1 wins any game, the probability that he wins the next is 0.4; otherwise the probability is 0.2. Find the probability that K1 wins

(a) the first two games,

(b) at least one of the first two games,

(c) the first three games,

(d) exactly one of the first three games.

The result of any game can be a win for K1, a win for K2, or a draw. The probability that any one game is drawn is 0.5, independent of the result of all previous games. Find the probability that, after two games,

(e) K1 won the first and K2 the second,

(f) each won one game,

(g) each has won the same number of games.

7 A fair cubical dice is thrown four times. Find the probability that

(a) all four scores are 4 or more,

(b) at least one score is less than 4,

(c) at least one of the scores is a 6.

8 The Chevalier du Meré's Problem. A seventeenth-century French gambler, the Chevalier du Meré, had run out of takers for his bet that, when a fair cubical dice was thrown four times, at least one 6 would be scored. (See Question 7(c).) He therefore changed the game to throwing a pair of fair dice 24 times. What is the probability that, out of these 24 throws, at least one is a double 6?

9 The Birthday Problem. What is the probability that, out of 23 randomly chosen people, at least two share a birthday? Assume that all 365 days of the year are equally likely and ignore leap years. (Hint: find the probabilities that two people have different birthdays, that three people have different birthdays, and so on.)

10 Given that $P(A) = 0.75$, $P(B \mid A) = 0.8$ and $P(B \mid A') = 0.6$, calculate $P(B)$ and $P(A \mid B)$.

11* For any events A and B, write $P(A \text{ and } B)$ and $P(B)$ in terms of $P(A)$, $P(A')$, $P(B \mid A)$ and $P(B \mid A')$. Deduce Bayes' theorem: $P(A \mid B) = \dfrac{P(A)P(B \mid A)}{P(A)P(B \mid A) + P(A')P(B \mid A')}$.

12* The Doctor's Dilemma. It is known that, among all patients displaying a certain set of symptoms, the probability that they have a particular rare disease is 0.001. A test for the disease has been developed. The test shows a positive result on 98% of the patients who have the disease and on 3% of patients who do not have the disease.

The test is given to a particular patient displaying the symptoms, and it records a positive result. Find the probability that the patient has the disease. Comment on your answer.

13* The Prosecutor's Fallacy. An accused prisoner is on trial. The defence lawyer asserts that, in the absence of further evidence, the probability that the prisoner is guilty is 1 in a million. The prosecuting lawyer produces a further piece of evidence and asserts that, if the prisoner were guilty, the probability that this evidence would be obtained is 999 in 1000, and if he were not guilty it would be only 1 in 1000; in other words, $P(\text{evidence} \mid \text{guilty}) = 0.999$, and $P(\text{evidence} \mid \text{not guilty}) = 0.001$. Assuming that the court admits the legality of the evidence, and that both lawyers' figures are correct, what is the probability that the prisoner is guilty? Comment on your answer.

Miscellaneous exercise 4

1 Bag A contains 1 red ball and 1 black ball, and bag B contains 2 red balls; all four balls are indistinguishable apart from their colour. One ball is chosen at random from A and is transferred to B. One ball is then chosen at random from B and is transferred to A.

  (a) Draw a tree diagram to illustrate the possibilities for the colours of the balls transferred from A to B and then from B to A.

  (b) Find the probability that, after both transfers, the black ball is in bag A.   (OCR)

2 The probability that an event A occurs is $P(A) = 0.3$. The event B is independent of A and $P(B) = 0.4$.

  (a) Calculate $P(A \text{ or } B \text{ or both occur})$.

  Event C is defined to be the event that neither A nor B occurs.

  (b) Calculate $P(C \mid A')$, where A' is the event that A does not occur.   (OCR, adapted)

3 Two cubical fair dice are thrown, one red and one blue. The scores on their faces are added together. Determine which, if either, is greater:

  (a) the probability that the total score will be 10 or more given that the red dice shows a 6,

  (b) the probability that the total score will be 10 or more given that at least one of the dice shows a 6.   (OCR)

Probability

1.

a) $P(X > 3) = P(4) + P(5) + P(6) = \frac{1}{6} + \frac{1}{6} + \frac{1}{6} = \frac{1}{2}$

f) $P(X > 3 \mid \text{prime} \mid \text{Both})$

b) $P(X > 3) = \frac{4}{6} = \frac{2}{3}$

c) $P(X = \text{odd}) = \frac{3}{6} = \frac{1}{2}$

d) $P(X = \text{prime}) = P(2) + P(3) + P(5) = \frac{3}{6} = \frac{1}{2}$

e) $P(X > 3, \text{prime}) = P(5) = \frac{1}{6}$

2.

a) $P(\text{Red}) = \frac{26}{52} = \frac{1}{2}$

b) $P(K, Q, J) = \frac{12}{52} = \frac{3}{13}$

c) $P(\text{Honour}) = \frac{20}{52} = \frac{5}{13}$

d) $P(\text{red hon.}) = \frac{10}{52} = \frac{5}{26}$

d) $P(\text{Red/honour/both}) = P \frac{1}{2} + \frac{8}{26}4 = \frac{9}{13}$

3.

a) $P(7) = P(1+6) + P(2+5) + P(3+4) + P(4+3) + P(5+2) + P(6+1) = \frac{6}{36} = \frac{1}{6}$

b) $P(\Sigma X \geq 8) = P(2+6) + P(3+6) + P(4+6) + P(5+6) + P(6+6) + P(3+5) +$
$P(4+4) + P(4+5) + P(5+5) + P(5+3) + P(6+3) + P(2+1) +$
$P(6+2) + P(6+3) + P(6+4) + P(6+5) +$
$= \frac{13}{36} = \frac{5}{12}$

c) $P(\Sigma X = \text{prime}) = P[\frac{1+1}{} + P(1+2) + P(1+4) + P(1+6) + P(2+1) + P(2+3) + P(2+5) +$
$+ P(3+2) + P(3+4) + P(4+1) + P(4+3) + P(5+2) + P(5+6) +$
$P(6+1) + P(6+5) +$
$= \frac{17}{36} = \frac{8}{12}$

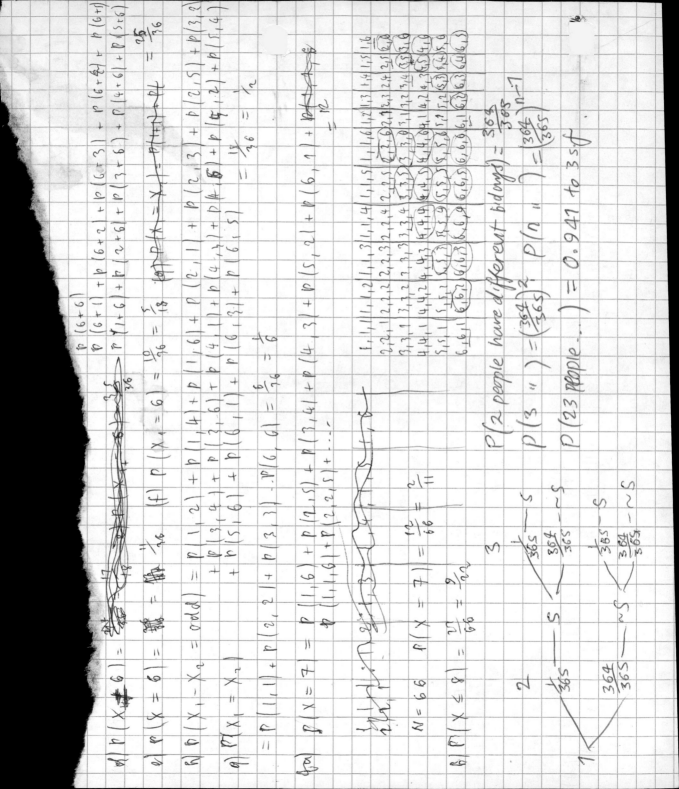

(a) $P(X \neq 6) =$

$P(6+6)$
$P(6+1) + P(6+2) + P(6+3) + P(6+4) + P(6+5) + P(5+6)$
$= \frac{25}{36}$

(a) $P(X \neq 6) = \frac{35}{36}$

(a) $P(X = 6) = \frac{17}{36}$

$P(1+6) + P(2+6) + P(3+6) + P(4+6) + P(5+6) + P(6+6) = \frac{10}{36} = \frac{5}{18}$

(b) $P(X_1 = 6) = P(X) = P(1) + P(2) + P(3) + P(4) + P(5) + P(6)$

(b) $P(X_1 = X_2 = \text{odd}) = P(1,2) + P(1,4) + P(1,6) + P(2,1) + P(2,3) + P(3,2)$
$+ P(3,4) + P(3,6) + P(4,1) + P(4,3) + P(4,5) + P(5,4)$
$+ P(5,6) + P(6,1) + P(6,3) + P(6,5)$

(c) $P[X_1 = X_2] = P(1,1) + P(2,2) + P(3,3) \cdots P(6,6)$
$= P(1,1) + P(2,2) + P(3,3) \cdots P(6,6)$
$= \frac{6}{36} = \frac{1}{6}$

(d) $P(X = 7) = P(1,6) + P(2,5) + P(3,4) + P(4,3) + P(5,2) + P(6,1) + \cdots$
$P(1,6) + P(1,6) + P(2,2,5) + \cdots$
$= \frac{6}{36} = \frac{1}{6}$

$N = 99$ $P(X = 7) = \frac{12}{99} = \frac{1}{2}$

(e) $P(X \leq 8) = \frac{27}{99} = \frac{9}{22}$

Birthday problem:

P(2 people have different birthdays) $= \frac{365}{365}$

$P(3 \;\;) = \left(\frac{364}{365}\right)^2$ $P(n \;\;) = \left(\frac{364}{365}\right)^{n-1}$

$P(23 \text{ people} \ldots) = 0.941$ to 3 s.f.

1
$\quad \frac{364}{365} \to S$
$\quad \frac{1}{365} \to \sim S$

2
$\quad \frac{364}{365} \to S$
$\quad \frac{1}{365} \to \sim S$

3
$\quad \frac{365}{365} \to S$
$\quad \frac{364}{365} \to \sim S$

4 Half of the A-level students in a community college study science and 30% study mathematics. Of those who study science, 40% study mathematics.

(a) What proportion of the A-level students study both mathematics and science?

(b) Calculate the proportion of those students who study mathematics but do not study science. (OCR)

5 Three friends, Ahmed, Benjamin and Chi, live in a town where there are only three cafés. They arrange to meet at a café one evening but do not specify the name of the café. The probabilities that they will each choose a particular café are independent. Ahmed lives close to Café Expresso and so the probability that he will choose to go there is $\frac{5}{9}$ whereas Café Kola and Café Pepi have equal chances of being visited by him.

Benjamin lives a long distance from Café Kola and the probability that he will choose this one is $\frac{1}{7}$, but he will choose either of the other two cafés with equal probability.

Each café has an equal chance of being visited by Chi.

(a) Show that the probability that the three friends meet at Café Expresso is $\frac{5}{63}$.

(b) Calculate the probability that

(i) the three friends will meet at the same café,

(ii) at most two friends will meet at the same café. (OCR)

6 Two events A and B are such that $P(A) = \frac{3}{4}$, $P(B \mid A) = \frac{1}{5}$ and $P(B' \mid A') = \frac{4}{7}$. By use of a tree diagram, or otherwise, find

(a) $P(A \text{ and } B)$,   (b) $P(B)$,   (c) $P(A \mid B)$.   (OCR, adapted)

7 Students have to pass a test before they are allowed to work in a laboratory. Students do not retake the test once they have passed it. For a randomly chosen student, the probability of passing the test at the first attempt is $\frac{1}{3}$. On any subsequent attempt, the probability of failing is half the probability of failing on the previous attempt. By drawing a tree diagram, or otherwise,

(a) show that the probability of a student passing the test in 3 attempts or fewer is $\frac{26}{27}$,

(b) find the conditional probability that a student passed at the first attempt, given that the student passed in 3 attempts or fewer. (OCR)

8 The probability of event A occurring is $P(A) = \frac{13}{25}$. The probability of event B occurring is $P(B) = \frac{9}{25}$. The conditional probability of A occurring given that B has occurred is $P(A \mid B) = \frac{5}{9}$.

(a) Determine the following probabilities.

(i) $P(A \text{ and } B)$ (ii) $P(B \mid A)$ (iii) $P(A \text{ or } B \text{ or both})$ (iv) $P(A' \mid B')$.

(b) Determine $P(A \text{ occurs or } B \text{ does not occur})$ showing your working. (OCR, adapted)

9 (a) The probability that an event A occurs is $P(A) = 0.4$. B is an event independent of A and $P(A \text{ or } B \text{ or both}) = 0.7$. Find $P(B)$.

(b) C and D are two events such that $P(D \mid C) = \frac{1}{5}$ and $P(C \mid D) = \frac{1}{4}$. Given that $P(C \text{ and } D \text{ occur}) = p$, express in terms of p (i) $P(C)$, (ii) $P(D)$.

(c) Given also that $P(C \text{ or } D \text{ or both occur}) = \frac{1}{5}$, find the value of p. (OCR, adapted)

10 A batch of forty tickets for an event at a stadium consists of ten tickets for the North stand, fourteen tickets for the East stand and sixteen tickets for the West stand. A ticket is taken from the batch at random and issued to a person, X. Write down the probability that X has a ticket for the North stand.

A second ticket is taken from the batch at random and issued to Y. Subsequently a third ticket is taken from the batch at random and issued to Z. Calculate the probability that

(a) both X and Y have tickets for the North stand,

(b) X, Y and Z all have tickets for the same stand,

(c) two of X, Y and Z have tickets for one stand and the other of X, Y and Z has a ticket for a different stand.   (OCR)

11 In a lottery there are 24 prizes allocated at random to 24 prize-winners. Ann, Ben and Cal are three of the prize-winners. Of the prizes, 4 are cars, 8 are bicycles and 12 are watches. Show that the probability that Ann gets a car and Ben gets a bicycle or a watch is $\frac{10}{69}$.

Giving each answer either as a fraction or as a decimal correct to 3 significant figures, find

(a) the probability that both Ann and Ben get cars, given that Cal gets a car,

(b) the probability that either Ann or Cal (or both) gets a car,

(c) the probability that Ann gets a car and Ben gets a car or a bicycle,

(d) the probability that Ann gets a car given that Ben gets either a car or a bicycle. (OCR)

12 In a certain part of the world there are more wet days than dry days. If a given day is wet, the probability that the following day will also be wet is 0.8. If a given day is dry, the probability that the following day will also be dry is 0.6.

Given that Wednesday of a particular week is dry, calculate the probability that

(a) Thursday and Friday of the same week are both wet days,

(b) Friday of the same week is a wet day.

In one season there were 44 cricket matches, each played over three consecutive days, in which the first and third days were dry. For how many of these matches would you expect that the second day was wet?   (OCR)

13 A study of the numbers of male and female children in families in a certain population is being carried out.

(a) A simple model is that each child in any family is equally likely to be male or female, and that the sex of each child is independent of the sex of any previous children in the family. Using this model calculate the probability that, in a randomly chosen family of 4 children,

(i)   there will be 2 males and 2 females,

(ii) there will be exactly 1 female given that there is at least 1 female.

(b) An alternative model is that the first child in any family is equally likely to be male or female, but that, for any subsequent children, the probability that they will be of the same sex as the previous child is $\frac{3}{5}$. Using this model, calculate the probability that, in a randomly chosen family of 4 children,

(i)   all four will be of the same sex,

(ii) no two consecutive children will be of the same sex,

(iii) there will be 2 males and 2 females.   (OCR, adapted)

14 A dice is known to be biased in such a way that, when it is thrown, the probability of a 6 showing is $\frac{1}{4}$. This biased dice and an ordinary fair dice are thrown. Find the probability that

 (a) the fair dice shows a 6 and the biased dice does not show a 6,

 (b) at least one of the two dice shows a 6,

 (c) exactly one of the two dice shows a 6, given that at least one of them shows a 6.

(OCR)

15 Spares of a particular component are produced by two firms, Bestbits and Lesserprod. Tests show that, on average, 1 in 200 components produced by Bestbits fail within one year of fitting, and 1 in 50 components produced by Lesserprod fail within one year of fitting. Given that 20 per cent of the components sold and fitted are made by Bestbits and 80 per cent by Lesserprod, what is the probability that a component chosen at random from those sold and fitted will fail within a year of fitting?

Find the proportion of components sold and fitted that would need to be made by Bestbits for this probability to be 0.01.   (OCR)

16 A game is played using a regular 12-faced fair dice, with faces labelled 1 to 12, a coin and a simple board with nine squares as shown in the diagram.

Initially, the coin is placed on the shaded rectangle. The game consists of rolling the dice and then moving the coin one rectangle towards **L** or **R** according to the outcome on the dice. If the outcome is a prime number (2, 3, 5, 7 or 11) the move is towards **R**, otherwise it is towards **L**. The game stops when the coin reaches either **L** or **R**. Find, giving your answers correct to 3 decimal places, the probability that the game

 (a) ends on the fourth move at **R**,

 (b) ends on the fourth move,

 (c) ends on the fifth move,

 (d) takes more than six moves.   (OCR)

17 You have n identical black balls, and n identical white balls, identical with the black balls except for their colour.

Box X contains 3 of the black balls, and $n-3$ white balls. Box Y contains $n-3$ black balls, and 3 white balls.

A ball is taken at random from box X and put into box Y. A ball is then taken at random from box Y.

 (a) Calculate in terms of n the probability that the ball taken from box Y is white.

 (b) Calculate in terms of n the probability that the first ball is black, given that the second ball is white.   (OCR)

5 Permutations and combinations

This chapter is about numbers of arrangements of different objects, and the number of ways you can choose different objects. When you have completed it, you should

- know what a permutation is, and be able to calculate with permutations
- know what a combination is, and be able to calculate with combinations
- be able to apply permutations and combinations to probability.

5.1 Permutations

In the last chapter you often had to count the number of outcomes in a sample space. When the number of outcomes is fairly small, this is quite straightforward, but suppose, for example, that you were to deal hands of 5 playing cards from a standard pack of 52 cards. The number of different hands which you might receive is very large and it would not be sensible to try to list all of them. It is necessary to find a method of counting the number of possible hands which avoids writing out a complete list.

It is useful to start with an easier situation. Suppose that you have the three letters A, B and C, one on each of three separate cards, and that you are going to arrange them in a line to form 'words'. How many three-letter words are there?

In this case the number of words is small enough for you to write them out in full.

$$ABC \quad ACB \quad BCA \quad BAC \quad CAB \quad CBA$$

You could also show the possible choices by using a tree diagram, as in Fig. 5.1.

You have 3 choices for the first letter:

either A, B or C.

Having chosen the first letter, you then have just 2 choices for the second letter:

B or C if A has been used,
C or A if B has been used,
A or B if C has been used.

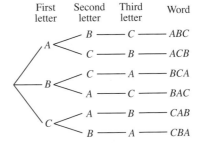

Fig. 5.1. Possible words made from the letters A, B and C.

Having chosen the first two letters, you then have only 1 choice for the third letter:

only C is left if A and B have been used,
only B is left if C and A have been used,
only A is left if B and C have been used.

So altogether there are $3 \times 2 \times 1 = 6$ possible words you can make with three letters.

Using a similar argument you can find the number of words which you can make from four letters A, B, C and D.

You have 4 possibilities for the first letter.
Having chosen the first letter, you then have 3 possibilities for the second letter.
Having chosen the first two letters, you then have 2 possibilities for the third letter.
You then have only 1 possibility for the last letter.

Therefore there are $4 \times 3 \times 2 \times 1 = 24$ possible words.

Each of these 24 possibilities is listed in Fig. 5.2.

ABCD	*BACD*	*CABD*	*DABC*
ABDC	*BADC*	*CADB*	*DACB*
ACBD	*BCAD*	*CBAD*	*DBAC*
ACDB	*BCDA*	*CBDA*	*DBCA*
ADBC	*BDAC*	*CDAB*	*DCAB*
ADCB	*BDCA*	*CDBA*	*DCBA*

Fig. 5.2. All possible arrangements of the letters A, B, C and D.

You can now generalise this result to the case where there are n distinct letters.

When you arrange n distinct letters in a line, the number of different 'words' you can make is

$$n \times (n-1) \times (n-2) \times \ldots \times 2 \times 1.$$

The argument and the result given above apply whenever n distinct objects are arranged in a line. The objects need not be letters. The different arrangements of the objects are called **permutations**.

It is useful to have a concise way of writing the expression

$$n \times (n-1) \times (n-2) \times \ldots \times 2 \times 1.$$

The expression $n \times (n-1) \times (n-2) \times \ldots \times 2 \times 1$ is called n **factorial** and written as $n!$.

The number of permutations of n distinct objects is $n!$, where

$$n! = n \times (n-1) \times (n-2) \times \ldots \times 2 \times 1. \qquad (5.1)$$

Table 5.3 shows how the number of permutations increases as the number of objects being arranged gets larger.

Number of objects, n	Number of permutations
1	$1 = 1$
2	$2 \times 1 = 2$
3	$3 \times 2 \times 1 = 6$
4	$4 \times 3 \times 2 \times 1 = 24$
5	$5 \times 4 \times 3 \times 2 \times 1 = 120$

Table 5.3. Number of permutations as n increases.

As you can see, the number of permutations increases very rapidly as the number of objects being arranged gets larger. For example,

$$8! = 8 \times 7 \times 6 \times 5 \times 4 \times 3 \times 2 \times 1 = 40\,320.$$

Your calculator will probably give you values of $n!$, but it can only approximate by using standard index form as n gets larger.

Suppose now that you have more letters than you need to make a word. For example, suppose that you have the seven letters A, B, C, D, E, F and G but that you want to make a four-letter word.

You have 7 choices for the first letter.
Having chosen the first letter, you have 6 choices for the second letter.
Having chosen the first two letters, you have 5 choices for the third letter.
Having chosen the first three letters, you have 4 choices for the fourth (and last) letter.

The number of permutations of 4 letters chosen from 7 letters (that is, the number of four-letter words) is therefore $7 \times 6 \times 5 \times 4$.

This result can be written concisely in terms of factorials.

$$7 \times 6 \times 5 \times 4 = \frac{7 \times 6 \times 5 \times 4 \times 3 \times 2 \times 1}{3 \times 2 \times 1} = \frac{7!}{3!} = \frac{7!}{(7-4)!}.$$

This is an illustration of a general rule.

The number of different permutations of r objects which can be made from n distinct objects is $\frac{n!}{(n-r)!}$. This number is usually given the special symbol ^nP_r.

The number ^nP_r of different permutations of r objects which can be made from n distinct objects is given by $^nP_r = \dfrac{n!}{(n-r)!}$.   (5.2)

On some calculators, this is written as $_nP_r$.

Example 5.1.1

Eight runners are hoping to take part in a race, but the track has only six lanes. In how many ways can six of the eight runners be assigned to lanes?

Using Equation 5.2, the number of permutations is

$$^8P_6 = \frac{8!}{(8-6)!} = \frac{8!}{2!} = \frac{8 \times 7 \times 6 \times 5 \times 4 \times 3 \times 2 \times 1}{2 \times 1} = 20\,160.$$

Notice that, if you try to use the formula $^nP_r = \dfrac{n!}{(n-r)!}$ to find the number of permutations of the eight letters $A, B, C, \dots, H$, you find that

$$^8P_8 = \frac{8!}{(8-8)!} = \frac{8!}{0!}.$$

But $0!$ cannot be defined using the relationship $n! - n \times (n-1) \times (n-2) \times \dots \times 2 \times 1$, so what does $0!$ mean? The answer is that it can be defined to be any convenient value. Recall that $^8P_8$ denotes the number of permutations of 8 objects when you have selected them from 8 distinct objects. But this has already been shown to be $8!$.

Therefore $\dfrac{8!}{0!}$ should equal $8!$.

This will only be true if $0! = 1$. The value of $0!$ is defined to be 1 to make the formula for ^nP_r consistent when $r = n$.

Example 5.1.2

Eight people, $A, B, \dots, H$, are arranged randomly in a line. What is the probability that (a) A and B are next to each other,   (b) A and B are not next to each other?

(a) There is a neat trick which helps to solve this problem. Imagine that A and B are stuck together in the order AB. There are then $7!$ ways to arrange the people in line. There are also another $7!$ ways to arrange them if A and B are stuck together in the order BA. There are therefore $2 \times 7!$ ways of arranging the eight people in line with A and B next to each other.

However, there are $8!$ ways of arranging the eight people in line if there are no restrictions.

The required probability is therefore $\dfrac{2 \times 7!}{8!} = \frac{2}{8} = \frac{1}{4}$.

(b) $\text{P}(A \text{ and } B \text{ are not together}) = 1 - \text{P}(A \text{ and } B \text{ are together})$,

so $\text{P}(A \text{ and } B \text{ are not together}) = 1 - \frac{1}{4} = \frac{3}{4}$.

If you need to find the probability that two objects are not together, it is usually a good idea to find first the probability that they are together.

In this section emphasis is placed on the fact that the objects being arranged have to be distinct. That is, you have to be able to identify each object uniquely. The next section shows how to tackle the permutation problem when the objects are not distinct.

5.2 Permutations when the objects are not distinct

Recall that there were $4! = 24$ permutations of the letters A, B, C and D. These were listed earlier in Fig. 5.2. Imagine that the A remains but that the letters B, C and D are all replaced by the letter Z. How many permutations will there be now?

Suppose that B is temporarily replaced by Z_1, C is replaced by Z_2 and D is replaced by Z_3 so that you can tell the Zs apart. Fig. 5.4 shows the permutations of A, Z_1, Z_2 and Z_3 using a different procedure from that used to write out Fig. 5.2.

Write the first permutation of A, Z_1, Z_2 and Z_3 at the top of the first column. Any permutation can be the first permutation. Leave A in the same position, but write the other permutations of Z_1, Z_2 and Z_3 underneath. Write a permutation not already used at the top of the next column, and repeat writing the other permutations of Z_1, Z_2 and Z_3 underneath while keeping A in the same position. Keep going until you have written all the permutations of A, Z_1, Z_2 and Z_3.

$$
\begin{array}{llll}
AZ_1Z_2Z_3 & Z_1AZ_2Z_3 & Z_1Z_2AZ_3 & Z_1Z_2Z_3A \\
AZ_1Z_3Z_2 & Z_1AZ_3Z_2 & Z_1Z_3AZ_2 & Z_1Z_3Z_2A \\
AZ_2Z_1Z_3 & Z_2AZ_1Z_3 & Z_2Z_1AZ_3 & Z_2Z_1Z_3A \\
AZ_2Z_3Z_1 & Z_2AZ_3Z_1 & Z_2Z_3AZ_1 & Z_2Z_3Z_1A \\
AZ_3Z_1Z_2 & Z_3AZ_1Z_2 & Z_3Z_1AZ_2 & Z_3Z_1Z_2A \\
AZ_3Z_2Z_1 & Z_3AZ_2Z_1 & Z_3Z_2AZ_1 & Z_3Z_2Z_1A \\
\end{array}
$$

Fig. 5.4. All permutations of the letters A, Z_1, Z_2 and Z_3.

There are $4!$ arrangements in Fig. 5.4. Each column has all the permutations of Z_1, Z_2 and Z_3, $3!$ in all, so there must be $\dfrac{4!}{3!} = 4$ columns altogether. Now replace Z_1, Z_2 and Z_3 by Z and you have the permutations of A, Z, Z and Z in the top row. These are

$$AZZZ, \qquad ZAZZ, \qquad ZZAZ, \qquad ZZZA.$$

You can generalise this argument. Suppose that you have n objects and r of them are identical. Then the number of arrangements in the table equivalent to Fig. 5.4 will be $n!$. When you write down the permutations in the columns corresponding to the arrangement at the top of the column, you find that there are $r!$ of them, so the table will have $r!$ rows. The number of columns (that is, the number of distinct permutations) is therefore $\dfrac{n!}{r!}$.

This result also generalises.

> The number of distinct permutations of n objects, of which p are identical to each other, and then q of the remainder are identical, and r of the remainder are identical, and so on is
>
> $$\frac{n!}{p! \times q! \times r! \times \ldots}, \qquad \text{where} \qquad p + q + r + \ldots = n.$$

Example 5.2.1

Find the number of distinct permutations of the letters of the word *MISSISSIPPI*.

The number of letters is 11, of which there are 4 *Ss*, 4 *Is*, 2 *Ps* and 1 *M*. The number of distinct permutations of the letters is therefore

$$\frac{11!}{4! \times 4! \times 2! \times 1!} = 34\,650 \,.$$

Exercise 5A

1   Seven different cars are to be loaded on to a transporter truck. In how many different ways can the cars be arranged?

2   How many numbers are there between 1245 and 5421 inclusive which contain each of the digits 1, 2, 4 and 5 once and once only?

3   An artist is going to arrange five paintings in a row on a wall. In how many ways can this be done?

4   Ten athletes are running in a 100-metre race. In how many different ways can the first three places be filled?

5   By writing out all the possible arrangements of $D_1 E_1 E_2 D_2$, show that there are $\frac{4!}{2!2!} = 6$ different arrangements of the letters of the word *DEED*.

6   A typist has five letters and five addressed envelopes. In how many different ways can the letters be placed in each envelope without getting every letter in the right envelope? If the letters are placed in the envelopes at random what is the probability that each letter is in its correct envelope?

7   How many different arrangements can be made of the letters in the word *STATISTICS*?

8   (a)   Calculate the number of arrangements of the letters in the word *NUMBER*.

     (b)   How many of the arrangements in part (a) begin and end with a vowel?

9   How many different numbers can be formed by taking one, two, three and four digits from the digits 1, 2, 7 and 8, if repetitions are not allowed?

    One of these numbers is chosen at random. What is the probability that it is greater than 200?

5.3 Combinations

In the last section you considered permutations (arrangements), for which the order of the objects is significant when you count the number of different possibilities. In some circumstances, however, the order of selection does not matter. For example, if you were dealt a hand of 13 cards from a standard pack of 52 playing cards, you would not be interested in the order in which you received the cards. When a selection is made from a set of objects and the order of selection is unimportant it is called a **combination**.

To see the difference between combinations and permutations consider what happens when you select three letters from the four letters A, B, C and D.

Here is a procedure for finding all the combinations. It starts by considering permutations, and gives you a method of counting the combinations.

Start with any permutation of three letters from A, B, C and D, and write it at the top of the first column. Write the other permutations of the same three letters underneath it. Write a permutation not already used at the top of the next column, and write the other permutations of the letters underneath. Keep on until you have used all the permutations of three letters from A, B, C and D.

The results are shown in Fig. 5.5.

ABC	*ABD*	*ACD*	*BCD*
ACB	*ADB*	*ADC*	*BDC*
BAC	*BAD*	*CAD*	*CBD*
BCA	*BDA*	*CDA*	*CDB*
CAB	*DAB*	*DAC*	*DBC*
CBA	*DBA*	*DCA*	*DCB*

Fig. 5.5. Procedure for finding the number of combinations.

Each column then corresponds to a single combination because the elements in any one column differ only in the order in which the letters are written. The permutations are all different, but they all give rise to the same combination at the head of the column. To count the combinations, it is sufficient to count the columns.

There are $^{4}P_{3}$ permutations of 3 objects from 4 objects, so there are $^{4}P_{3}$ elements in total in Fig. 5.5.

Each column has $3!$ elements, so, by dividing, you find that there must be $\dfrac{^{4}P_{3}}{3!}$ columns, which means $\dfrac{^{4}P_{3}}{3!}$ combinations. As $^{4}P_{3} = \dfrac{4!}{(4-3)!}$,

$$\frac{^{4}P_{3}}{3!} = \frac{4!}{(4-3)! \times 3!} = \frac{4!}{1! \times 3!} = \frac{4 \times 3 \times 2 \times 1}{1 \times (3 \times 2 \times 1)} = 4 \,.$$

So there are 4 combinations of three letters from the four letters A, B, C and D.

You can apply this reasoning and this calculation to finding the number of combinations of r objects taken from n objects. In the table which corresponds to Fig. 5.5, there would be $^{n}P_{r}$ elements in total, and each column would have $r!$ elements. There would therefore be $\dfrac{^{n}P_{r}}{r!}$ columns, which corresponds to $\dfrac{^{n}P_{r}}{r!}$ combinations of r objects taken from n objects.

Writing ^nP_r in factorials as $\dfrac{n!}{(n-r)!}$ leads to a simpler expression to remember: the number of combinations of r objects taken from n objects is $\dfrac{n!}{(n-r)! \times r!}$.

The number of combinations of r objects chosen from n distinct objects is given the symbol $\dbinom{n}{r}$, which is often read as 'n choose r'. The older symbols, $_nC_r$ and ^nC_r are also used, and your calculator probably uses one of them.

> A **combination** is a selection in which the order of the objects selected is unimportant.
>
> The number of different combinations of r objects selected from n distinct objects is $\dbinom{n}{r}$, where $\dbinom{n}{r} = \dfrac{n!}{(n-r)! \times r!}$.

Example 5.3.1

The manager of a football team has a squad of 16 players. He needs to choose 11 to play in a match. How many possible teams can be chosen?

This example is not entirely realistic because players will not be equally capable of playing in every position, but it does show how many possible teams there are. It is important to decide whether this question is about permutations or combinations. Clearly the important issue here is the people in the team and not their order of selection. Therefore this question is about combinations rather than permutations.

$$\text{The number of teams is } \binom{16}{11} = \frac{16!}{(16-11)! \times 11!} = \frac{16!}{5! \times 11!} = 4368.$$

The number of teams is surprisingly large.

You may notice in Example 5.3.1 that if you had chosen the 5 players to drop out of the squad of 16 players, you would in effect be selecting the 11 by another method. You can select the 5 players in $\dbinom{16}{5}$ ways, and

$$\binom{16}{5} = \frac{16!}{(16-5)! \times 5!} = \frac{16!}{11! \times 5!},$$

which is clearly equal to $\dbinom{16}{11}$.

When you come to calculate a number like $\dbinom{16}{11}$ or $\dbinom{16}{5}$, you can take a short cut. Since

$$16! = 16 \times 15 \times \ldots \times 12 \times 11 \times 10 \times \ldots \times 2 \times 1,$$

you can cancel the $11 \times 10 \times \ldots \times 2 \times 1$ in the numerator with the $11!$ in the denominator.

Therefore you can write down immediately that

$$\binom{16}{5} = \frac{16 \times 15 \times \ldots \times 12}{5!},$$

where you need to make sure that you multiply 5 numbers in the numerator if the denominator is $5!$.

In general,

$$\binom{n}{r} = \frac{\overbrace{n \times (n-1) \times \ldots \times (n-r+1)}^{r \text{ factors}}}{r!}.$$

Example 5.3.2

A team of 5 people, which must contain 3 men and 2 women, is chosen from 8 men and 7 women. How many different teams can be selected?

The number of different teams of 3 men which can be selected from 8 is $\binom{8}{3}$.

The number of different teams of 2 women which can be selected from 7 is $\binom{7}{2}$.

Any of the $\binom{8}{3}$ men's teams can join up with any of the $\binom{7}{2}$ women's teams to make an acceptable team of 5. Therefore you need to multiply these two quantities together to find the number of different teams possible.

The number of possible teams is

$$\binom{8}{3} \times \binom{7}{2} = \frac{8 \times 7 \times 6}{1 \times 2 \times 3} \times \frac{7 \times 6}{1 \times 2} = 56 \times 21 = 1176.$$

You can now apply some of these counting methods to probability examples.

Example 5.3.3

Five cards are dealt without replacement from a standard pack of 52 cards. Find the probability that exactly 3 of the 5 cards are hearts.

The sample space is very large. It would consist of a list of all possible sets of 5 cards which you could choose from the 52 cards in the pack. You do not need such a list, however. All that you need to know is how many different sets of cards the sample space contains. You are choosing 5 objects from 52, so the number of unrestricted choices is $\binom{52}{5}$, because the order of selection is irrelevant.

Let A be the event that exactly 3 cards of the 5 dealt out are hearts. The method used to find the number of outcomes in the event A is very similar to the technique used in Example 5.3.2.

There are $\binom{13}{3}$ 'teams' of 3 hearts.

There are $\binom{39}{2}$ 'teams' of 2 'non-hearts'.

Therefore the number of sets of 5 cards with exactly 3 hearts is $\binom{13}{3} \times \binom{39}{2}$

The probability that event A happens is $\dfrac{\binom{13}{3} \times \binom{39}{2}}{\binom{52}{5}} = 0.0815$, correct to 3 significant figures.

Exercise 5B

1 How many different three-card hands can be dealt from a pack of 52 cards?

2 From a group of 30 boys and 32 girls, two girls and two boys are to be chosen to represent their school. How many possible selections are there?

3 A history exam paper contains eight questions, four in Part A and four in Part B. Candidates are required to attempt five questions. In how many ways can this be done if

   (a) there are no restrictions,

   (b) at least two questions from Part A and at least two questions from Part B must be attempted?

4 A committee of three people is to be selected from four women and five men. The rules state that there must be at least one man and one woman on the committee. In how many different ways can the committee be chosen?

   Subsequently one of the men and one of the women marry each other. The rules also state that a married couple may not both serve on the committee. In how many ways can the committee be chosen now?

5 A box of one dozen eggs contains one that is bad. If three eggs are chosen at random, what is the probability that one of them will be bad?

6 In a game of bridge the pack of 52 cards is shared equally between all four players. What is the probability that one particular player has no hearts?

7 A bag contains 20 chocolates, 15 toffees and 12 peppermints. If three sweets are chosen at random, what is the probability that they are

   (a) all different,   (b) all chocolates,

   (c) all the same,   (d) all not chocolates?

8 Show that $\binom{n}{r} = \binom{n}{n-r}$.

9 Show that the number of permutations of n objects of which r are of one kind and $n - r$ are of another kind is $\binom{n}{r}$.

5.4   Applications of permutations and combinations

In Example 5.1.2 you were asked to find the number of ways that eight people could stand in a line when two people had to stand next to each other. This was an example in which you were asked to find the number of permutations or combinations of a set of objects with some extra condition included. This section will show you how to answer such questions.

Example 5.4.1

Find the number of ways of arranging 6 women and 3 men to stand in a row so that all 3 men are standing together.

> You can make this problem simpler by thinking of the 3 men as a single unit. Imagine tying them together for example! You would then have 7 items (or units), the 6 individual women and the block of 3 men.
>
> So one possible arrangement would be
>
> $$W_1 \quad W_3 \quad W_5 \quad W_6 \quad W_2 \quad W_4 \quad M_1 M_3 M_2 \, ,$$
>
> where W_3, for example, represents the third woman.
>
> The number of permutations of these 7 units is $7!$. However, for each of these permutations the men could be arranged (inside the rope) in $3!$ different ways. Therefore the total number of permutations in which the 6 women and 3 men can be arranged so that the 3 men are standing together is $7! \times 3! = 30\,240$.

Example 5.4.2

Find the number of ways of arranging 6 women and 3 men in a row so that no two men are standing next to one another.

> You can ensure that no two men stand next to one another in the following way.
>
> Arrange the 6 women to stand in a line with a space between each pair of them and two extra spaces, one at each end of the line. One such arrangement is
>
> Space 1   Space 2   Space 3   Space 4   Space 5   Space 6   Space 7
> ↓ W_1 ↓ W_2 ↓ W_5 ↓ W_4 ↓ W_6 ↓ W_3 ↓
>
> There are $6!$ arrangements of the 6 women. For any of these $6!$ arrangements you can now pick a space in which to place the first man M_1. This can be done in 7 ways.
>
> Here is the arrangement above with one of the men, M_1, placed in Space 2.
>
> Space 1   Space 3   Space 4   Space 5   Space 6   Space 7
> ↓ W_1 M_1 W_2 ↓ W_5 ↓ W_4 ↓ W_6 ↓ W_3 ↓
>
> By using a similar argument you can see that there will be 6 choices for the position of M_2 and 5 choices for the position of M_3. Once the 3 men have been placed the remaining spaces can be 'closed up' or simply ignored. By using this method you can guarantee that no two men can stand next to one another. Also all possible arrangements will be counted using this method.

Therefore the number of permutations in which no two men stand next to one another is $6! \times 7 \times 6 \times 5 = 151\,200$.

It should be clear that you multiply $6!$ by 7, 6 and 5 because for every one of the $6!$ arrangements of the women there will be 7 spaces to choose for M_1, and then 6 places to choose for M_2, and then 5 places to choose for M_3.

It is also worth noting that the answers to Examples 5.4.1 and 5.4.2 when added together do not give $9!$, which is the total number of arrangements of 9 people without any restriction at all. This is because there is a third possibility. If two men were standing together and the third man was separated from these two by some women, then it would not be the case that all the men were together but neither would it be the case that the three men were all apart from one another.

Example 5.4.3

A group of 12 people consisting of 6 married couples is arranged at random in a line for a photograph. Find the probability that each wife is standing next to her husband.

The number of unrestricted arrangements is $12!$. Each of them is equally likely.

If each husband and wife 'couple' is to stand together, then you can consider each couple as a unit. There are therefore 6 such units.

The number of permutations of these units is $6!$.

But the first couple H_1W_1 can be arranged in $2!$ ways, either H_1W_1 or W_1H_1. This applies equally to couples $2, 3, 4, 5$ and 6. Therefore the number of arrangements in which each couple stands together is $6! \times (2!)^6$.

Hence P(each couple stands together) $= \dfrac{6! \times (2!)^6}{12!} = \dfrac{1}{10\,395} = 9.62 \times 10^{-5}$, correct to 3 significant figures.

Example 5.4.4

Four letters are to be selected from the letters in the word *RIGIDITY*. How many different combinations are there?

The problem here is that the letters are not all distinct since there are three *I*s. Therefore the answer is not $\binom{8}{4}$. In order to deal with this problem a useful strategy is to split it into different cases depending on the number of *I*s chosen.

Case 1   Combinations with no *I*s

In this case you are selecting 4 letters from the 5 letters R, G, D, T, Y, so the number of combinations is $\binom{5}{4} = 5$.

These are the combinations with no *I*. Remember that since this is a problem about combinations you are not interested in the order. All that matters here is which 'team' of letters you choose. The possible teams are

RGDT   RGDY   RGTY   RDTY   GDTY.

Case 2   Combinations with one *I*

In this case you are selecting 3 letters from the 5 letters R, G, D, T, Y, together with one *I*, so the number of combinations is $\binom{5}{3} = 10$. Here are the combinations with one *I*:

> RGDI   RGTI   RGYI   RDTI   RDYI
> RTYI   GDTI   GDYI   GTYI   DTYI.

Case 3   Combinations with two *I*s

In this case you are selecting 2 letters from the 5 letters R, G, D, T, Y, together with two *I*s, so the number of combinations is $\binom{5}{2} = 10$. Here they are:

> RGII   RDII   RTII   RYII   GDII
> GTII   GYII   DTII   DYII   TYII.

Case 4   Combinations with three *I*s.

In this case you are selecting 1 letter from the 5 letters R, G, D, T, Y, together with three *I*s, so the number of combinations is $\binom{5}{1} = 5$. Here they are:

> RIII   GIII   DIII   TIII   YIII .

The total number of distinct combinations of four letters selected from the letters of the word *RIGIDITY* is $5 + 10 + 10 + 5 = 30$. All 30 combinations have been listed above.

Exercise 5C

1   The letters of the word *CONSTANTINOPLE* are written on 14 cards, one on each card. The cards are shuffled and then arranged in a straight line.

(a)   How many different possible arrangements are there?

(b)   How many arrangements begin with *P*?

(c)   How many arrangements start and end with *O*?

(d)   How many arrangements are there where no two vowels are next to each other?

2   A coin is tossed 10 times.

(a)   How many different sequences of heads and tails are possible?

(b)   How many different sequences containing six heads and four tails are possible?

(c)   What is the probability of getting six heads and four tails?

3   Eight cards are selected with replacement from a standard pack of 52 playing cards, with 12 picture cards, 20 odd cards and 20 even cards.

(a)   How many different sequences of eight cards are possible?

(b)   How many of the sequences in part (a) will contain three picture cards, three odd-numbered cards and two even-numbered cards?

(c)   Use parts (a) and (b) to determine the probability of getting three picture cards, three odd-numbered cards and two even-numbered cards if eight cards are selected with replacement from a standard pack of 52 playing cards.

4 Eight women and five men are standing in a line.

    (a) How many arrangements are possible if any individual can stand in any position?

    (b) In how many arrangements will all five men be standing next to one another?

    (c) In how many arrangements will no two men be standing next to one another?

5 Each of the digits 1, 1, 2, 3, 3, 4, 6 is written on a separate card. The seven cards are then laid out in a row to form a 7-digit number.

    (a) How many distinct 7-digit numbers are there?

    (b) How many of these 7-digit numbers are even?

    (c) How many of these 7-digit numbers are divisible by 4?

    (d) How many of these 7-digit numbers start and end with the same digit?

6 Three families, the Mehtas, the Mupondas and the Lams, go to the cinema together to watch a film. Mr and Mrs Mehta take their daughter Indira, Mr and Mrs Muponda take their sons Paul and John, and Mrs Lam takes her children Susi, Kim and Lee. The families occupy a single row with eleven seats.

    (a) In how many ways could the eleven people be seated if there were no restriction?

    (b) In how many ways could the eleven people sit down so that the members of each family are all sitting together?

    (c) In how many of the arrangements will no two adults be sitting next to one another?

7 The letters of the word *POSSESSES* are written on nine cards, one on each card. The cards are shuffled and four of them are selected and arranged in a straight line.

    (a) How many possible selections are there of four letters?

    (b) How many arrangements are there of four letters?

Miscellaneous exercise 5

1 The judges in a 'Beautiful Baby' competition have to arrange 10 babies in order of merit. In how many different ways could this be done? Two babies are to be selected to be photographed. In how many ways can this selection be made?

2 In how many ways can a committee of four men and four women be seated in a row if

    (a) they can sit in any position,

    (b) no one is seated next to a person of the same sex?

3 How many distinct arrangements are there of the letters in the word *ABRACADABRA*?

4 Six people are going to travel in a six-seater minibus but only three of them can drive. In how many different ways can they seat themselves?

5 There are eight different books on a bookshelf: three of them are hardbacks and the rest are paperbacks.

    (a) In how many different ways can the books be arranged if all the paperbacks are together and all the hardbacks are together?

    (b) In how many different ways can the books be arranged if all the paperbacks are together?

6 Four boys and two girls sit in a line on stools in front of a coffee bar.

(a) In how many ways can they arrange themselves so that the two girls are together?

(b) In how many ways can they sit if the two girls are not together? (OCR)

7 Ten people travel in two cars, a saloon and a Mini. If the saloon has seats for six and the Mini has seats for four, find the number of different ways in which the party can travel, assuming that the order of seating in each car does not matter and all the people can drive. (OCR)

8 Giving a brief explanation of your method, calculate the number of different ways in which the letters of the word *TRIANGLES* can be arranged if no two vowels may come together. (OCR)

9 I have seven fruit bars to last the week. Two are apricot, three fig and two peach. I select one bar each day. In how many different orders can I eat the bars?

If I select a fruit bar at random each day, what is the probability that I eat the two apricot ones on consecutive days?

10 A class contains 30 children, 18 girls and 12 boys. Four complimentary theatre tickets are distributed at random to the children in the class. What is the probability that

(a) all four tickets go to girls,

(b) two boys and two girls receive tickets? (OCR)

11 (a) How many different 7-digit numbers can be formed from the digits $0, 1, 2, 2, 3, 3, 3$ assuming that a number cannot start with 0 ?

(b) How many of these numbers will end in 0? (OCR)

12 Calculate the number of ways in which three girls and four boys can be seated on a row of seven chairs if each arrangement is to be symmetrical. (OCR)

13 Find the number of ways in which

(a) 3 people can be arranged in 4 seats,

(b) 5 people can be arranged in 5 seats.

In a block of 8 seats, 4 are in row A and 4 are in row B. Find the number of ways of arranging 8 people in the 8 seats given that 3 specified people must be in row A. (OCR)

14 Eight different cards, of which four are red and four are black, are dealt to two players so that each receives a hand of four cards.

Calculate

(a) the total number of different hands which a given player could receive,

(b) the probability that each player receives a hand consisting of four cards all of the same colour. (OCR)

15 A piece of wood of length 10 cm is to be divided into 3 pieces so that the length of each piece is a whole number of cm, for example 2 cm, 3 cm and 5 cm.

(a) List all the different sets of lengths which could be obtained.

(b) If one of these sets is selected at random, what is the probability that the lengths of the pieces could be lengths of the sides of a triangle? (OCR)

16 Nine persons are to be seated at three tables holding 2, 3 and 4 persons respectively. In how many ways can the groups sitting at the tables be selected, assuming that the order of sitting at the tables does not matter? (OCR)

17 (a) Calculate the number of different arrangements which can be made using all the letters of the word *BANANA*.

  (b) The number of combinations of 2 objects from n is equal to the number of combinations of 3 objects from n. Determine n. (OCR)

18 A 'hand' of 5 cards is dealt from an ordinary pack of 52 playing cards. Show that there are nearly 2.6 million distinct hands and that, of these, 575 757 contain no card from the heart suit.

  On three successive occasions a card player is dealt a hand containing no heart. What is the probability of this happening? What conclusion might the player justifiably reach? (OCR)

19* Notice that $7! \times 6! = 10!$. Find three integers, m, n and r, where $r > 10$, for which $m! \times n! = r!$.

6 Probability distributions

This chapter introduces the idea of a discrete random variable. When you have completed it, you should

- understand what a discrete random variable is
- know the properties of a discrete random variable
- be able to construct a probability distribution table for a discrete random variable.

6.1 Discrete random variables

Most people have played board games at some time. Here is an example.

Game A   A turn consists of throwing a dice and then moving a number of squares equal to the score on the dice.

'The number of squares moved in a turn' is a variable because it can take different values, namely 1, 2, 3, 4, 5 and 6. However, the value taken at any one turn cannot be predicted, but depends on chance. For these reasons 'the number of squares moved in a turn' is called a 'random variable'.

> A **random variable** is a quantity whose value depends on chance.

The 'number of squares moved in a turn' is a **discrete** random variable because there are clear steps between the different possible values it can take.

Although you cannot predict the result of the next throw of the dice, you do know that, if the dice is fair, the probability of getting each value is $\frac{1}{6}$. A convenient way of expressing this information is to let X stand for 'the number of squares moved in a turn'. Then, for example, $P(X = 3) = \frac{1}{6}$ means 'the probability that X takes the value 3 is $\frac{1}{6}$'. Generalising, $P(X = x)$ means 'the probability that the variable X takes the value x'.

Note how the capital letter stands for the variable itself and the small letter stands for the value which the variable takes.

This notation is used in Table 6.1 to give the possible values for the number of squares moved and the probability of each value. This table is called the 'probability distribution' of X.

x	1	2	3	4	5	6	Total
$P(X = x)$	$\frac{1}{6}$	$\frac{1}{6}$	$\frac{1}{6}$	$\frac{1}{6}$	$\frac{1}{6}$	$\frac{1}{6}$	1

Table 6.1. Probability distribution of X, the number of squares moved in a turn for a single throw of a dice.

> The **probability distribution** of a discrete random variable is a listing of
> the possible values of the variable and the corresponding probabilities.

In some board games, a dice is used in a more complicated way in order to decide how many squares a person should move. Here are two different examples.

Game *B*   A person is allowed a second throw of the dice if a 6 is thrown, and, in this case, moves a number *Y* of squares equal to the sum of the two scores obtained.

Game *C*   The dice is thrown twice and the number, *W*, of squares moved is the sum of the two scores.

Fig. 6.2 is a tree diagram illustrating Game *B*. As *Y* is the number of squares moved in a turn, it can take the values $1, 2, 3, 4, 5, 7, 8, 9, 10, 11$ and 12. The probability of each of the first five values is $\frac{1}{6}$, as in the previous game. In order to score 7, you have to score 6 followed by 1. Since the two events are independent, the probability of scoring a 6 followed by a 1 is found by multiplying the two probabilities:

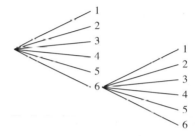

Fig. 6.2. Tree diagram for Game *B*.

$$P(Y = 7) = P(6 \text{ on first throw}) \times P(1 \text{ on second throw})$$
$$= \tfrac{1}{6} \times \tfrac{1}{6} = \tfrac{1}{36}.$$

The probability that *Y* takes each of the values $8, 9, 10, 11$ and 12 will also be $\frac{1}{36}$. Table 6.3 gives the probability distribution of *Y*.

y	1	2	3	4	5	7	8	9	10	11	12	Total
$P(Y=y)$	$\frac{1}{6}$	$\frac{1}{6}$	$\frac{1}{6}$	$\frac{1}{6}$	$\frac{1}{6}$	$\frac{1}{36}$	$\frac{1}{36}$	$\frac{1}{36}$	$\frac{1}{36}$	$\frac{1}{36}$	$\frac{1}{36}$	1

Table 6.3. Probability distribution of *Y*, the number of squares moved in Game *B*.

The possible values of *W* in Game *C* can be found by constructing a table as shown in Fig. 6.4.

		First throw					
		1	2	3	4	5	6
	1	2	3	4	5	6	7
	2	3	4	5	6	7	8
Second	3	4	5	6	7	8	9
throw	4	5	6	7	8	9	10
	5	6	7	8	9	10	11
	6	7	8	9	10	11	12

Fig. 6.4. Possible total scores when two individual scores are added in Game *C*.

There are 36 outcomes in the table and they are all equally likely, so, for example, $P(W = 6) = \frac{5}{36}$ and $P(W = 7) = \frac{6}{36}$. Table 6.5 gives the probability distribution of W. The fractions could have been cancelled but in their present forms it is easier to see the shape of the distribution.

w	2	3	4	5	6	7	8	9	10	11	12	Total
$P(W = w)$	$\frac{1}{36}$	$\frac{2}{36}$	$\frac{3}{36}$	$\frac{4}{36}$	$\frac{5}{36}$	$\frac{6}{36}$	$\frac{5}{36}$	$\frac{4}{36}$	$\frac{3}{36}$	$\frac{2}{36}$	$\frac{1}{36}$	1

Table 6.5. Probability distribution of W, the number of squares moved in Game C.

Fig. 6.6 allows you to compare the probability distributions of X, Y and W.

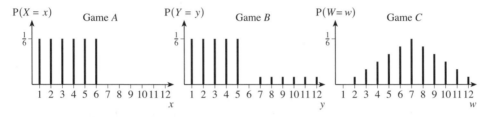

Fig. 6.6. Comparing the probability distributions of Games A, B and C.

Looking at Fig. 6.6, which method of scoring will take you round the board most quickly and which most slowly? (A method for finding the answer to this question by calculation is given in Example 8.1.1.)

Examples 6.1.1 and 6.1.2 illustrate some other probability distributions.

Example 6.1.1

A bag contains two red and three blue marbles. Two marbles are selected at random without replacement and the number, X, of blue marbles is counted. Find the probability distribution of X.

Fig. 6.7 is a tree diagram illustrating this situation. R_1 denotes the event that the first marble is red and R_2 the event that the second marble is red. Similarly B_1 and B_2 stand for the events that the first and second marbles respectively are blue. X can take the values 0, 1 and 2.

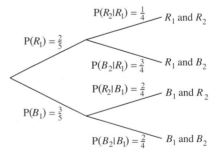

Fig. 6.7. Tree diagram for Example 6.1.1.

$$P(X = 0) = P(R_1 \text{ and } R_2)$$
$$= P(R_1) \times P(R_2 \mid R_1)$$
$$= \tfrac{2}{5} \times \tfrac{1}{4} = \tfrac{2}{20} = \tfrac{1}{10}.$$

$$P(X = 1) = P(B_1 \text{ and } R_2) + P(R_1 \text{ and } B_2)$$
$$= P(B_1) \times P(R_2 \mid B_1) + P(R_1) \times P(B_2 \mid R_1)$$
$$= \tfrac{3}{5} \times \tfrac{2}{4} + \tfrac{2}{5} \times \tfrac{3}{4} = \tfrac{12}{20} = \tfrac{3}{5}.$$

$$P(X = 2) = P(B_1 \text{ and } B_2)$$
$$= P(B_1) \times P(B_2 \mid B_1)$$
$$= \frac{3}{5} \times \frac{2}{4} = \frac{6}{20} = \frac{3}{10}.$$

Here is the probability distribution of X.

x	0	1	2	Total
$P(X = x)$	$\frac{1}{10}$	$\frac{3}{5}$	$\frac{3}{10}$	1

Example 6.1.2

A random variable, X, has the probability distribution shown below.

x	1	2	3	4
$P(X = x)$	0.1	0.2	0.3	0.4

Two observations are made of X and the random variable Y is equal to the larger minus the smaller; if the two observations are equal, Y takes the value 0. Find the probability distribution of Y. Which value of Y is most likely?

The following table gives the values for X and the corresponding value of Y. Since the two observations of X are independent, you find the probability of each pair by multiplying the probabilities for the two X values, as shown in the last column of the table.

First value of X	Second value of X	Y	Probability
1	1	0	$0.1 \times 0.1 = 0.01$
1	2	1	$0.1 \times 0.2 = 0.02$
1	3	2	$0.1 \times 0.3 = 0.03$
1	4	3	$0.1 \times 0.4 = 0.04$
2	1	1	$0.2 \times 0.1 = 0.02$
2	2	0	$0.2 \times 0.2 = 0.04$
2	3	1	$0.2 \times 0.3 = 0.06$
2	4	2	$0.2 \times 0.4 = 0.08$
3	1	2	$0.3 \times 0.1 = 0.03$
3	2	1	$0.3 \times 0.2 = 0.06$
3	3	0	$0.3 \times 0.3 = 0.09$
3	4	1	$0.3 \times 0.4 = 0.12$
4	1	3	$0.4 \times 0.1 = 0.04$
4	2	2	$0.4 \times 0.2 = 0.08$
4	3	1	$0.4 \times 0.3 = 0.12$
4	4	0	$0.4 \times 0.4 = 0.16$

This table shows that Y takes the values 0, 1, 2 and 3. You can find the total probability for each value of Y by adding the individual probabilities:

$$P(Y = 0) = 0.01 + 0.04 + 0.09 + 0.16 = 0.30,$$
$$P(Y = 1) = 0.02 + 0.02 + 0.06 + 0.06 + 0.12 + 0.12 = 0.40,$$
$$P(Y = 2) = 0.03 + 0.08 + 0.03 + 0.08 = 0.22,$$
$$P(Y = 3) = 0.04 + 0.04 = 0.08.$$

So Y has the probability distribution shown below.

y	0	1	2	3	Total
$P(Y = y)$	0.30	0.40	0.22	0.08	1

The most likely value of Y is 1, because it has the highest probability.

Exercise 6A

1 A fair coin is thrown four times. The random variable X is the number of heads obtained. Tabulate the probability distribution of X.

2 Two fair dice are thrown simultaneously. The random variable D is the difference between the smaller and the larger score, or zero if they are the same. Tabulate the probability distribution of D.

3 A fair dice is thrown once. The random variable X is related to the number N thrown on the dice as follows. If N is even, then X is half N; otherwise X is double N. Tabulate the probability distribution of X.

4 Two fair dice are thrown simultaneously. The random variable H is the highest common factor of the two scores. Tabulate the probability distribution of H, combining together all the possible ways of obtaining the same value.

5 When a four-sided dice is thrown, the score is the number on the bottom face. Two fair four-sided dice, each with faces numbered 1 to 4, are thrown simultaneously. The random variable M is the product of the two scores multiplied together. Tabulate the probability distribution of M, combining together all the possible ways of obtaining the same value.

6 A bag contains six red and three green counters. Two counters are drawn from the bag, without replacement. Tabulate the probability distribution of the number of green counters obtained.

7 Satish picks a card at random from an ordinary pack. If the card is an ace, he stops; if not, he continues to pick cards at random, without replacement, until either an ace is picked, or four cards have been drawn. The random variable C is the total number of cards drawn. Construct a tree diagram to illustrate the possible outcomes of the experiment, and use it to calculate the probability distribution of C.

8* Obtain the probability distribution of the total score when three cubical dice are thrown simultaneously.

9 If you have access to a spreadsheet, use it to draw diagrams to illustrate the probability distributions of the total number of heads obtained when $3, 4, 5, \ldots$ fair coins are thrown.

6.2 An important property of a probability distribution

You have probably noticed that, in all the probability distributions considered so far, the sum of the probabilities is 1. This must always be the case, because one of the outcomes must happen. This is an important property of a probability distribution and a useful check that you have found the probabilities correctly.

> For any random variable, X, the sum of the probabilities is 1; that is, $\sum P(X = x) = 1$.

Example 6.2.1
The table below gives the probability distribution of the random variable T.
Find   (a) the value of c,   (b) $P(T \leqslant 3)$,   (c) $P(T > 3)$.

t	1	2	3	4	5
$P(T = t)$	c	$2c$	$2c$	$2c$	c

(a) Since the probabilities must sum to 1,

$$c + 2c + 2c + 2c + c = 1, \quad \text{so} \quad 8c = 1, \quad \text{giving} \quad c = \tfrac{1}{8}.$$

(b) $P(T \leqslant 3) = P(T = 1) + P(T = 2) + P(T = 3) = c + 2c + 2c = 5c = \tfrac{5}{8}.$

(c) $P(T > 3) = P(T = 4) + P(T = 5) = 2c + c = 3c = \tfrac{3}{8}.$

Example 6.2.2
A computer is programmed to give single-digit numbers X between 0 and 9 inclusive in such a way that the probability of getting an odd digit $(1, 3, 5, 7, 9)$ is half the probability of getting an even digit $(0, 2, 4, 6, 8)$. Find the probability distribution of X.

Let the probability of getting an even digit be c. Then the probability of getting an odd digit is $\tfrac{1}{2}c$.

Since the probabilities must sum to 1,

$$\sum P(X = x) = c + \tfrac{1}{2}c + c + \tfrac{1}{2}c + c + \tfrac{1}{2}c + c + \tfrac{1}{2}c + c + \tfrac{1}{2}c = 1,$$

which gives $\tfrac{15}{2}c = 1$; that is, $c = \tfrac{2}{15}$.

The probability distribution of X is $P(X = x) = \tfrac{1}{15}$ for $x = 1, 3, 5, 7$ and 9 and $P(X = x) = \tfrac{2}{15}$ for $x = 0, 2, 4, 6$ and 8.

Exercise 6B

1 In the following probability distribution, c is a constant. Find the value of c.

x	0	1	2	3
$P(X = x)$	$\frac{1}{4}$	$\frac{1}{5}$	$\frac{1}{2}$	c

2 In the following probability distribution, d is a constant. Find the value of d.

x	0	1	2	3
$P(X = x)$	d	0.1	0.2	0.4

3 In the following probability distribution, d is a constant. Find the value of d.

x	0	1	2	3	4
$P(X = x)$	d	0.2	0.15	0.2	$2d$

4 The score S on a spinner is a random variable with distribution given by $P(S = s) = k$ $(s = 1, 2, 3, 4, 5, 6, 7, 8)$, where k is a constant. Find the value of k.

5 A cubical dice is biased so that the probability of an odd number is three times the probability of an even number. Find the probability distribution of the score.

6 A cubical dice is biased so that the probability of any particular score between 1 and 6 (inclusive) being obtained is proportional to that score. Find the probability of scoring a 1.

7 For a biased cubical dice the probability of any particular score between 1 and 6 (inclusive) being obtained is inversely proportional to that score. Find the probability of scoring a 1.

8 In the following probability distribution, c is a constant. Find the value of c.

x	0	1	2	3
$P(X = x)$	0.6	0.16	c	c^2

6.3 Using a probability distribution as a model

So far, the discussion of probability distributions in this chapter has been very mathematical. At this point it may be helpful to point out the practical application of probability distributions. Probability distributions are useful because they provide models for experiments. Consider again the random variable X, the score on a dice, whose probability distribution was given in Table 6.1. Suppose you actually threw a dice 360 times. Since the values 1, 2, 3, 4, 5 and 6 have equal probabilities, you would expect them to occur with approximately equal frequencies of, in this case, $\frac{1}{6} \times 360 = 60$. It is very unlikely that all the observed frequencies will be exactly equal to 60. However, if the model is a suitable one, the observed frequencies should be close to the expected values.

What conclusion would you draw about the dice if the observed frequencies were not close to the expected values?

Now look at the random variable Y, whose probability distribution was given in Table 6.3. For this variable the values are not equally likely and so you would not expect to observe approximately equal frequencies. In Section 4.1 you met the idea that

$$\text{relative frequency} = \frac{\text{frequency}}{\text{total frequency}} \approx \text{probability}.$$

You can rearrange this equation to give an expression for the frequencies you would expect to observe:

$$\text{frequency} \approx \text{total frequency} \times \text{probability}.$$

For 360 observations of Y, the expected frequencies will be about $360 \times \frac{1}{6} = 60$ for $y = 1, 2, 3, 4, 5$ and $360 \times \frac{1}{36} = 10$ for $y = 7, 8, 9, 10, 11$ and 12.

What will the expected frequencies be for 360 observations of the random variable W, whose probability distribution is given in Table 6.5?

Exercise 6C

1 A card is chosen at random from a pack and replaced. This experiment is carried out 520 times. State the expected number of times on which the card is

(a) a club,

(b) an ace,

(c) a picture card (K, Q, J)

(d) either an ace or a club or both,

(e) neither an ace nor a club.

2 The biased dice of Exercise 6B Question 5 is rolled 420 times. State how many times you would expect to obtain

(a) a one,

(b) an even number,

(c) a prime number.

3 The table below gives the cumulative probability distribution for a random variable R. 'Cumulative' means that the probability given is $P(R \leqslant r)$, not $P(R = r)$.

r	0	1	2	3	4	5
$P(R \leqslant r)$	0.116	0.428	0.765	0.946	0.995	1.000

One hundred observations of R are made. Calculate the expected frequencies of each outcome, giving each answer to the nearest whole number.

4* A random variable G has a probability distribution given by the following formulae:

$$P(G = g) = \begin{cases} 0.3 \times (0.7)^g & \text{for } g = 1, 2, 3, 4, \\ k & \text{for } g = 5, \\ 0 & \text{for all other values of } g. \end{cases}$$

Find the value of k, and find the expected frequency of the result $G = 3$ when 1000 independent observations of G are made.

Miscellaneous exercise 6

1 Three cards are selected at random, without replacement, from a shuffled pack of 52 playing cards. Using a tree diagram, find the probability distribution of the number of honours $(A, K, Q, J, 10)$ obtained.

2 An electronic device produces an output of 0, 1 or 3 volts, each time it is operated, with probabilities $\frac{1}{2}$, $\frac{1}{3}$ and $\frac{1}{6}$ respectively. The random variable X denotes the result of adding the outputs for two such devices which act independently.

   (a) Tabulate the possible values of X with their corresponding probabilities.

   (b) In 360 independent operations of the device, state on how many occasions you would expect the outcome to be 1 volt.   (OCR, adapted)

3 The probabilities of the scores on a biased dice are shown in the table below.

Score	1	2	3	4	5	6
Probability	k	$\frac{1}{9}$	$\frac{1}{9}$	$\frac{1}{9}$	$\frac{1}{9}$	$\frac{1}{2}$

   (a) Find the value of k.

   Two players, Hazel and Ross, play a game with this biased dice and a fair dice. Hazel chooses one of the two dice at random and rolls it. If the score is 5 or 6 she wins a point.

   (b) Calculate the probability that Hazel wins a point.

   (c) Hazel chooses a dice, rolls it and wins a point. Find the probability that she chose the biased dice.   (OCR)

4 In an experiment, a fair cubical dice was rolled repeatedly until a six resulted, and the number of rolls was recorded. The experiment was conducted 60 times.

   (a) Show that you would expect to get a six on the first roll ten times out of the 60 repetitions of the experiment.

   (b) Find the expected frequency for two rolls correct to one decimal place.

                                    (OCR, adapted)

5 The probability distribution of the random variable Y is given in the following table, where c is a constant.

y	1	2	3	4	5
$P(Y = y)$	c	$3c$	c^2	c^2	$\frac{15}{32}$

   Prove that there is only one possible value of c, and state this value.

7 The binomial distribution

This chapter introduces you to a discrete probability distribution called the binomial distribution. When you have completed it, you should

- know the conditions necessary for a random variable to have a binomial distribution
- be able to calculate probabilities for a binomial distribution
- know what the parameters of a binomial distribution are.

7.1 The binomial distribution

The spinner in Fig. 7.1 is an equilateral triangle. When it is spun it comes to rest on one of its three edges. Two of the edges are white and one is black. In Fig. 7.1 the spinner is resting on the black edge. This will be described as 'showing black'.

Fig. 7.1. A triangular spinner.

The spinner is fair, so the probability that the spinner shows black is $\frac{1}{3}$ and the probability that it shows white is $\frac{2}{3}$.

Suppose now that the spinner is spun on 5 separate occasions. Let the random variable X be the number of times out of 5 that the spinner shows black.

To derive the probability distribution of X, it is helpful to define some terms. The act of spinning the spinner once is called a **trial**. A simple way of describing the result of each trial is to call it a **success** (s) when the spinner shows black, and a **failure** (f) when the spinner shows white. So X could now be defined as the number of successes in the 5 trials.

The event $\{X = 0\}$ would mean that the spinner did not show black on any of its 5 spins. The notation f_1 will be used to mean that the first trial resulted in a failure, f_2 will mean that the second trial resulted in a failure, and so on, giving

$$P(X = 0) = P(\text{there are 5 failures}) = P(f_1 f_2 f_3 f_4 f_5).$$

Since the outcomes of the trials are independent,

$$P(f_1 f_2 f_3 f_4 f_5) = P(f_1) \times P(f_2) \times P(f_3) \times P(f_4) \times P(f_5)$$
$$= \tfrac{2}{3} \times \tfrac{2}{3} \times \tfrac{2}{3} \times \tfrac{2}{3} \times \tfrac{2}{3} = \tfrac{32}{243}.$$

The probability $P(X = 1)$ is more complicated to calculate. The event $\{X = 1\}$ means that there is one success and also four failures. One possible sequence of a success and four failures is $s_1 f_2 f_3 f_4 f_5$ (where s_1 denotes the event that the first trial was a success).

The probability that the first trial is a success and the other four trials are failures is

$$P(s_1 f_2 f_3 f_4 f_5) = P(s_1) \times P(f_2) \times P(f_3) \times P(f_4) \times P(f_5)$$

$$= \tfrac{1}{3} \times \tfrac{2}{3} \times \tfrac{2}{3} \times \tfrac{2}{3} \times \tfrac{2}{3}$$

$$= \left(\tfrac{1}{3}\right)\left(\tfrac{2}{3}\right)^4 = \tfrac{16}{243}.$$

However there are four other possible sequences for the event $\{X = 1\}$. They are

$$f_1 s_2 f_3 f_4 f_5 \quad f_1 f_2 s_3 f_4 f_5 \quad f_1 f_2 f_3 s_4 f_5 \quad f_1 f_2 f_3 f_4 s_5.$$

Therefore

$$P(X = 1) = P(s_1 f_2 f_3 f_4 f_5) + P(f_1 s_2 f_3 f_4 f_5) + P(f_1 f_2 s_3 f_4 f_5)$$

$$+ P(f_1 f_2 f_3 s_4 f_5) + P(f_1 f_2 f_3 f_4 s_5)$$

$$= \left(\tfrac{1}{3}\right) \times \left(\tfrac{2}{3}\right)^4 + \left(\tfrac{2}{3}\right) \times \left(\tfrac{1}{3}\right) \times \left(\tfrac{2}{3}\right)^3 + \left(\tfrac{2}{3}\right)^2 \times \left(\tfrac{1}{3}\right) \times \left(\tfrac{2}{3}\right)^2$$

$$+ \left(\tfrac{2}{3}\right)^3 \times \left(\tfrac{1}{3}\right) \times \left(\tfrac{2}{3}\right) + \left(\tfrac{2}{3}\right)^4 \times \left(\tfrac{1}{3}\right)$$

$$= 5 \times \left(\tfrac{1}{3}\right) \times \left(\tfrac{2}{3}\right)^4 = \tfrac{80}{243}.$$

Notice that the probability for each individual sequence is the same as for any other sequence, namely $\left(\tfrac{1}{3}\right)\left(\tfrac{2}{3}\right)^4$, and that the 5 in the last line corresponds to the number of different sequences which give $X = 1$. You could have counted the number of sequences by using an argument involving combinations. There are 5 positions in each sequence and one of the positions must be filled with a success (s) and the remaining four must all be failures (f). The choice of which position to place the s in can be made in any one of $\binom{5}{1}$ ways.

Therefore $P(X = 1) = \binom{5}{1} \times \left(\tfrac{1}{3}\right) \times \left(\tfrac{2}{3}\right)^4$.

Similarly you could find that for $X = 2$ there are sequences such as $s_1 s_2 f_3 f_4 f_5$ and $f_1 s_2 f_3 s_4 f_5$. To see how many of these sequences there are, consider the following argument. There are 5 positions which have to be filled with 2 ss and 3 fs. After you choose the places in which to put the 2 ss, there is then no choice as to where the fs go.

There are 5 places to choose from for the 2 ss. From Section 5.3, you have seen that the number of choices is $\binom{5}{2}$. Each of these choices has probability $\left(\tfrac{1}{3}\right)^2 \times \left(\tfrac{2}{3}\right)^3$. Using these results $P(X = 2) = \binom{5}{2} \times \left(\tfrac{1}{3}\right)^2 \times \left(\tfrac{2}{3}\right)^3$.

Continuing in this way, you can find the distribution of X, given in Table 7.2.

x	$P(X = x)$	
0	$\left(\frac{2}{3}\right)^5$	$= \frac{32}{243}$
1	$\binom{5}{1} \times \left(\frac{1}{3}\right) \times \left(\frac{2}{3}\right)^4$	$= \frac{80}{243}$
2	$\binom{5}{2} \times \left(\frac{1}{3}\right)^2 \times \left(\frac{2}{3}\right)^3$	$= \frac{80}{243}$
3	$\binom{5}{3} \times \left(\frac{1}{3}\right)^3 \times \left(\frac{2}{3}\right)^2$	$= \frac{40}{243}$
4	$\binom{5}{4} \times \left(\frac{1}{3}\right)^4 \times \left(\frac{2}{3}\right)$	$= \frac{10}{243}$
5	$\binom{5}{5} \times \left(\frac{1}{3}\right)^5$	$= \frac{1}{243}$

Table 7.2. Probability distribution for the number of times out of 5 that the spinner shows black.

Notice that $\sum_{x=0}^{5} P(X = x)$ is 1. This is a useful check for the probabilities in any distribution table.

Notice also that as $\left(\frac{1}{3}\right)^0 = 1$ and $\left(\frac{2}{3}\right)^0 = 1$ you could write $P(X = 0)$ as $\binom{5}{0} \times \left(\frac{1}{3}\right)^0 \times \left(\frac{2}{3}\right)^5$, and $P(X = 5)$ as $\binom{5}{5} \times \left(\frac{1}{3}\right)^5 \times \left(\frac{2}{3}\right)^0$. These results enable you to write $P(X = x)$ as a formula:

$$P(X = x) = \binom{5}{x} \times \left(\frac{1}{3}\right)^x \times \left(\frac{2}{3}\right)^{5-x}.$$

However the formula on its own is not sufficient, because you must also give the values for which the formula is defined. In this case x can take integer values from 0 to 5 inclusive. So a more concise definition of the distribution of X than Table 7.2 would be

$$P(X = x) = \binom{5}{x} \times \left(\frac{1}{3}\right)^x \times \left(\frac{2}{3}\right)^{5-x} \qquad \text{for } x = 0, 1, 2, \ldots, 5.$$

Although the case of the spinner is not important in itself, it is an example of an important and frequently occurring situation.

- A single trial has just two possible outcomes (often called success, s, and failure, f).
- There is a fixed number of trials, n.
- The outcome of each trial is independent of the outcome of all the other trials.
- The probability of success at each trial, p, is constant.

The random variable X, which represents the number of successes in n trials of this experiment, is said to have a **binomial distribution**.

A consequence of the last condition is that the probability of failure will also be a constant, equal to $1-p$. This probability is usually denoted by q, which means that $q=1-p$.

In a binomial distribution, the random variable X has a probability distribution given by

$$P(X = x) = \binom{n}{x} p^x q^{n-x} \quad \text{for } x = 0, 1, 2, \ldots, n.$$

You will see the reason for the name 'binomial' a little later. Provided you are given the values of n and p, you can evaluate all of the probabilities in the distribution table. The values of n and p are therefore the essential pieces of information about the probability distribution. In the example, n was 5 and p was $\frac{1}{3}$. You did not need to be told q, because its value is always $1-p$, so in the example the value of q was $\frac{2}{3}$.

The values of n and p are called the **parameters** of the binomial distribution. You need to know the parameters of a probability distribution to calculate the probabilities numerically.

To denote that a random variable X has a binomial distribution with parameters n and p, you write $X \sim B(n,p)$. So for the probability distribution in Table 7.2 you write $X \sim B\left(5, \frac{1}{3}\right)$.

Example 7.1.1
Given that $X \sim B\left(8, \frac{1}{4}\right)$, find   (a) $P(X = 6)$,   (b) $P(X \leq 2)$,   (c) $P(X > 0)$.

(a) Using the binomial probability formula with $n = 8$ and $p = \frac{1}{4}$ you get

$$P(X = 6) = \binom{8}{6} \times \left(\frac{1}{4}\right)^6 \times \left(\frac{3}{4}\right)^2 = 28 \times \left(\frac{1}{4}\right)^6 \times \left(\frac{3}{4}\right)^2 = 0.003\,85,$$

correct to 3 significant figures.

(b) $P(X \leq 2) = P(X = 0) + P(X = 1) + P(X = 2)$

$$= \binom{8}{0}\left(\frac{1}{4}\right)^0\left(\frac{3}{4}\right)^8 + \binom{8}{1}\left(\frac{1}{4}\right)^1\left(\frac{3}{4}\right)^7 + \binom{8}{0}\left(\frac{1}{4}\right)^2\left(\frac{3}{4}\right)^6$$

$$= 0.1001\ldots + 0.2669\ldots + 0.3114\ldots$$

$$= 0.6785\ldots = 0.679, \text{correct to 3 significant figures.}$$

(c) The easiest way to find $P(X > 0)$ is to use the fact that $P(X > 0)$ is the complement of $P(X = 0)$.

So $P(X > 0) = 1 - P(X = 0)$

$$= 1 - \binom{8}{0}\left(\frac{1}{4}\right)^0\left(\frac{3}{4}\right)^8 \qquad \text{(from part (b))}$$

$$= 1 - 0.1001\ldots$$

$$= 0.8998\ldots = 0.900, \text{correct to 3 significant figures.}$$

To check that the binomial formula does represent a probability distribution you must show that $\sum_{x=0}^{n} P(X = x) = 1$. Consider the example involving the spinner, but use p and q instead of $\frac{1}{3}$ and $\frac{2}{3}$ respectively. Table 7.3 shows the distribution.

x	$P(X = x)$	
0	q^5	$= q^5$
1	$\binom{5}{1} \times p \times q^4$	$= 5pq^4$
2	$\binom{5}{2} \times p^2 \times q^3$	$= 10p^2q^3$
3	$\binom{5}{3} \times p^3 \times q^2$	$= 10p^3q^2$
4	$\binom{5}{4} \times p^4 \times q$	$= 5p^4q$
5	p^5	$= p^5$

Table 7.3. Probability distribution for the number of times out of 5 that the spinner shows black.

If you sum the probabilities in the right column you get

$$\sum_{x=0}^{5} P(X = x) = q^5 + 5pq^4 + 10p^2q^3 + 10p^3q^2 + 5p^4q + p^5.$$

The right side of this equation is the binomial expansion of $(q + p)^5$ (see P1 Chapter 9). You could check for yourself by multiplying out $(q + p)(q + p)(q + p)(q + p)(q + p)$, so

$$\sum_{x=0}^{5} P(X = x) = (q + p)^5 = 1^5 = 1.$$

You can use a similar argument to show that

$$\sum_{x=0}^{n} P(X = x) = \sum_{x=0}^{n} \left[\binom{n}{x} \times p^x \times q^{n-x} \right] = (q + p)^n = 1^n = 1.$$

The individual probabilities in the binomial distribution are the terms of the binomial expansion of $(q + p)^n$: these are two similar uses of the word 'binomial'.

On the next page there is a summary of the binomial distribution.

Binomial distribution

- A single trial has exactly two possible outcomes (success and failure) and these are mutually exclusive.
- A fixed number, n, of trials takes place.
- The outcome of each trial is independent of the outcome of all the other trials.
- The probability of success at each trial is constant.

The random variable X, which represents the number of successes in the n trials of this experiment, has a probability distribution given by

$$P(X = x) = \binom{n}{x} p^x q^{n-x} \qquad \text{for } x = 0, 1, 2, \ldots, n, \qquad (7.1)$$

where p is the probability of success and $q = 1 - p$ is the probability of failure.

When the random variable X satisfies these conditions, $X \sim B(n, p)$.

Exercise 7A

In this exercise give probabilities correct to 4 decimal places.

1 The random variable X has a binomial distribution with $n = 6$ and $p = 0.2$. Calculate
  (a) $P(X = 3)$,   (b) $P(X = 4)$,   (c) $P(X = 6)$.

2 Given that $Y \sim B\left(7, \frac{2}{3}\right)$, calculate
  (a) $P(Y = 4)$,   (b) $P(Y = 6)$,   (c) $P(Y = 0)$.

3 Given that $Z \sim B(9, 0.45)$, calculate
  (a) $P(Z = 3)$,   (b) $P(Z = 4 \text{ or } 5)$,   (c) $P(Z \geqslant 7)$.

4 Given that $D \sim B(12, 0.7)$, calculate
  (a) $P(D < 4)$,   (b) the smallest value of d such that $P(D > d) < 0.90$.

5 Given that $H \sim B\left(9, \frac{1}{2}\right)$, calculate the probability that H is
  (a) exactly 5,   (b) 5 or 6,   (c) at least 8,   (d) more than 2.

6 Given that $S \sim B\left(7, \frac{1}{6}\right)$, find the probability that S is
  (a) exactly 3,   (b) at least 4.

7* If $X \sim B(n, p)$, show that $P(X = r + 1) = P(X = r) \times \dfrac{p(n-r)}{q(r+1)}$ for $r = 0, 1, \ldots, n - 1$.

If you have access to a spreadsheet, use this formula to construct tables for binomial probabilities.

Why is it better to use this formula than to calculate $\binom{n}{r} p^r q^{n-r}$ directly?

8* Use the formula of Question 7 to prove that the mode of a binomial distribution (that is, the value of r with the highest probability) satisfies $(n+1)p-1 \leqslant \text{mode} \leqslant (n+1)p$.

When is there equality?

7.2 Using the binomial distribution as a model

Before using the binomial distribution as a model for a situation you need to convince yourself that all the conditions are satisfied. The following example illustrates some of the problems that can occur.

Example 7.2.1

A school car park has 5 parking spaces. A student decides to do a survey to see whether this is enough. At the same time each day, she observes the number of spaces which are filled. Let X be the number of spaces filled at this time on a randomly chosen day. Is it reasonable to model the distribution of the random variable X with a binomial distribution?

> She looks at each parking space to see whether it is occupied or not. This represents a single trial.
>
> Are there exactly two outcomes for each trial (parking space), and are these mutually exclusive? In other words, is each parking space either occupied by a single car or not? The answer will usually be yes, but sometimes poorly parked vehicles will give the answer no.
>
> Are there a fixed number of trials? The answer is yes. On each day there are 5 parking spaces available so the number of trials is 5.
>
> Are the trials independent? This is not likely. Drivers may be less inclined to park in one of the centre spaces if it is surrounded by cars, because getting out of their own car may be more difficult.
>
> Is the probability p of success (in this case a parking space being filled by a car) constant? Probably not, because people may be more likely to choose the space closest to the school entrance, for example.

You can see that, when you are proposing to model a practical situation with a binomial distribution, many of the assumptions may be questionable and some may not be valid at all. In this case, however, provided you are aware that the binomial model is far from perfect, you could still use it as a reasonable approximation. You might also have realised that you do not know the value of p in this example, so you would have to estimate it. To do this you would divide the total number of cars observed by the total number of available car parking spaces, which in this case is

$5 \times$ (the number of days for which the survey was carried out).

Example 7.2.2

State whether a binomial distribution could be used in each of the following problems. If the binomial distribution is an acceptable model, define the random variable clearly and state its parameters.

(a) A fair cubical dice is rolled 10 times. Find the probability of getting three 4s, four 5s and three 6s.

(b) A fair coin is spun until a head occurs. Find the probability that eight spins are necessary, including the one on which the head occurs.

(c) A jar contains 49 balls numbered 1 to 49. Six of the balls are selected at random. Find the probability that four of the six have an even score.

> (a) In this case you are interested in three different outcomes: a 4, a 5 and a 6. A binomial distribution depends on having only two possible outcomes, success and failure, so it cannot be used here.

> (b) The binomial distribution requires a fixed number of trials, n, and this is not the case here, since the number of trials is unknown. In fact, the number of trials is the random variable of interest here.

> (c) Whether a binomial model is appropriate or not depends on whether the selection of the balls is done with replacement or without replacement. If the selection is without replacement, then the outcome of each trial will not be independent of all the other trials. If the selection is with replacement, then define the random variable X to be the number of balls with an even score out of six random selections. X will then have a binomial distribution with parameters 6 and $\frac{24}{49}$. You write this as $X \sim B\left(6, \frac{24}{49}\right)$. You are assuming, of course, that the balls are thoroughly mixed before each selection and that every ball has an equal chance of being selected.

Example 7.2.3

A card is selected at random from a standard pack of 52 playing cards. The suit of the card is recorded and the card is replaced. This process is repeated to give a total of 16 selections, and on each occasion the card is replaced in the pack before another selection is made. Calculate the probability that

(a) exactly five hearts occur in the 16 selections,

(b) at least three hearts occur.

> Let X be the number of hearts in 16 random selections (with replacement) of a playing card from a pack. Then X satisfies all the conditions for a binomial distribution.

> - Each trial consists of selecting a card from the pack, with replacement.
> - Each trial has exactly two possible outcomes, and these are mutually exclusive; getting a heart is a success and not getting a heart is a failure.

You may think that there are 52 possible outcomes for each trial, but you are only interested in whether the card is a heart or not a heart.

> - The outcome of each trial is independent of any other trial. This is true since each card is replaced before the next one is selected. But you must ensure that each selection is random and that the cards are thoroughly shuffled before each selection.

- The probabilities of success and failure are constant. As the cards are replaced, P(selecting a heart) = P(success) = $\frac{1}{4}$ and P(not selecting a heart) = P(failure) = $\frac{3}{4}$, so this condition is fulfilled.

X therefore has a binomial distribution with parameters $n = 16$ and $p = \frac{1}{4}$. That is,

$$X \sim B\left(16, \tfrac{1}{4}\right).$$

(a) Using the binomial formula,

$$P(X = 5) = \binom{16}{5} \times \left(\tfrac{1}{4}\right)^5 \times \left(\tfrac{3}{4}\right)^{11} = 0.180, \text{ correct to 3 significant figures.}$$

(b) To find $P(X \geqslant 3)$, use the fact that $P(X \geqslant 3) = 1 - P(X \leqslant 2)$.

$$P(X \geqslant 3) = 1 - P(X \leqslant 2)$$
$$= 1 - \binom{16}{0}\left(\tfrac{1}{4}\right)^0\left(\tfrac{3}{4}\right)^{16} - \binom{16}{1}\left(\tfrac{1}{4}\right)^1\left(\tfrac{3}{4}\right)^{15} - \binom{16}{2}\left(\tfrac{1}{4}\right)^2\left(\tfrac{3}{4}\right)^{14}$$
$$= 1 - 0.010\,02 - 0.053\,45 - 0.133\,63\ldots$$
$$= 1 - 0.197\,11$$
$$= 0.802\,88\ldots = 0.803, \text{ correct to 3 significant figures.}$$

7.3 Practical activities

1 Penalties or shots

(a) Select a group of students and ask them each to take either 8 penalties at football or 8 shots at basketball. For each student record the number of successful penalties or shots.

(b) Does the binomial distribution provide a reasonable model for these results? Is it necessary to use the same goalkeeper for all of the football penalties?

(c) Does the skill level of each person matter if the binomial distribution is to be a reasonable model? Is the basketball example more likely to be fitted by a binomial model than the football example?

Exercise 7B

1 In a certain school, 30% of the students are in the age group 16–19.

(a) Ten students are chosen at random. What is the probability that fewer than four of them are in the 16–19 age group?

(b) If the ten students were chosen by picking ten who were sitting together at lunch, explain why a binomial distribution might no longer have been suitable.

2 A factory makes large quantities of coloured sweets, and it is known that on average 20% of the sweets are coloured green. A packet contains 20 sweets. Assuming that the packet forms a random sample of the sweets made by the factory, calculate the probability that exactly seven of the sweets are green.

If you knew that, in fact, the sweets could have been green, red, orange or brown, would it have invalidated your calculation?

3   Eggs produced at a farm are packaged in boxes of six. Assume that, for any egg, the probability that it is broken when it reaches the retail outlet is 0.1, independent of all other eggs. A box is said to be bad if it contains at least two broken eggs. Calculate the probability that a randomly selected box is bad.

Ten boxes are chosen at random. Find the probability that just two of these boxes are bad.

It is known that, in fact, breakages are more likely to occur after the eggs have been packed into boxes, and while they are being transported to the retail outlet. Explain why this fact is likely to invalidate the calculation.

4   On a particular tropical island, the probability that there is a hurricane in any given month can be taken to be 0.08. Use a binomial distribution to calculate the probability that there is a hurricane in more than two months of the year. State two assumptions needed for a binomial distribution to be a good model. Why may one of the assumptions not be valid?

5   It is given that, at a stated time of day, 35% of the adults in the country are wearing jeans. At that time, a sample of twelve adults is selected. Use a binomial distribution to calculate the probability that exactly five out of these twelve are wearing jeans. Explain carefully two assumptions that must be made for your calculation to be valid. (If you say 'sample is random' you must explain what this means in the context of the question.)

6   Explain why a binomial distribution would not be a good model in the following problem. (Do not attempt any calculation.)

Thirteen cards are chosen at random from an ordinary pack. Find the probability that there are four clubs, four diamonds, three hearts and two spades.

7   Explain why the binomial distribution $B(6, 0.5)$ would not be a good model in each of the following situations. (Do not attempt any calculations.)

(a)   It is known that 50% of the boys in a certain school are over 170 cm in height. They are arranged, for a school photograph, in order of ascending height. A group of six boys standing next to each other is selected at random. Find the probability that exactly three members of the sample are over 170 cm in height.

(b)   It is known that, on average, the temperature in London reaches at least $20\,°C$ on exactly half the days in the year. A day is picked at random from each of the months January, March, May, July, September and November. Find the probability that the temperature in London reaches $20\,°C$ on exactly three of these six days.

8   A bag contains six red and four green counters. Four counters are selected at random, without replacement. The events A, B, C and D represent obtaining a red counter on the first, second, third and fourth selection, respectively.

Use a tree diagram to show that $P(A) = P(B) = P(C) = P(D) = 0.6$.

Explain why the total number of red counters could not be well modelled by the distribution $B(4, 0.6)$.

The purpose of this and the preceding question is to illustrate that the properties 'the probability of a success is constant' and 'the outcomes are independent' are not the same, and you should try to distinguish carefully between them. Notice also that 'the outcomes are independent' is not the same thing as 'sampling with replacement'.

Miscellaneous exercise 7

1 The probability of a novice archer hitting a target with any shot is 0.3. Given that the archer shoots six arrows, find the probability that the target is hit at least twice.   (OCR)

2 A computer is programmed to produce at random a single digit from the list $0, 1, 2, 3, 4, 5,$ $6, 7, 8, 9$. The program is run twenty times. Let Y be the number of zeros that occur.

(a) State the distribution of Y and give its parameters.

(b) Calculate $P(Y < 3)$.

3 A dice is biased so that the probability of throwing a 6 is 0.2. The dice is thrown eight times. Let X be the number of '6's thrown.

(a) State the distribution of X and give its parameters.

(b) Calculate $P(X > 3)$.

4 Joseph and four friends each have an independent probability 0.45 of winning a prize. Find the probability that

(a) exactly two of the five friends win a prize,

(b) Joseph and only one friend win a prize.   (OCR)

5 A bag contains two biased coins: coin A shows Heads with probability 0.6, and coin B shows Heads with probability 0.25. A coin is chosen at random from the bag, and tossed three times.

(a) Find the probability that the three tosses of the coin show two Heads and one Tail in any order.

(b) Find the probability that the coin chosen was coin A, given that the three tosses result in two Heads and one Tail.   (OCR)

6 (a) A fair coin is tossed 4 times. Calculate the probabilities that the tosses result in $0, 1, 2,$ 3 and 4 heads.

(b) A fair coin is tossed 8 times. Calculate the probability that the first 4 tosses and the last 4 tosses result in the same number of heads.

(c) Two teams each consist of 3 players. Each player in a team tosses a fair coin once and the team's score is the total number of heads thrown. Find the probability that the teams have the same score.   (OCR)

7 State the conditions under which the binomial distribution may be used for the calculation of probabilities.

The probability that a girl chosen at random has a weekend birthday in 1993 is $\frac{2}{7}$. Calculate the probability that, among a group of ten girls chosen at random,

(a) none has a weekend birthday in 1993,

(b) exactly one has a weekend birthday in 1993.

Among 100 groups of ten girls, how many groups would you expect to contain more than one girl with a weekend birthday in 1993?   (OCR)

8 Show that, when two fair dice are thrown, the probability of obtaining a 'double' is $\frac{1}{6}$, where a 'double' is defined as the same score on both dice. Four players play a board game which requires them to take it in turns to throw two fair dice. Each player throws the two dice once in each round. When a double is thrown the player moves forward six squares. Otherwise the player moves forward one square. Find

(a) the probability that the first double occurs on the third throw of the game,

(b) the probability that exactly one of the four players obtains a double in the first round,

(c) the probability that a double occurs exactly once in 4 of the first 5 rounds.   (OCR)

9 Six hens are observed over a period of 20 days and the number of eggs laid each day is summarised in the following table.

Number of eggs	3	4	5	6
Number of days	2	2	10	6

Show that the mean number of eggs per day is 5.

It may be assumed that a hen never lays more than one egg in any day. State one other assumption that needs to be made in order to consider a binomial model, with $n = 6$, for the total number of eggs laid in a day. State the probability that a randomly chosen hen lays an egg on a given day.

Calculate the expected frequencies of 3, 4, 5 and 6 eggs.   (OCR)

10 A Personal Identification Number (PIN) consists of 4 digits in order, each of which is one of the digits $0, 1, 2, \dots, 9$. Susie has difficulty remembering her PIN. She tries to remember it and writes down what she thinks it is. The probability that the first digit is correct is 0.8 and the probability that the second digit is correct is 0.86. The probability that the first two digits are correct is 0.72. Find

(a) the probability that the second digit is correct given that the first digit is correct,

(b) the probability that the first digit is correct and the second digit is incorrect,

(c) the probability that the first digit is incorrect and the second digit is correct,

(d) the probability that the second digit is incorrect given that the first digit is incorrect.

The probability that all four digits are correct is 0.7. On 12 separate occasions Susie writes down independently what she thinks is her PIN. Find the probability that the number of occasions on which all four digits are correct is less than 10.   (OCR)

8 Expectation and variance of a random variable

This chapter shows you how to calculate the mean and variance of a discrete random variable. When you have completed it, you should

- know the meaning of the notation $E(X)$ and $Var(X)$
- be able to calculate the mean, $E(X)$, of a random variable X
- be able to calculate the variance, $Var(X)$, of a random variable X
- be able to use the formulae $E(X) = np$ and $Var(X) = np(1-p)$ for a binomial distribution.

8.1 Expectation

A computer is programmed to produce a sequence of integers, X, from 0 to 3 inclusive, with probabilities as shown below.

x	0	1	2	3
$P(X = x)$	0.4	0.3	0.2	0.1

Suppose that a sequence of 100 integers is produced by the computer. What would you expect the mean of these 100 values to be? It is not possible to answer this question exactly because you cannot tell how often each value will actually turn up in the sequence. However, it is possible to obtain an *estimate* of the mean value. You can estimate the frequency with which each integer occurs using

$$\text{frequency} \approx \text{total frequency} \times \text{probability}$$

(see Section 6.3). You might expect there to be about $100 \times 0.4 = 40$ '0's, $100 \times 0.3 = 30$ '1's, $100 \times 0.2 = 20$ '2's and $100 \times 0.1 = 10$ '3's. The sum of these integers would be

$$(0 \times 40) + (1 \times 30) + (2 \times 20) + (3 \times 10) = 100$$

so their mean would be $\frac{100}{100} = 1$.

If you look at this calculation carefully, you will see that it is independent of the number of integers in the sequence. For example, if you had a sequence of 1000 integers, then the sum of the integers would be 10 times as great, but the estimate of the mean would stay the same.

The same result can be obtained more directly by multiplying each value by its probability and summing. Using p_i as a shortened form of $P(X = x_i)$, this gives

$$\sum x_i p_i = (0 \times 0.4) + (1 \times 0.3) + (2 \times 0.2) + (3 \times 0.1) = 1.$$

The value which has just been calculated is a theoretical mean. It is denoted by μ (which is read as 'mu'), the Greek letter m, standing for 'mean'. The new symbol is used in order to distinguish the mean of a probability distribution from $\bar{x}$, the mean of a data set. The mean, μ, of a probability distribution does not represent the mean of a finite sequence of numbers. It is the value to which the mean tends as the length of the sequence gets larger and larger, or, as mathematicians say, 'tends to infinity'. In practice, it is helpful to think of μ as the mean you would expect for a very very long sequence. For this reason, μ is often called the **expectation** or **expected value** of X and is denoted by $E(X)$.

The expectation of a random variable X is defined by $E(X) = \mu = \sum x_i p_i$.

Example 8.1.1

Find the expected value of each of the variables X, Y and W, which have the probability distributions given below.

(a)

x	1	2	3	4	5	6	Total
$P(X = x)$	$\frac{1}{6}$	$\frac{1}{6}$	$\frac{1}{6}$	$\frac{1}{6}$	$\frac{1}{6}$	$\frac{1}{6}$	1

(b)

y	1	2	3	4	5	7	8	9	10	11	12	Total
$P(Y = y)$	$\frac{1}{6}$	$\frac{1}{6}$	$\frac{1}{6}$	$\frac{1}{6}$	$\frac{1}{6}$	$\frac{1}{36}$	$\frac{1}{36}$	$\frac{1}{36}$	$\frac{1}{36}$	$\frac{1}{36}$	$\frac{1}{36}$	1

(c)

w	2	3	4	5	6	7	8	9	10	11	12	Total
$P(W = w)$	$\frac{1}{36}$	$\frac{2}{36}$	$\frac{3}{36}$	$\frac{4}{36}$	$\frac{5}{36}$	$\frac{6}{36}$	$\frac{5}{36}$	$\frac{4}{36}$	$\frac{3}{36}$	$\frac{2}{36}$	$\frac{1}{36}$	1

(a) $E(X) = \sum x_i p_i = \left(1 \times \frac{1}{6}\right) + \left(2 \times \frac{1}{6}\right) + \left(3 \times \frac{1}{6}\right) + \left(4 \times \frac{1}{6}\right) + \left(5 \times \frac{1}{6}\right) + \left(6 \times \frac{1}{6}\right) = 3\frac{1}{2}$.

You may have spotted that there is a quicker way to find the mean in this example. Since the distribution is symmetrical about $3\frac{1}{2}$, the mean must equal $3\frac{1}{2}$.

(b) This distribution is not symmetrical and so the mean has to be calculated.

$$E(Y) = \sum y_i p_i = \left(1 \times \frac{1}{6}\right) + \left(2 \times \frac{1}{6}\right) + \left(3 \times \frac{1}{6}\right) + \left(4 \times \frac{1}{6}\right) + \left(5 \times \frac{1}{6}\right) + \left(7 \times \frac{1}{36}\right)$$

$$+ \left(8 \times \frac{1}{36}\right) + \left(9 \times \frac{1}{36}\right) + \left(10 \times \frac{1}{36}\right) + \left(11 \times \frac{1}{36}\right) + \left(12 \times \frac{1}{36}\right)$$

$$= (1 + 2 + 3 + 4 + 5) \times \frac{1}{6} + (7 + 8 + 9 + 10 + 11 + 12) \times \frac{1}{36}$$

$$= 15 \times \frac{1}{6} + 57 \times \frac{1}{36} = 4\frac{1}{12}.$$

(c) As in part (a), the probability distribution is symmetrical, in this case about 7, so $E(W) = 7$.

The variables X, Y and W were discussed in Section 6.1 in connection with the number of squares moved in a turn at three different board games. This calculation shows that you move round the board fastest in Game C and slowest in Game A.

Example 8.1.2

A random variable R has the probability distribution shown below.

r	1	2	3	4
$P(R = r)$	0.1	a	0.3	b

Given that $E(R) = 3$, find a and b.

Since $\sum P(R = r) = 1$,

$$0.1 + a + 0.3 + b = 1, \quad \text{so} \quad a + b = 0.6.$$

Also $E(R) = 3$, so $\sum rP(R = r) = 3$,

$$1 \times 0.1 + 2 \times a + 3 \times 0.3 + 4 \times b = 3, \quad \text{so} \quad 2a + 4b = 2.$$

Solving these two equations simultaneously gives $a = 0.2$ and $b = 0.4$.

8.2 The variance of a random variable

Example 8.1.1 showed that the random variables X, Y and W have different means. If you compare the probability distributions (which are illustrated in Fig. 6.6), you will see that X, Y and W also have different degrees of spread. Just as the spread in a data set can be measured by the standard deviation or variance, so it is possible to define a corresponding measure of spread for a random variable. The symbol used for the standard deviation of a random variable is σ (a small Greek s, read as 'sigma') and its square, σ^2, the variance of a random variable, is denoted by $\text{Var}(X)$.

Before deriving a formula for $\text{Var}(X)$, it is helpful to look at another method of arriving at the formula for $E(X)$. Suppose that you had a sequence of n integers produced by the computer described in Section 8.1, and that the sequence contained f_1 '0's, f_2 '1's, f_3 '2's and f_4 '3's. The mean for these n integers is given by

$$\bar{x} = \frac{\sum x_i f_i}{n} = \frac{0 \times f_1}{n} + \frac{1 \times f_2}{n} + \frac{2 \times f_3}{n} + \frac{3 \times f_4}{n}.$$

The right side of the expression can be written slightly differently in the form

$$\bar{x} = 0 \times \frac{f_1}{n} + 1 \times \frac{f_2}{n} + 2 \times \frac{f_3}{n} + 3 \times \frac{f_4}{n} = \sum \left(x_i \times \frac{f_i}{n} \right).$$

Now consider what happens as n becomes very large: the value of $\bar{x}$ tends to μ, and the ratio $\frac{f_i}{n}$, which is the relative frequency, tends to the corresponding theoretical probability, p_i. This gives

$$\mu = E(X) = \sum x_i p_i. \tag{8.1}$$

which was the result obtained in Section 8.1.

Now consider the formula given in Equation 3.3 for the variance of a data set. Replacing $\sum f_i$ by n and rearranging gives

$$\text{variance} = \frac{\sum (x_i - \bar{x})^2 f_i}{n} = \sum (x_i - \bar{x})^2 \times \frac{f_i}{n}.$$

Again consider what happens when n becomes large. The ratio $\frac{f_i}{n}$ tends to p_i, and $\bar{x}$ tends to μ, giving

$$\sigma^2 = \text{Var}(X) = \sum (x_i - \mu)^2 p_i. \tag{8.2}$$

Alternatively, starting from Equation 3.4 for the variance of a data set, replacing $\sum f_i$ by n and rearranging gives

$$\text{variance} = \frac{\sum x_i^2 f_i}{n} - \bar{x}^2 = \sum x_i^2 \times \frac{f_i}{n} - \bar{x}^2.$$

When n becomes large, $\frac{f_i}{n}$ tends to p_i and $\bar{x}$ tends to μ, giving

$$\sigma^2 = \text{Var}(X) = \sum x_i^2 p_i - \mu^2. \tag{8.3}$$

The **variance** of a random variable X is defined by

$$\sigma^2 = \text{Var}(X) = \sum (x_i - \mu)^2 p_i = \sum x_i^2 p_i - \mu^2.$$

The **standard deviation** of a random variable is σ, the square root of $\text{Var}(X)$.

In practice it is usually simpler to calculate $\text{Var}(X)$ from Equation 8.3 rather than from Equation 8.2.

Example 8.2.1

Calculate the standard deviation of the random variable X in Example 8.1.1, using Equation 8.3.

First calculate $\sum x_i^2 p_i$:

$$\sum x_i^2 p_i = \left(1^2 \times \tfrac{1}{6}\right) + \left(2^2 \times \tfrac{1}{6}\right) + \left(3^3 \times \tfrac{1}{6}\right) + \left(4^2 \times \tfrac{1}{6}\right) + \left(5^2 \times \tfrac{1}{6}\right) + \left(6^2 \times \tfrac{1}{6}\right)$$
$$= \left(1^2 + 2^2 + 3^2 + 4^2 + 5^2 + 6^2\right) \times \tfrac{1}{6} = 91 \times \tfrac{1}{6} = 15\tfrac{1}{6}.$$

From Example 8.1.1, $\mu = \text{E}(X) = 3\tfrac{1}{2}$.

Using Equation 8.3:

$$\sigma^2 = \text{Var}(X) = \sum x_i^2 p_i - \mu^2 = 15\tfrac{1}{6} - \left(3\tfrac{1}{2}\right)^2 = \tfrac{35}{12}.$$

Then calculate the standard deviation:

$$\sigma = \sqrt{\tfrac{35}{12}} = 1.71 \text{, correct to 3 significant figures.}$$

The standard deviations for the random variables Y and W in Example 8.1.1 are

$\sqrt{\tfrac{10\,395}{1296}} = 2.83$ *and* $\sqrt{\tfrac{35}{6}} = 2.42$ *respectively, both given to 3 significant figures.*

You could check these values. If you look again at Fig. 6.6 you will see how the size of the standard deviation is related to the degree of spread of the distribution. Although Y and W have very similar ranges, W has a smaller standard deviation because the probability distribution rises to a peak at the centre.

Example 8.2.2

In a certain field, each mushroom which is growing gives rise to a number X of mushrooms in the following year. None of the mushrooms present in one year survives until the next year. The random variable X has the following probability distribution.

x	0	1	2
$P(X = x)$	0.2	0.6	0.2

If there were two mushrooms present in one year, find the probability distribution of Y, the number of mushrooms present in the following year. Hence find the mean and variance of Y.

The possible values of Y are given below, where the first value of X is the value of X for one mushroom, and the second value of X is the value of X for the second mushroom.

		First value of X		
		0	1	2
	0	0	1	2
Second value of X	1	1	2	3
	2	2	3	4

The corresponding probabilities are given below.

		First value of X		
		0	1	2
	0	0.2×0.2	0.2×0.6	0.2×0.2
Second value of X	1	0.6×0.2	0.6×0.6	0.6×0.2
	2	0.2×0.2	0.2×0.6	0.2×0.2

Combining these two sets of results gives the probability distribution of Y, from which $E(Y)$ and $Var(Y)$ can be found.

y	$P(Y = y)$	$yP(Y = y)$	$y^2 P(Y = y)$
0	0.04	0	0
1	$0.12 + 0.12 = 0.24$	0.24	0.24
2	$0.04 + 0.36 + 0.04 = 0.44$	0.88	1.76
3	$0.12 + 0.12 = 0.24$	0.72	2.16
4	0.04	0.16	0.64
	Totals: $\sum P(Y = y) = 1$	$\sum yP(Y = y) = 2$	$\sum y^2 P(Y = y) = 4.8$

From the last row of the table $\sum yP(Y = y) = 2$, and $\sum y^2 P(Y = y) = 4.8$.

Then $E(Y) = \sum yP(Y = y) = 2$, and

$$Var(Y) = \sum y^2 P(Y = y) - (E(Y))^2 = 4.8 - 2^2 = 0.8.$$

Exercise 8A

In this exercise all variables are discrete. Give numerical answers to 4 significant figures when appropriate.

1 Find the mean of the random variables X and Y which have the following probability distributions.

(a)

x	0	1	2	3	4
$P(X = x)$	$\frac{1}{8}$	$\frac{3}{8}$	$\frac{1}{8}$	$\frac{1}{4}$	$\frac{1}{8}$

(b)

y	-2	-1	0	1	2	3
$P(Y = y)$	0.15	0.25	0.3	0.05	0.2	0.05

2 The random variable T has the probability distribution given in the following table.

t	1	2	3	4	5	6	7
$P(T = t)$	0.1	0.2	0.1	0.2	0.1	0.2	0.1

Find $E(T)$ and $Var(T)$.

3 Find the exact expectation and variance of the random variable Y, which has the following probability distribution.

y	3	4	5	6	7
$P(Y = y)$	$\frac{1}{18}$	$\frac{5}{18}$	$\frac{7}{18}$	$\frac{1}{18}$	$\frac{4}{18}$

4 The six faces of a fair cubical dice are numbered $1, 2, 2, 3, 3$ and 3. When the dice is thrown once, the score is the number appearing on the top face. This is denoted by X.

(a) Find the mean and standard deviation of X.

(b) The dice is thrown twice and Y denotes the sum of the scores obtained. Find the probability distribution of Y. Hence find $E(Y)$ and $Var(Y)$.

5 A construction company can bid for one of two possible projects and the finance director has been asked to advise on which to choose. She estimates that project A will yield a profit of $150\,000$ with probability 0.5, a profit of $250\,000$ with probability 0.2 and a loss of $100\,000$ with probability 0.3. Project B will yield a profit of $100\,000$ with probability 0.6, a profit of $200\,000$ with probability 0.3 and a loss of $50\,000$ with probability 0.1. Determine which project the finance director should support.

6 Some of the eggs at a market are sold in boxes of six. The number, X, of broken eggs in a box has the probability distribution given in the following table.

x	0	1	2	3	4	5	6
$P(X = x)$	0.80	0.14	0.03	0.02	0.01	0	0

(a) Find the expectation and variance of X.

(b) Find the expectation and variance of the number of unbroken eggs in a box.

(c) Comment on the relationship between your answers to part (a) and part (b).

7 Find $E(H)$ and $Var(H)$ for the H defined in Exercise 6A Question 4.

8 The random variable X has the probability distribution given in the following table.

x	1	2	3	4	5
$P(X = x)$	a	0.3	0.2	0.1	0.2

Find the values of a, μ and σ for the distribution.

9 The random variable Y has the probability distribution given in the following table.

y	2	3	4	5	6	7
$P(Y = y)$	0.05	0.25	a	b	0.1	0.3

Given that $E(Y) = 4.9$, show that $a = b$, and find the standard deviation of Y.

10 A game is played by throwing a fair dice until either a 6 is obtained or four throws have been made. Let X denote the number of throws made. Find

(a) the probability distribution of X,   (b) the standard deviation of X.

The number of 6s obtained in the game is denoted by Y. Find $E(Y)$.

If the player throws a 6 in the course of the game, then the player wins 100 points. If a 6 is not thrown, then 150 points are lost. Find the expectation of the number of points received by a player after one game.

11 The dice of Question 4 is thrown and then an unbiased coin is thrown the number of times indicated by the score on the dice. Let H denote the number of heads obtained.

(a) Show that $P(H = 2) = \frac{13}{48}$.

(b) Tabulate the probability distribution of H.

(c) Show that $E(H) = \frac{1}{2}E(X)$, where X denotes the score on the dice.

(d) Calculate $Var(H)$.

8.3 The expectation and variance of a binomial distribution

Suppose that you want to find the mean and variance of the random variable X, where $X \sim B\left(3,\frac{1}{4}\right)$. One way would be to write out the probability distribution and calculate $E(X)$ and $Var(X)$ using Equations 8.1 and 8.3.

Example 8.3.1
Calculate $E(X)$ and $Var(X)$ for $X \sim B\left(3,\frac{1}{4}\right)$ from the probability distribution.

The probability distribution is found using the binomial probability formula

$$P(X = x) = \binom{n}{x}p^x(1-p)^{n-x} \text{ (see Equation 7.1)}.$$

x	$P(X = x)$	$xP(X = x)$	$x^2P(X = x)$
0	$\binom{3}{0}\left(\frac{1}{4}\right)^0\left(\frac{3}{4}\right)^3 = \frac{27}{64}$	0	0
1	$\binom{3}{1}\left(\frac{1}{4}\right)^1\left(\frac{3}{4}\right)^2 = \frac{27}{64}$	$\frac{27}{64}$	$\frac{27}{64}$
2	$\binom{3}{2}\left(\frac{1}{4}\right)^2\left(\frac{3}{4}\right)^1 = \frac{9}{64}$	$\frac{18}{64}$	$\frac{36}{64}$
3	$\binom{3}{3}\left(\frac{1}{4}\right)^3\left(\frac{3}{4}\right)^0 = \frac{1}{64}$	$\frac{3}{64}$	$\frac{9}{64}$

Totals: $\sum p_i = 1 \quad \sum x_i p_i = \frac{48}{64} \quad \sum x_i^2 p_i = \frac{72}{64}$

Remember that p_i is the same as $P(X = x_i)$.

$$\mu = E(X) = \sum x_i p_i = \frac{48}{64} = \frac{3}{4}.$$

$$\sigma^2 = Var(X) = \sum x_i^2 p_i - \mu^2 = \frac{72}{64} - \left(\frac{3}{4}\right)^2 = \frac{36}{64} = \frac{9}{16}.$$

There is, however, a quicker method for doing these calculations. If you consider the general case $X \sim B(n,p)$, then the mean would be given by $\sum x_i p_i = \sum x\binom{n}{x}p^x(1-p)^{n-x}$.

Each term in this sum depends on the parameters n and p and so it would be reasonable to assume that $E(X)$ also depends on n and p. Although this sum looks very complicated, it can be shown that it simplifies to np.

The working is not shown here, but intuitively you might expect this result, since in n trials

number of successes ≈ number of trials × probability of success at a single trial

$$= n \times p = np.$$

Now $\sum x_i^2 p_i$ also depends on n and p and so, therefore, does $\text{Var}(X)$. It can be shown that $\text{Var}(X) = np(1-p) - npq$, where $q = 1-p$.

> For a random variable with a binomial distribution, $X \sim \text{B}(n,p)$,
>
> $$E(X) = np, \tag{8.4}$$
> $$\text{Var}(X) = np(1-p) = npq, \quad \text{where } q = 1-p. \tag{8.5}$$

Example 8.3.2

Calculate $E(X)$ and $\text{Var}(X)$ for $X \sim \text{B}\left(3, \frac{1}{4}\right)$ using Equations 8.4 and 8.5.

Using Equations 8.4 and 8.5,

$$E(X) = \mu = np = 3 \times \tfrac{1}{4} = \tfrac{3}{4},$$
$$\text{Var}(X) = \sigma^2 = np(1-p) = 3 \times \tfrac{1}{4} \times \tfrac{3}{4} = \tfrac{9}{16}.$$

You can see that the second method is much quicker than the first. The formulae for calculating the mean and variance of a binomial distribution are particularly useful when n is large, as in the following example.

Example 8.3.3

Nails are sold in packets of 100. Occasionally a nail is faulty. The number of faulty nails in a randomly chosen packet is denoted by X. Assuming that faulty nails occur independently and at random, calculate the mean and standard deviation of X, given that the probability of any nail being faulty is 0.04.

Since faulty nails occur independently and at random and with a fixed probability, the distribution of X can be modelled by the binomial distribution with $n = 100$ and $p = 0.04$. Therefore

$$E(X) = \mu = np = 100 \times 0.04 = 4,$$
$$\text{Var}(X) = \sigma^2 = np(1-p) = 100 \times 0.04 \times 0.96 = 3.84.$$

Therefore $\sigma = \sqrt{3.84} = 1.96$, correct to 3 significant figures.

To calculate μ and σ using Equations 8.1 and 8.3 you have to write out a probability distribution with 101 terms!

The following examples give further illustrations of the use of Equations 8.4 and 8.5.

Example 8.3.4
(a) Given that $X \sim B(10,0.3)$, find $E(X)$ and $Var(X)$.
(b) For $X \sim B(10,0.3)$, calculate $P(\mu - \sigma < X < \mu + \sigma)$.

   (a) Since $n = 10$ and $p = 0.3$,

$$E(X) = \mu = np = 10 \times 0.3 = 3,$$
$$Var(X) = \sigma^2 = np(1-p) = 10 \times 0.3 \times 0.7 = 2.1.$$

   (b) $\quad P(\mu - \sigma < X < \mu + \sigma) = P\left(\mu - \sqrt{2.1} < X < \mu + \sqrt{2.1}\right)$
$$= P(3 - 1.44... < X < 3 + 1.44...)$$
$$= P(1.55... < X < 4.44...)$$
$$= P(X = 2) + P(X = 3) + P(X = 4)$$
$$= \binom{10}{2}0.3^2 0.7^8 + \binom{10}{3}0.3^3 0.7^7 + \binom{10}{4}0.3^4 0.7^6$$
$$= 0.2334... + 0.2668... + 0.2001... = 0.7004....$$

   Thus $P(\mu - \sigma < X < \mu + \sigma) = 0.700$, correct to 3 significant figures.

Example 8.3.5
Given that $Y \sim B(n,p)$, and $E(Y) = 24$ and $Var(Y) = 8$, find the values of n and p.

   Using Equations 8.4 and 8.5,

$$E(Y) = np = 24 \quad \text{and} \quad Var(Y) = np(1-p) = 8.$$

   Substituting the value of np from the first equation into the second equation gives:

$$24(1-p) = 8, \quad \text{so} \quad 1-p = \tfrac{1}{3} \quad \text{and} \quad p = \tfrac{2}{3}.$$

   Using $np = 24$,

$$n = \frac{24}{p} = \frac{24}{\tfrac{2}{3}} = 24 \times \tfrac{3}{2} = 36.$$

Exercise 8B

1 Given that $X \sim B(20,0.14)$, calculate
   (a) $E(X)$ and $Var(X)$,   (b) $P(X \leq E(X))$.

2 A batch of capsules of a certain drug contains 2% of damaged capsules. A bottle contains 42 of these capsules. Calculate the mean and standard deviation of the number of damaged capsules in such a bottle, assuming that each capsule was randomly selected for inclusion in the bottle.

3 In a certain examination 35% of all candidates pass. Calculate the expectation and variance of the number of passes in a group of 30 randomly chosen candidates who take the examination.

4 The random variable X has a binomial distribution with mean 3 and variance 2.25. Find $P(X=3)$.

5 The random variables X and Y are such that $X \sim B(n,p)$ and $Y \sim B(m,p)$. Given that $E(X)=3$, $Var(X)=2.4$ and $E(Y)=2$, find $Var(Y)$.

6 For the random variable Y, for which $Y \sim B(16,0.8)$, calculate $P(Y > \mu + \sigma)$.

Miscellaneous exercise 8

1 The number of times a certain factory machine breaks down each working week has been recorded over a long period. From these data, the following probability distribution for the number, X, of weekly breakdowns was produced.

x	0	1	2	3	4	5	6
$P(X=x)$	0.04	0.24	0.28	0.16	0.16	0.08	0.04

(a) Find the mean and standard deviation of X.

(b) What would be the expected total number of breakdowns that will occur over the next 48 working weeks?

2 Some of the eggs sold in a store are packed in boxes of 10. For any egg, the probability that it is cracked is 0.05, independently of all other eggs. A shelf contains 80 of these boxes. Calculate the expected value of the number of boxes on the shelf which do not contain a cracked egg.

3 The random variable X is such that $X \sim B(5,p)$. Given that $P(X=0)=0.010\,24$, find the values of $E(X)$, $Var(X)$ and $P(X=E(X))$.

4 The independent random variables X and Y have the following probability distributions.

x	0	1	2	3
$P(X=x)$	0.3	0.2	0.4	0.1

y	3	4	5
$P(Y=y)$	0.5	0.2	0.3

Find $E(X)$, $Var(X)$, $E(Y)$ and $Var(Y)$.

The sum of one random observation of X and one random observation of Y is denoted by Z.

(a) Obtain the probability distribution of Z.

(b) Show that $E(Z)=E(X)+E(Y)$ and $Var(Z)=Var(X)+Var(Y)$.

5 A possible criterion for an outlier of a set of data is if it lies outside the interval from $\mu-2\sigma$ to $\mu+2\sigma$. For a set of observations of a random variable X, where $X \sim B(20,0.4)$, determine whether the following values constitute outliers according to this criterion.

(a) 2   (b) 5   (c) 10   (d) 15

Find $P(X < \mu-2\sigma)$ and $P(X > \mu+2\sigma)$.

6 An absent-minded mathematician is attempting to log on to a computer, which is done by typing the correct password. Unfortunately he can't remember his password. If he types the wrong password he tries again. The computer allows a maximum of four attempts altogether. For each attempt the probability of success is 0.4, independently of all other attempts.

   (a) Calculate the probability that he logs on successfully.

   (b) The total number of attempts he makes, successful or not, is denoted by X (so that the possible values of X are $1, 2, 3$ or 4). Tabulate the probability distribution of X.

   (c) Calculate the expectation and variance of X.   (OCR)

7 A committee of six men and four women appoints two of its members to represent it. Assuming that each member is equally likely to be appointed, obtain the probability distribution of the number of women appointed. Find the expected number of women appointed.

8 The discrete random variable X takes the values $1, 2, 3, 4$ and 5 only, with the probabilities shown in the table.

x	1	2	3	4	5
$P(X = x)$	a	0.3	0.1	0.2	b

   (a) Given that $E(X) = 2.34$. show that $a = 0.34$, and find the value of b.

   (b) Find $\text{Var}(X)$.

9* The number of eggs, X, laid by the female tawny owl (*Strix aluco*) has the probability distribution given in the following table.

x	2	3	4
$P(X = x)$	0.1	0.2	0.7

For any egg, the probability that it is hatched is 0.8, independently of all other eggs. Let Y denote the number of hatched eggs in a randomly chosen nest.

   (a) Obtain the probability distribution of Y.

   (b) Find $E(Y)$ and $\text{Var}(Y)$.

9 The normal distribution

This chapter investigates a very commonly occurring distribution, called the normal distribution. When you have completed it, you should

- understand the use of the normal distribution to model a continuous random variable
- be able to use the normal distribution function tables accurately
- be able to solve problems involving the normal distribution
- be able to find a relationship between x, μ and σ given the value of $P(X > x)$ or its equivalent
- recall conditions under which the normal distribution can be used as an approximation to the binomial distribution
- be able to solve problems using the normal approximation, with a continuity correction.

9.1 Modelling continuous variables

In Section 6.1, you met the idea of a discrete random variable and its probability distribution. An example is given in Table 9.1, which shows the probability distribution of the outcome of a single throw of a dice. The table lists each possible value of the variable together with its associated probability.

x	1	2	3	4	5	6
$P(X = x)$	$\frac{1}{6}$	$\frac{1}{6}$	$\frac{1}{6}$	$\frac{1}{6}$	$\frac{1}{6}$	$\frac{1}{6}$

Table 9.1. Probability distribution of the outcome of a single throw of a dice.

Is it possible to specify the distribution of a continuous random variable in the same way? Consider the lengths, in millimetres, of 50 leaves that have fallen from a coffee tree.

60	31	72	57	99	46	68	47	54	57
42	48	39	40	67	89	70	68	42	54
52	50	85	56	50	53	57	83	79	63
63	72	57	53	90	52	58	47	34	102
70	60	94	43	85	67	78	66	57	44

Although at first sight it appears that the length of a leaf takes discrete values, this is only because the length has been measured to a given degree of accuracy. For example, when the length is given as 63 mm, it means that the length, l, of the leaf lies in the interval $62.5 \leqslant l < 63.5$. This suggests that a probability model for the length, L, of a leaf should give the probability that L lies in a certain interval rather than that L takes a particular value. Thus the approach to modelling continuous variables must be different from that used for discrete variables.

The way in which the length of the leaves is distributed can be illustrated by a histogram. First, the data are assembled into a grouped frequency table, as in Table 9.2.

Length (mm)	Frequency	Relative frequency	Class boundaries	Class width	Relative frequency density
30–39	3	0.06	29.5–39.5	10	0.006
40–49	9	0.18	39.5–49.5	10	0.018
50–59	15	0.30	49.5–59.5	10	0.030
60–69	9	0.18	59.5–69.5	10	0.018
70–79	6	0.12	69.5–79.5	10	0.012
80–89	4	0.08	79.5–89.5	10	0.008
90–99	3	0.06	89.5–99.5	10	0.006
100–109	1	0.02	99.5–109.5	10	0.002

Table 9.2. Grouped frequency table for the coffee tree leaves.

The third column of this table gives the relative frequencies: these are found by dividing each frequency by the total frequency, in this case 50. The relative frequency gives the experimental probability that the length of a leaf lies in a given interval. The fourth and fifth columns give the class boundaries and class widths respectively. The last column gives the **relative frequency density**: this is found by dividing the relative frequency by the class width. The data are illustrated by the histogram in Fig. 9.3.

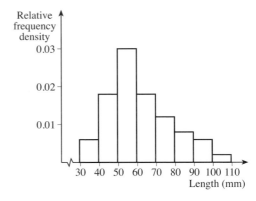

Fig. 9.3. Histogram of the data in Table 9.2.

A histogram is usually plotted with frequency density rather than *relative* frequency density on the vertical axis. The reason for using relative frequency density here is that area then represents *relative* frequency and hence experimental probability. It follows that the total area of the histogram must be equal to 1. The histogram can be used to give other experimental probabilities. For example, the shaded area in Fig. 9.4 gives the probability that the length, L, lies in the interval $54.5 \leqslant L < 71.5$. This area is equal to $5 \times 0.03 + 10 \times 0.018 + 2 \times 0.012 = 0.354$.

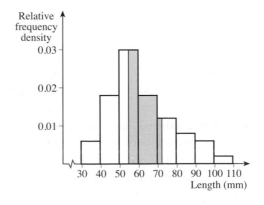

Fig. 9.4. Histogram of the data in Table 9.2.

If you want the probability that $L = 51.2$, say, the answer is zero. Although it is theoretically possible for L to equal 51.2 exactly, that is 51.200 000 …, the probability is actually zero. This means that $P(51 < L < 53) = P(51 \leqslant L < 53) = P(51 < L \leqslant 53) = P(51 \leqslant L \leqslant 53)$. This is characteristic of continuous distributions.

The probabilities calculated from the histogram in Fig. 9.4 could be used to model the length of a coffee tree leaf. However, the model is crude; first, because of the limited amount of data and, secondly, because of the small number of classes into which the leaves are assembled and the resulting 'steps' in the histogram. Collecting more data and reducing the class width can improve the model. Table 9.5 gives the frequency table for 100 leaves, with the size of the class widths halved. This table is illustrated by the histogram in Fig. 9.6. The area of this histogram is again 1 but the steps in the histogram are smaller.

Length (mm)	Frequency	Relative frequency	Class boundaries	Class width	Relative frequency density
30–34	2	0.02	29.5–34.5	5	0.004
35–39	4	0.04	34.5–39.5	5	0.008
40–44	7	0.07	39.5–44.5	5	0.014
45–49	10	0.10	44.5–49.5	5	0.020
50–54	14	0.14	49.5–54.5	5	0.028
55–59	15	0.15	54.5–59.5	5	0.030
60–64	13	0.13	59.5–64.5	5	0.026
65–69	9	0.09	64.5–69.5	5	0.018
70–74	8	0.08	69.5–74.5	5	0.016
75–79	7	0.07	74.5–79.5	5	0.014
80–84	4	0.04	79.5–84.5	5	0.008
85–89	3	0.03	84.5–89.5	5	0.006
90–94	2	0.02	89.5–94.5	5	0.004
95–99	1	0.01	94.5–99.5	5	0.002
100–104	1	0.01	99.5–104.5	5	0.002

Table 9.5. Grouped frequency table for the lengths of 100 coffee tree leaves.

The model could be further refined by repeating the process of collecting more data and reducing the class width. If this process were to be continued indefinitely, then the outline of the histogram would become a smooth curve instead of a series of steps. The sort of curve which you might expect is shown in Fig. 9.7. Since the distribution of the leaf length is approximately symmetrical, a symmetrical curve would seem appropriate. The axis of symmetry of the curve will be positioned at the mean length. The curve gives a model for the

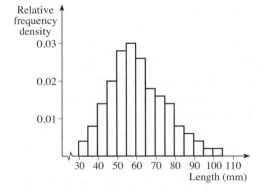

Fig. 9.6. Histogram of data in Table 9.5

length of a coffee tree leaf. The probability that the length of a leaf lies between the values a and b is given by the area under the curve between a and b, as shown in Fig. 9.8.

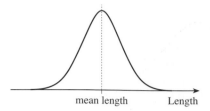

Fig. 9.7. Distribution of coffee tree leaf length.

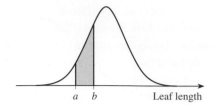

Fig. 9.8. Shaded area gives the probability that leaf length lies between a and b.

9.2   The normal distribution

The histograms of many other variables have features in common with Fig. 9.6.

(a) The distribution has a modal class somewhere in the middle of the range of values.
(b) The distribution is approximately symmetrical.
(c) The frequency density tails off fairly rapidly as the values of the variable move further away from the modal class.

This is just the sort of histogram which you would expect for the dimensions and masses of physical objects. Most of the values are close to the 'average' with just a few very large and a few very small values.

If the histogram of a variable shows these properties, then a bell-shaped curve, like that in Fig. 9.7, provides a suitable model. This model is called the **normal distribution**.

*The normal distribution is sometimes called the **Gaussian distribution** after Carl Friedrich Gauss (1777–1855), who introduced it in connection with the theory of errors. Although many continuous variables are normally distributed, many are not. Since the latter are in no way 'abnormal', the name 'Gaussian' is sometimes preferred.*

Although the curves for different variables that are normally distributed will have a similar bell shape, they will have different locations and spread. For example, the mean length of orange tree leaves will be different from that of coffee tree leaves and so will the dispersion. In order to specify the distribution completely, you need to give the mean, μ, and the variance, σ^2. The notation $X \sim N(\mu, \sigma^2)$ is used to denote a continuous variable which is normally distributed with mean, μ, and variance, σ^2.

Fig. 9.9 illustrates how the appearance of the normal distribution varies for different values of the parameters, μ and σ^2. Look at the top diagram. The curve for X_1 is centred on the mean 13, while that for X_2 is centred on the mean 20. The curves have the same spread because the variance is 9 for both variables. Now look at the bottom diagram. Both curves are centred on the mean 15, but the spread for X_2 is greater than that for X_1 because it has the greater variance. The area under all the curves is the same and equal to 1. This is why the curve for X_2 is flatter than that for X_1 in the bottom diagram.

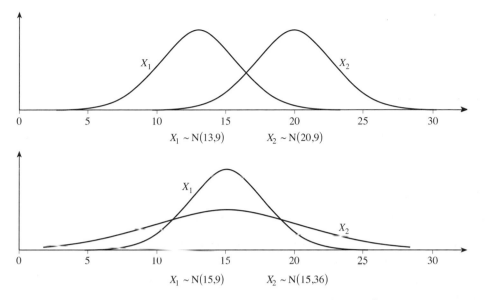

$$X_1 \sim N(13,9) \qquad X_2 \sim N(20,9)$$

$$X_1 \sim N(15,9) \qquad X_2 \sim N(15,36)$$

Fig. 9.9. Normal distributions with different values of μ and σ^2.

For any variable which is normally distributed, about $\frac{2}{3}$ of the values lie within 1 standard deviation of the mean, about 95% of values lie within 2 standard deviations of the mean and nearly all the values lie within 3 standard deviations of the mean. These properties are illustrated in Fig. 9.10. You can check that the diagrams in Fig. 9.9 also show these properties.

The curve of the distribution $X \sim N(\mu,\sigma^2)$ can be described mathematically by the function

$$f(x) = \frac{1}{\sigma\sqrt{2\pi}}\, e^{-\frac{(x-\mu)^2}{2\sigma^2}}$$

for all real values of x.

You will see that this curve extends from $-\infty$ to $+\infty$, which implies that x can take negative values. The length of a leaf, for example, can never be negative. However, the curve falls away so sharply that the probability that the normal model would predict a negative value for the length of a leaf is negligible.

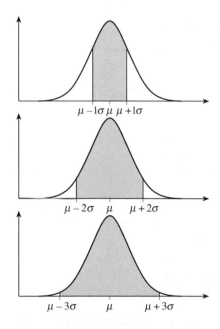

Fig. 9.10. Properties of the normal distribution: top, approximately $\frac{2}{3}$ of values lie within $\pm 1\sigma$ of the mean; middle, approximately 95% of values lie within $\pm 2\sigma$ of the mean; bottom, nearly all the values lie within $\pm 3\sigma$ of the mean.

9.3 The standard normal distribution

Probabilities for a variable which is normally distributed can be found from tables. At first sight this might appear impossible because a different table would be needed for each distribution, depending on the values of its parameters. However, it turns out that if the variable is **standardised** then one table is sufficient for all normal distributions. The standardised value, Z, is calculated from the value of the variable X by

$$Z = \frac{X - \mu}{\sigma}. \qquad (9.1)$$

You can see that Z measures the deviation of X from the mean, μ, in units of the standard deviation, σ. The random variable Z has a distribution which is $N(0,1)$. This is called the **standard normal distribution**. It is illustrated in Fig. 9.11. Like all other normal distributions, about $\frac{2}{3}$ of the values lie within 1 standard deviation of the mean, that is between -1 and 1, about 95% of values lie within 2 standard deviations of the mean, that is between -2 and 2, and nearly all the values lie within 3 standard deviations of the mean, that is between -3 and 3.

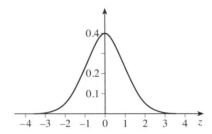

Fig. 9.11. Graph of the standard normal distribution.

If $X \sim N(\mu,\sigma^2)$ and $Z = \dfrac{X - \mu}{\sigma}$, then $Z \sim N(0,1)$.

The discussion which follows explains why $Z \sim N(0,1)$.

Suppose that the random variable X has a normal distribution with parameters μ and σ^2. Then the bell-shaped curve of the normal distribution will be centred on μ.

Let $Y = X - \mu$. Then the distribution of Y will have a typical bell shape but it will be centred on 0, rather than μ, because all the values have been reduced by μ.

The spreads of the two distributions are identical, so $Y \sim N(0,\sigma^2)$. Fig. 9.12 shows the relation between the distributions of X and Y.

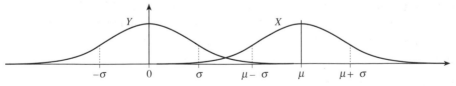

Fig. 9.12. Normal ditributions for $X \sim N(\mu,\sigma^2)$ and $Y \sim N(0,\sigma^2)$, where $Y = X - \mu$.

Now let $Z = \dfrac{Y}{\sigma}$. This has the effect of altering the spread of the distribution since when $Y = \pm\sigma$, then $Z = \pm 1$. Also when $Y = \pm 2\sigma$, then $Z = \pm 2$, and when $Y = \pm 3\sigma$, then $Z = \pm 3$. So, as Fig. 9.13 shows, Z has a standard normal distribution.

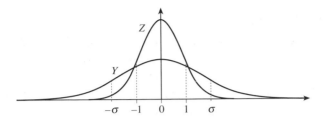

Fig. 9.13. Normal ditributions for $Y \sim N\left(0,\sigma^2\right)$ and $Z \sim N(0,1)$.

On page 172 there is a table of areas under the standard normal distribution. The table gives the value of $\Phi(z)$, the **normal distribution function**, where $\Phi(z) = P(Z \leqslant z)$. The shaded region in Fig. 9.14 shows the area tabulated.

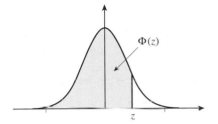

Fig. 9.14. The function $\Phi(z)$.

The symbol Φ, pronounced 'fi', is the Greek letter 'F'.

If your calculator has a routine which gives you the area under the standard normal distribution, then you should use this rather than the table.

To see what the numbers in the normal distribution function table mean, consider the value $\Phi(2)$. From the table on page 172, $\Phi(2) = 0.9772$. This means that for a random variable Z with a $N(0,1)$ distribution, $P(Z \leqslant 2) = 0.9772$. Fig. 9.15 illustrates this situation.

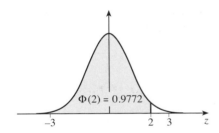

Fig. 9.15. $\Phi(2) = 0.9772$.

The table enables you to find $P(Z \leqslant z)$ for values of z, given correct to 3 decimal places, from $z = 0$ up to $z = 3$. Table 9.16 is taken from the table on page 172.

z	0	1	2	3	4	5	6	7	8	9	1	2	3	4	5	6	7	8	9
0.6	0.7257	0.7291	**0.7324**	0.7357	0.7389	0.7422	0.7454	0.7486	0.7517	0.7549	3	7	10	**13**	16	19	23	26	29

Table 9.16. Extract from the normal distribution function table on page 172.

Suppose that you wish to use the table to find $P(Z \leqslant 0.624)$, where $Z \sim N(0,1)$. The first two digits 0.6 of 0.624 indicate that you must look in the row labelled 0.6 in the z-column. The digit in the second decimal place is 2, so now look at the entry in the first column marked 2, giving the value 0.7324. The digit in the third decimal place is 4, so you must add 13 ten-thousandths (from the '4' column on the right) to 0.7324, giving 0.7337. Thus

$$P(Z \leqslant 0.624) = 0.7337.$$

To find the area between two values, $z = a$ and $z = b$, use the fact that the area between $z = a$ and $z = b$ can be written as

(area between $z = a$ and $z = b$) = (area up to $z = b$) − (area up to $z = a$).

In symbols,

$$P(a \leqslant Z \leqslant b) = P(Z \leqslant b) - P(Z \leqslant a) = \Phi(b) - \Phi(a).$$

For example,

$$P(1.20 \leqslant Z \leqslant 2.34) = \Phi(2.34) - \Phi(1.20) = 0.9904 - 0.8849 = 0.1055.$$

It is sensible to round all answers obtained from the table to 3 decimal places since the entries are given correct to 4 decimal places. So write

$$P(1.20 \leqslant Z \leqslant 2.34) = \Phi(2.34) - \Phi(1.20) = 0.9904 - 0.8849$$
$$= 0.1055 = 0.106, \text{correct to 3 decimal places.}$$

Notice that the table does not give the values of $\Phi(z)$ for negative values of z. The reason is that you can deduce the value of $\Phi(z)$ for negative z from the symmetry of the distribution.

The diagrams in Fig. 9.17 show how to calculate $P(Z \leqslant -1.2)$.

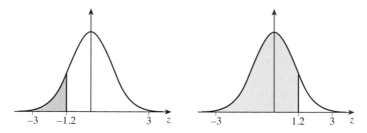

Fig. 9.17. Diagram showing how to calculate $\Phi(z)$ when z is negative.

Fig. 9.17 shows that the area shaded in the left diagram is equal to the area unshaded under the graph in the right diagram. Since the total area, shaded and unshaded, under the graph in each diagram is equal to 1,

$$\Phi(-1.2) = 1 - \Phi(1.2) = 1 - 0.8849$$
$$= 0.1151 = 0.115, \text{correct to 3 decimal places.}$$

This is an example of the identity

$$\Phi(-z) \equiv 1 - \Phi(z),$$

which applies for all values of z.

This identity means that it is not necessary to tabulate values of $\Phi(z)$ for negative values of z.

If you are using a calculator, you may not need to use the formula $\Phi(-z) \equiv 1 - \Phi(z)$ because the calculator gives output for negative values of z. But whichever method you use, table or calculator, make sure that you show your working clearly.

It will help to draw a sketch of the region whose area you are finding. Sketches will be drawn in this section but omitted in following sections. However, you are advised always to make a sketch.

Example 9.3.1
The random variable Z is such that $Z \sim N(0,1)$. Find the following probabilities.

(a) $P(0.7 \leqslant Z < 1.4)$ (b) $P(Z \leqslant -2.3)$ (c) $P(Z > 0.732)$ (d) $P(-1.4 \leqslant Z \leqslant 1)$

(a) $P(0.7 \leqslant Z < 1.4) = \Phi(1.4) - \Phi(0.7)$
$= 0.9192 - 0.7580$
$= 0.1612$
$= 0.161$, correct to 3 decimal places.

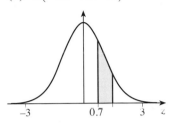

(b) Using the identity $\Phi(-z) \equiv 1 - \Phi(z)$,
$P(Z \leqslant -2.3) = 1 - P(Z \leqslant 2.3)$
$= 1 - \Phi(2.3)$
$= 1 - 0.9893$
$= 0.0107$
$= 0.011$, correct to 3 decimal places.

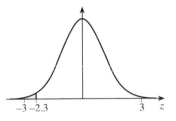

(c) $P(Z > 0.732) = 1 - P(Z \leqslant 0.732)$
$= 1 - \Phi(0.732)$
$= 1 - (0.7673 + 0.0006)$
$= 1 - 0.7679 = 0.2321$
$= 0.232$, correct to 3 decimal places.

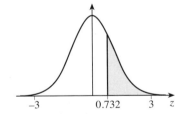

(d) $P(-1.4 \leqslant Z \leqslant 1) = P(Z \leqslant 1) - P(Z \leqslant -1.4)$
$= P(Z \leqslant 1) - (1 - P(Z \leqslant 1.4))$
$= P(Z \leqslant 1) - 1 + P(Z \leqslant 1.4)$
$= 0.8413 - 1 + 0.9192$
$= 0.7605$
$= 0.761$, correct to 3 decimal places.

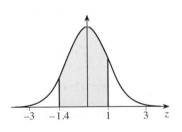

A rough sketch of the graph of the $N(0,1)$ *distribution with the ends of the sketch marked as –3 and 3 can give you some indication of whether your answer is approximately correct.*

It is also sometimes necessary to use the table 'in reverse'. For example, if you know the probability of $P(Z \geqslant k)$, you may need to find the corresponding value of k. As the function Φ is one–one (see P1 Section 11.6) you can always use the table in this way.

Example 9.3.2

The random variable Z is such that $Z \sim N(0,1)$. Use the normal distribution function table to find

(a) the value of s such that $P(Z \leqslant s) = 0.7$,

(b) the value of t such that $P(Z > t) = 0.8$.

(a) In this case you need to use the table in reverse. You know that $\Phi(s) = 0.7$.

From the table,

$$\Phi(0.524) = 0.6999 \quad \text{and} \quad \Phi(0.525) = 0.7002,$$

so $s = 0.524$, correct to 3 decimal places.

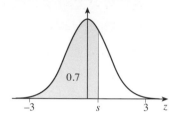

(b) From the diagram (*right*), it is clear that the value of t such that $P(Z > t) = 0.8$ is negative.

Since the value of t is negative, it cannot be found directly from the normal distribution function table.

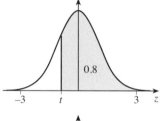

However, from the diagram (*below*), $t = -v$ where $P(Z \leqslant v) = 0.8$, using symmetry.

You know that $\Phi(v) = 0.8$.

From the table, $\Phi(0.842) = 0.8000$, so $v = 0.842$, and hence $t = \pm 0.842$, correct to 3 decimal places.

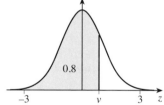

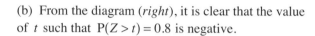

Exercise 9A

In this exercise use either your calculator or the table on page 172.

1 $Z \sim N(0,1)$. Find the following probabilities.

(a) $P(Z < 1.23)$ (b) $P(Z \leqslant 2.468)$ (c) $P(Z < 0.157)$

(d) $P(Z \geqslant 1.236)$ (e) $P(Z > 2.378)$ (f) $P(Z \geqslant 0.588)$

(g) $P(Z > -1.83)$ (h) $P(Z \geqslant -2.057)$ (i) $P(Z > -0.067)$

(j) $P(Z \leqslant -1.83)$ (k) $P(Z < -2.755)$ (l) $P(Z \leqslant -0.206)$

(m) $P(Z < 1.645)$ (n) $P(Z \geqslant 1.645)$ (o) $P(Z > -1.645)$

(p) $P(Z \leqslant -1.645)$

2 The random variable Z is distributed such that $Z \sim N(0,1)$. Find these probabilities.

(a) $P(1.15 < Z < 1.35)$ (b) $P(1.111 \leqslant Z \leqslant 2.222)$

(c) $P(0.387 < Z < 2.418)$ (d) $P(0 \leqslant Z < 1.55)$

(e) $P(-1.815 < Z < 2.333)$ (f) $P(-0.847 < Z \leqslant 2.034)$

3 The random variable Z is distributed such that $Z \sim N(0,1)$. Find these probabilities.

(a) $P(-2.505 < Z < 1.089)$

(b) $P(-0.55 \leqslant Z \leqslant 0)$

(c) $P(-2.82 < Z < -1.82)$

(d) $P(-1.749 \leqslant Z \leqslant -0.999)$

(e) $P(-2.568 < Z < -0.123)$

(f) $P(-1.96 \leqslant Z < 1.96)$

(g) $P(-2.326 < Z < 2.326)$

(h) $P(|Z| \leqslant 1.3)$

(i) $P(|Z| > 2.4)$

4 The random variable $Z \sim N(0,1)$. In each part, find the value of s, t, u or v.

(a) $P(Z < s) = 0.6700$

(b) $P(Z < t) = 0.8780$

(c) $P(Z < u) = 0.9842$

(d) $P(Z < v) = 0.8455$

(e) $P(Z > s) = 0.4052$

(f) $P(Z > t) = 0.1194$

(g) $P(Z > u) = 0.0071$

(h) $P(Z > v) = 0.2241$

(i) $P(Z > s) = 0.9977$

(j) $P(Z > t) = 0.9747$

(k) $P(Z > u) = 0.8496$

(l) $P(Z > v) = 0.5$

(m) $P(Z < s) = 0.0031$

(n) $P(Z < t) = 0.0142$

(o) $P(Z < u) = 0.0468$

(p) $P(Z < v) = 0.4778$

(q) $P(-s < Z < s) = 0.90$

(r) $P(-t < Z < t) = 0.80$

(s) $P(-u < Z < u) = 0.99$

(t) $P(|Z| < v) = 0.50$

9.4 Standardising a normal distribution

The standardisation equation (9.1)

$$Z = \frac{X - \mu}{\sigma}$$

allows you to change a statement about a $N(\mu, \sigma^2)$ distribution into an equivalent statement about a $N(0,1)$ distribution.

To see how standardisation works, consider finding the probability $P(X \leqslant 230)$, where $X \sim N(205, 20^2)$

Using the standardisation equation, $Z = \frac{1}{20}(X - 205)$, you know that $Z \sim N(0,1)$.

Then

$$P(X \leqslant 230) = P\left(Z \leqslant \tfrac{1}{20}(230 - 205)\right)$$

$$= P(Z \leqslant 1.25)$$

$$= \Phi(1.25)$$

$$= 0.8944$$

$$= 0.894, \text{ correct to 3 decimal places.}$$

Example 9.4.1

Given that $X \sim N(4,25)$, find the following probabilities.

(a) $P(X < 4.5)$ (b) $P(5 \leq X \leq 6)$ (c) $P(2 \leq X \leq 7)$ (d) $P(X > 1)$

Let $Z = \frac{1}{5}(X - 4)$. Then $Z \sim N(0,1)$.

(a) $P(X < 4.5) = P\left(Z < \frac{1}{5}(4.5 - 4)\right) = P(Z < 0.1)$

$= \Phi(0.1) = 0.5398$

$= 0.540$, correct to 3 decimal places.

(b) $P(5 \leq X \leq 6) = P\left(\frac{1}{5}(5 - 4) \leq Z \leq \frac{1}{5}(6 - 4)\right) = P(0.2 \leq Z \leq 0.4)$

$= P(Z \leq 0.4) - P(Z \leq 0.2)$

$= \Phi(0.4) - \Phi(0.2)$

$= 0.6554 - 0.5793 = 0.0761$

$= 0.076$, correct to 3 decimal places.

(c) $P(2 \leq X \leq 7) = P\left(\frac{1}{5}(2 - 4) \leq Z \leq \frac{1}{5}(7 - 4)\right) = P(-0.4 \leq Z \leq 0.6)$

$= P(Z \leq 0.6) - P(Z \leq -0.4)$

$= \Phi(0.6) - \Phi(-0.4)$

$= \Phi(0.6) - (1 - \Phi(0.4))$

$= 0.7257 - (1 - 0.6554) = 0.3811$

$= 0.381$, correct to 3 decimal places.

(d) $P(X > 1) = P\left(Z > \frac{1}{5}(1 - 4)\right) = P(Z > -0.6)$

$= P(Z < 0.6)$ (by symmetry)

$= \Phi(0.6) = 0.7257$

$= 0.726$, correct to 3 decimal places.

Example 9.4.2

Given that $X \sim N(6,4)$, find, correct to 3 significant figures, the values of s and t such that

(a) $P(X \leq s) = 0.6500$,   (b) $P(X > t) = 0.8200$.

Let $Z = \frac{1}{2}(X - 6)$. Then $Z \sim N(0,1)$.

(a) The statement $P(X \leq s) = 0.6500$ is equivalent to $P\left(Z \leq \frac{1}{2}(s - 6)\right) = 0.6500$.

Therefore $\Phi\left(\frac{1}{2}(s - 6)\right) = 0.6500$.

From the table,

$\Phi(0.385) = 0.6498$ and $\Phi(0.386) = 0.6502$.

Therefore, by interpolation, $\Phi(0.3855) = 0.6500$, so $\frac{1}{2}(s - 6) = 0.3855$ giving

$s = 6 + 2 \times 0.3855 = 6.771$, which is 6.77, correct to 3 significant figures.

(b) The statement $P(X > t) = 0.8200$ is equivalent to $P\!\left(Z > \tfrac{1}{2}(t-6)\right) = 0.8200$,
The problem is now similar to Example 9.3.2(b).

The value of $\tfrac{1}{2}(t-6)$ which you are looking for is negative. Let $v = -\tfrac{1}{2}(t-6)$.
Then by symmetry, $P(Z \leqslant v) = 0.8200$. Therefore $v = \Phi^{-1}(0.8200)$, and from the
table $v = 0.9155$.

This means that $-\tfrac{1}{2}(t-6) = 0.9155$. Rearranging, $t = 6 + 2 \times (-0.9155) = 4.169$,
which is 4.17, correct to 3 significant figures.

Exercise 9B

You are strongly advised to draw rough sketches for these questions.

1 Given that $X \sim N(20,16)$, find the following probabilities.

   (a) $P(X \leqslant 26)$ (b) $P(X > 30)$ (c) $P(X \geqslant 17)$ (d) $P(X < 13)$

2 Given that $X \sim N(24,9)$, find the following probabilities.

   (a) $P(X \leqslant 29)$ (b) $P(X > 31)$ (c) $P(X \geqslant 22)$ (d) $P(X < 16)$

3 Given that $X \sim N(50,16)$, find the following probabilities.

   (a) $P(54 \leqslant X \leqslant 58)$ (b) $P(40 < X \leqslant 44)$ (c) $P(47 < X < 57)$

   (d) $P(39 \leqslant X < 53)$ (e) $P(44 \leqslant X \leqslant 56)$

4 The random variable X can take negative and positive values. X is distributed normally
   with mean 3 and variance 4. Find the probability that X has a negative value.

5 The random variable X has a normal distribution. The mean is μ (where $\mu > 0$) and the
   variance is $\tfrac{1}{4}\mu^2$.

   (a) Find $P(X > 1.5\mu)$.   (b) Find the probability that X is negative.

6 Given that $X \sim N(44,25)$, find s, t, u and v correct to 2 decimal places when

   (a) $P(X \leqslant s) = 0.9808$,   (b) $P(X \geqslant t) = 0.7704$,

   (c) $P(X \geqslant u) = 0.0495$,   (d) $P(X \leqslant v) = 0.3336$.

7 Given that $X \sim N(15,4)$, find s, t, u, v and w correct to 2 decimal places when

   (a) $P(X \leqslant s) = 0.9141$,   (b) $P(X \geqslant t) = 0.5746$,   (c) $P(X \geqslant u) = 0.1041$,

   (d) $P(X \leqslant v) = 0.3924$,   (e)* $P(|X - 15| < w) = 0.9$.

8 Given that $X \sim N(35.4,12.5)$, find the values of s, t, u and v correct to 1 decimal place
   when

   (a) $P(X < s) = 0.96$,   (b) $P(X > t) = 0.9391$,

   (c) $P(X > u) = 0.2924$,   (d) $P(X < v) = 0.1479$.

9   X has a normal distribution with mean 32 and variance σ^2. Given that the probability that
    X is less than 33.14 is 0.6406, find σ^2. Give your answer correct to 2 decimal places.

10   X has a normal distribution, and $P(X > 73.05) = 0.0289$. Given that the variance of the distribution is 18, find the mean.

11   X is distributed normally, $P(X \geqslant 59.1) = 0.0218$ and $P(X \geqslant 29.2) = 0.9345$. Find the mean and standard deviation of the distribution, correct to 3 significant figures.

12   $X \sim N(\mu, \sigma^2)$, $P(X \geqslant 9.81) = 0.1587$ and $P(X \leqslant 8.82) = 0.0116$. Find μ and σ, correct to 3 significant figures.

9.5   Modelling with the normal distribution

The normal distribution is often used as a model for practical situations. In the following examples, you need to translate the given information into the language of the normal distribution before you can solve the problem.

Example 9.5.1

Look back to the data on lengths given in Table 9.2, and to the associated histogram in Fig. 9.3. Assuming that the distribution is normal, how many of the 50 leaves would you expect to be in the interval $59.5 \leqslant l \leqslant 69.5$?

You can check that the mean and the standard deviation of the original data on page 133 are 61.4 and 16.8, correct to 1 decimal place.

Using a random variable, L with a $N(61.4, 16.8^2)$ distribution you can calculate the expected frequency for each class.

Given that $L \sim N(61.4, 16.8^2)$, let $Z = \dfrac{L - 61.4}{16.8}$. Then $Z \sim N(0,1)$.

$$P(59.5 \leqslant L \leqslant 69.5) = P\left(\frac{59.5 - 61.4}{16.8} \leqslant Z \leqslant \frac{69.5 - 61.4}{16.8} \right)$$
$$= P(-0.113... \leqslant Z \leqslant 0.482...)$$
$$= \Phi(0.482...) - \Phi(-0.113...)$$
$$= \Phi(0.482...) - (1 - \Phi(0.113...)) \quad \text{(using symmetry)}$$
$$= 0.6851 - (1 - 0.5450) = 0.2301.$$

This means that the expected frequency for the class $59.5 \leqslant l \leqslant 69.5$ is $50 \times 0.2301 = 11.5$, correct to 1 decimal place.

Therefore in a group of 50 leaves you would expect about 11 or 12 leaves to have lengths in the class $59.5 \leqslant l \leqslant 69.5$.

The observed frequency was actually 9. Does this mean that the $N(61.4, 16.8^2)$ distribution is a poor model for these data? To answer this question sensibly, you really need to calculate the expected frequencies for all eight classes.

Using the method shown above find the expected frequencies for the remaining seven classes and then review the results to consider whether the $N(61.4, 16.8^2)$ distribution is a suitable model for these data.

Example 9.5.2

Two friends Sarah and Hannah often go to the Post Office together. They travel on Sarah's scooter. Sarah always drives Hannah to the Post Office and drops her off there. Sarah then drives around until she is ready to pick Hannah up some time later. Their experience has been that the time Hannah takes in the Post Office can be approximated by a normal distribution with mean 6 minutes and standard deviation 1.3 minutes. How many minutes after having dropped Hannah off should Sarah return if she wants to be at least 95% certain that Hannah will not keep her waiting?

Let T be the time Hannah takes in the Post Office on a randomly chosen trip. Then $T \sim \mathrm{N}(6, 1.3^2)$.

Let t be the number of minutes after dropping Hannah off when Sarah returns; you then need to find t such that $\mathrm{P}(T \leqslant t) \geqslant 0.95$.

After standardising, this expression becomes

$$\mathrm{P}\left(Z \leqslant \frac{t-6}{1.3}\right) \geqslant 0.95 \quad \text{or} \quad \Phi\left(\frac{t-6}{1.3}\right) \geqslant 0.95 .$$

Therefore $\dfrac{t-6}{1.3} \geqslant \Phi^{-1}(0.95) = 1.645$, which, on rearranging, gives $t \geqslant 8.1385\ldots$.

Sarah should not return for at least 8.14 minutes, correct to 3 significant figures, if she wants to be at least 95% sure that Hannah will not keep her waiting.

Example 9.5.3

A biologist has been collecting data on the heights of a particular species of cactus (*Notocactus rutilans*). He has observed that 34.2% of the cacti are below 12 cm in height and 18.4% of the cacti are above 16 cm in height. He assumes that the heights are normally distributed. Find the mean and standard deviation of the distribution.

Let the mean and standard deviation of the distribution be μ and σ respectively. Then, if H is the height of a randomly chosen cactus of this species,

$$H \sim \mathrm{N}(\mu, \sigma^2).$$

The biologist's observations can now be written

$$\mathrm{P}(H < 12) = 0.342 \quad \text{and} \quad \mathrm{P}(H > 16) = 0.184 .$$

After standardising using $Z = \dfrac{H - \mu}{\sigma}$, these equations become

$$\mathrm{P}\left(Z < \frac{12 - \mu}{\sigma}\right) = 0.342 \quad \text{and} \quad \mathrm{P}\left(Z > \frac{16 - \mu}{\sigma}\right) = 0.184 .$$

Writing $\dfrac{12 - \mu}{\sigma} = s$ and $\dfrac{16 - \mu}{\sigma} = t$, the two equations become

$P(Z < s) = 0.342$ and $P(Z > t) = 0.184$

or, in terms of the normal distribution function,

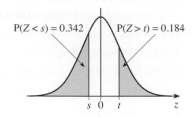

$\Phi(s) = 0.342$ and $1 - \Phi(t) = 0.184$.

This information is summarised in the diagram.

Using the table, after writing $s = -v$, gives $\Phi(v) = 0.658$, $v = 0.407$ and $s = -0.407$.

Since $1 - \Phi(t) = 0.184$, $\Phi(t) = 0.816$ giving $t = 0.900$.

Therefore $s = \dfrac{12 - \mu}{\sigma} = -0.407$ and $t = \dfrac{16 - \mu}{\sigma} = 0.900$.

These give the two simultaneous equations

$$12 - \mu = -0.407\sigma,$$
$$16 - \mu = 0.900\sigma.$$

Solving these equations gives $\mu = 13.2$ and $\sigma = 3.06$, correct to 3 significant figures.

9.6 Practical activities

1 Leaves   Collect about 50 fallen leaves from a bush and measure the length of each leaf. You may need to consider what 'length' means, but any consistently applied definition should be satisfactory. Summarise the data in a grouped frequency table similar to Table 9.2 and calculate estimates of the mean length and the standard deviation. Use a normal distribution with the estimated mean and standard deviation to calculate expected frequencies for each class and compare these expected frequencies with the observed frequencies. Was the normal distribution a good model? You could repeat this experiment with a larger number of leaves, say 100. Does this have any effect upon your conclusions?

2 Other situations   You can investigate a number of other situations to see whether or not they show normal characteristics: weight, height, foot length, finger length etc. for people of the same age and gender; masses of pebbles in sample of gravel, lengths of nails of the 'same' size; heights jumped in the Practical activities for Chapter 1; the error (plus or minus) in bisecting a line 30 cm long by eye; masses of coins of various ages (measured very accurately on a scientific balance); lengths of songs in minutes taken from a CD.

Exercise 9C

1   The time spent waiting for a prescription to be prepared at a chemist's shop is normally distributed with mean 15 minutes and standard deviation 2.8 minutes. Find the probability that the waiting time is

(a) more than 20 minutes,   (b) less than 8 minutes,

(c) between 10 minutes and 18 minutes.

2 The heights of a group of sixteen-year-old girls are normally distributed with mean 161.2 cm and standard deviation 4.7 cm. Find the probability that one of these girls will have height

(a) more than 165 cm,   (b) less than 150 cm,

(c) between 165 cm and 170 cm,   (d) between 150 cm and 163 cm.

In a sample of 500 girls of this age estimate how many will have heights in each of the above four ranges.

3 The lengths of replacement car wiper blades are normally distributed with mean of 25 cm and standard deviation 0.2 cm. For a batch of 200 wiper blades estimate how many would be expected to be

(a) 25.3 cm or more in length,   (b) between 24.89 cm and 25.11 cm in length,

(c) between 24.89 cm and 25.25 cm in length.

4 The time taken by a garage to replace worn-out brake pads follows a normal distribution with mean 90 minutes and standard deviation 5.8 minutes.

(a) Find the probability that the garage takes longer than 105 minutes.

(b) Find the probability that the garage takes less than 85 minutes.

(c) The garage claims to complete the replacements in 'a to b minutes'. If this claim is to be correct for 90% of the repairs, find a and b correct to 2 significant figures, based on a symmetrical interval centred on the mean.

5 The fluorescent light tubes made by the company Well-lit have lifetimes which are normally distributed with mean 2010 hours and standard deviation 20 hours. The company decides to promote its sales of the tubes by guaranteeing a minimum life of the tubes, replacing free of charge any tubes that fail to meet this minimum life. If the company wishes to have to replace free only 3% of the tubes sold, find the guaranteed minimum it must set.

6 The lengths of sweetpea flower stems are normally distributed with mean 18.2 cm and standard deviation 2.3 cm.

(a) Find the probability that the length of a flower stem is between 16 cm and 20 cm.

(b) 12% of the flower stems are longer than h cm. 20% of the flower stems are shorter than k cm. Find h and k.

(c) Stem lengths less than 14 cm are unacceptable at a florist's shop. In a batch of 500 sweetpeas estimate how many would be unacceptable.

7 The T-Q company makes a soft drink sold in '330 ml' cans. The actual volume of drink in the cans is distributed normally with standard deviation 2.5 ml.

To ensure that at least 99% of the cans contain more than 330 ml, find the volume that the company should supply in the cans on average.

8 The packets in which sugar is sold are labelled '1 kg packets'. In fact the mass of sugar in a packet is distributed normally with mean mass 1.08 kg.

Sampling of the packets of sugar shows that just 2.5% are 'underweight' (that is, contain less than the stated mass of 1 kg).

Find the standard deviation of the distribution.

9 The life of the Powerhouse battery has a normal distribution with mean 210 hours. It is found that 4% of these batteries operate for more than 222 hours.

Find the variance of the distribution, correct to 2 significant figures.

10 In a statistics examination, 15% of the candidates scored more than 63 marks and 10% of the candidates scored less than 32 marks. Assuming that the marks were distributed normally find the mean mark and the standard deviation.

9.7 The normal distribution as an approximation to the binomial distribution

If you were asked to estimate the probability that a school of 1000 students contains more than 150 left-handed students, how would you try to solve such a problem? Perhaps one sensible approach would be to take a reasonably large sample, say of size 50, and count the number of left-handed students in the sample. From this information you could estimate the probability that a randomly chosen student is left-handed.

For example, if your sample contains 8 left-handed people you would estimate the probability that a randomly chosen person is left-handed as $\frac{8}{50}$, or 0.16. If you define L as the number of left-handed people in a random sample of 1000 people, you could then use the distribution B(1000,0.16) as a model for the distribution of L. You only need to find $P(L > 150)$. This is given by

$$P(L > 150) = 1 - P(L \leqslant 150) = 1 - P(L = 0) - P(L = 1) - P(L = 2) - \ldots - P(L = 150)$$

$$= 1 - \binom{1000}{0}0.16^0 \, 0.84^{1000} - \binom{1000}{1}0.16^1 \, 0.84^{999}$$

$$- \binom{1000}{2}0.16^2 \, 0.84^{998} - \ldots - \binom{1000}{150}0.16^{150}0.84^{850}.$$

To calculate this is horrendous; there are 151 separate calculations to be carried out.

Fortunately there is an approximate method which uses the normal distribution and involves far less work. This section shows how to carry out such approximations.

Fig. 9.18 shows bar charts of the binomial distribution for different values of n and p.

The diagrams in the top row of Fig. 9.18 show $p = 0.1$, with three values of n, 12, 20 and 60. When $n = 12$ and $p = 0.1$ the bar chart is positively skewed. However, as n gets larger, the bar chart becomes more symmetrical and bell-shaped in appearance.

The diagrams in the bottom row of Fig. 9.18 show that when $p = \frac{1}{2}$ the shape of the bar chart resembles the bell shape that you associate with a normal distribution. This is true even when n is quite small as the diagram for $n = 12$ and $p = \frac{1}{2}$ shows.

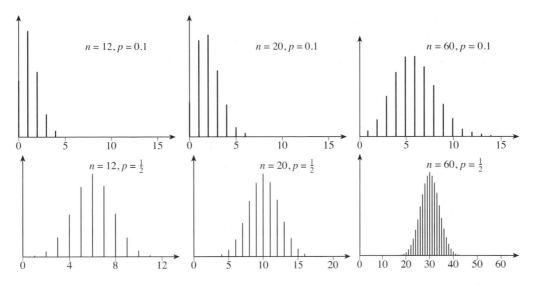

Fig. 9.18. Bar charts showing the binomial distribution for different values of n and p.

You should be able to see that if a third row of bar charts were drawn with $p = 0.9$ for the three values of n, 12, 20 and 60, then each bar chart would be the mirror image of the corresponding bar chart in the first row, about the vertical line $x = \frac{1}{2}n$. Thus, the bar chart for $n = 12$ and $p = 0.9$ is the mirror image of that for $n = 12$ and $p = 0.1$.

Summarising these observations you find that if $X \sim B(n,p)$ and n is sufficiently large, then the distribution of X is approximately normal. If p is close to 0 or 1, then n must be larger than if p is close to $\frac{1}{2}$.

There is a simple condition which you can use to test whether a binomial distribution can reasonably be approximated by a normal distribution.

> If $X \sim B(n,p)$, and if $np > 5$ and $nq > 5$, where $q = 1 - p$, then the distribution of X can reasonably be approximated by a normal distribution.

Notice that if $p = \frac{1}{2}$, then the conditions $np > 5$ and $nq > 5$ will be satisfied when $n > 10$. You saw that when $n = 12$ and $p = \frac{1}{2}$ the normal approximation would be reasonable.

On the other hand, if $p = 0.1$ or if $p = 0.9$, then only when $n > 50$ will *both* $np > 5$ *and* $nq > 5$ be satisfied. You saw that for a $B(60,0.1)$ distribution the normal approximation seemed satisfactory. A normal approximation would still be satisfactory for a $B(60,0.9)$ distribution because the bar chart representing this distribution is a mirror image of the one representing a $B(60,0.1)$ distribution.

If the normal distribution is a good approximation to a binomial distribution you would imagine that the normal curve would nearly pass through the tops of the bars on the bar chart. In this case it seems reasonable to suppose that the two distributions have the same mean and variance.

But you know that if $X \sim B(n,p)$, then $E(X) = np$ and $\text{Var}(X) = npq$. The approximating normal distribution should therefore also have mean np and variance npq. That is, the distribution of X is approximated by a $N(np, npq)$ distribution.

Summarising:

> If $X \sim B(n,p)$, and if $np > 5$ and $nq > 5$, where $q = 1 - p$,
> then X can reasonably be approximated by $V \sim N(np, npq)$.

For example, if $X \sim B\left(60, \frac{1}{2}\right)$, then the distribution of X can be approximated by the normal distribution with mean $\mu = 60 \times \frac{1}{2} = 30$ and variance $\sigma^2 = 60 \times \frac{1}{2} \times \frac{1}{2} = 15$. So the distribution $X \sim B\left(60, \frac{1}{2}\right)$ can be approximated by the distribution $V \sim N(30, 15)$.

If you have access to a computer, see whether you can draw the bar charts in Fig. 9.18 using a spreadsheet. Experiment with values of n and p and check whether the bar charts look 'normally distributed' whenever the conditions $np > 5$ and $nq > 5$ are satisfied.

Note that the normal approximation is $N(np, npq)$, and not $N(np, nq)$.

But how does the normal approximation work in practice? There seems immediately to be a problem since, for example,

$$P(X = 31) = \binom{60}{31} \times 0.5^{31} \times 0.5^{29} \neq 0,$$

whereas

$$P(V = 31) = 0$$

since V has a continuous distribution.

In fact, $P(V = v) = 0$ for any $v = 0, 1, 2, \ldots, 60$, so a little more work is needed in order to make the connection between the binomial distribution and the normal distribution useful.

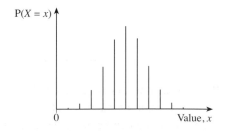

Usually discrete distributions are represented by bar charts in which each bar is separate from the next bar and in which the height of the bar is proportional to the probability of that particular value, as in Fig. 9.19.

Fig. 9.19. Bar chart showing the distribution of a discrete random variable, X.

In order to compare the binomial distribution with the normal distribution it is more helpful to draw a bar chart that looks similar to a histogram. You widen each of the bars by a $\frac{1}{2}$ unit on either side so that each is still centred on an integer value but the blocks now touch. Each block has an area proportional to the probability of the integer on which it is centred. The resulting diagram is more suitable for comparison with the normal distribution as you can see in Fig. 9.20.

The possible values which a $B(n,p)$ distribution can take are $0, 1, 2, \ldots, n$, whereas the $N(np,npq)$ distribution can take all real values. In particular, this means that the normal distribution can take values greater than n or less than 0. This would seem to indicate that a normal distribution is not a satisfactory approximation to a binomial distribution. However, the area below the normal curve for x-values above n or below 0 will be very small indeed and so, although it is possible for the

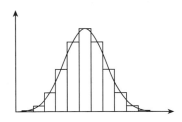

Fig. 9.20. Comparison between the binomial distribution and the normal distribution.

$N(np,npq)$ distribution to be greater than n or less than 0, it is very unlikely indeed and you do not need to worry about the fact that a normal distribution can take all real values.

Fig. 9.21a and Fig. 9.21b show how you can make the relationship between the normal approximation and the binomial distribution more precise.

You can see that the probability which is represented by the shaded rectangular region in Fig. 9.21a can be approximated by the shaded region in Fig. 9.21b, which resembles a trapezium and which is the area under the normal curve between 30.5 and 31.5.

In other words, $P(X = 31) \approx P(30.5 < V < 31.5)$.

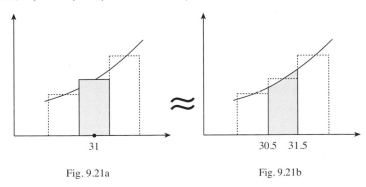

Fig. 9.21a   Fig. 9.21b

The normal distribution approximates to the binomial distribution.

If you wanted to calculate $P(X \leqslant 26)$ you would calculate the total area of all the blocks up to and including the block at $x = 26$. This area is best approximated by the area under the normal curve up to $v = 26.5$. That is,

$$P(X \leqslant 26) \approx P(V \leqslant 26.5).$$

The 'extra' 0.5 which appears is necessary because you are approximating a discrete distribution by a continuous distribution. It is called a **continuity correction** and it is needed in order to make the approximation as accurate as possible.

Example 9.7.1

The random variable X has a $B\left(60,\frac{1}{2}\right)$ distribution. For each of the following binomial probabilities describe the region under the approximating normal curve whose area gives the best estimate.

(a) $P(X \leqslant 12)$ (b) $P(X = 16)$ (c) $P(X < 22)$

(d) $P(X > 18)$ (e) $P(12 < X \leqslant 34)$ (f) $P(12 \leqslant X < 21)$

Since $X \sim B\left(60,\frac{1}{2}\right)$, it can be approximated by the distribution of V where $V \sim N(30,15)$.

(a) To find $P(X \leqslant 12)$ you need to find the total area of the blocks for $x = 0, 1, 2, \ldots, 12$. The area under the normal curve which best approximates to this is the area for which $v \leqslant 12.5$, so $P(X \leqslant 12) \approx P(V \leqslant 12.5)$.

(b) To find $P(X = 16)$ you need to find the total area of the block for $x = 16$. The area under the normal curve which best approximates to this is the area between $v = 15.5$ and $v = 16.5$, so $P(X = 16) \approx P(15.5 \leqslant V \leqslant 16.5)$.

(c) To find $P(X < 22)$ you need to find the total area of the blocks for $x = 0, 1, 2, \ldots, 21$. The area under the normal curve which best approximates to this is the area for which $v \leqslant 21.5$, so $P(X < 22) \approx P(V \leqslant 21.5)$.

(d) To find $P(X > 18)$ you need to find the total area of the blocks for $x = 19, \ldots, 60$. The area under the normal curve which best approximates to this is the area for which $v \geqslant 18.5$, so $P(X > 18) \approx P(V \geqslant 18.5)$.

(e) To find $P(12 < X \leqslant 34)$ you need to find the total area of the blocks for $x = 13, 14, \ldots, 34$. The area under the normal curve which best approximates to this is between $v = 12.5$ and $v = 34.5$, so $P(12 < X \leqslant 34) \approx P(12.5 \leqslant V \leqslant 34.5)$.

(f) To find $P(12 \leqslant X < 21)$ you need to find the total area of the blocks for $x = 12, 13, \ldots, 20$. The area under the normal curve which best approximates to this is between $v = 11.5$ and $v = 20.5$, so $P(12 \leqslant X < 21) \approx P(11.5 \leqslant V \leqslant 20.5)$.

The best way to work with the normal approximation to the binomial distribution using the continuity correction is to draw a sketch of the situation each time it arises. Do not try to learn the results in Example 9.7.1.

Notice that there was no need in Example 9.7.1 to test the validity of the normal approximation to the binomial distribution, because it had already been verified in the discussion which preceded the example. That is not the case in the next example.

Example 9.7.2

A random variable X has a binomial distribution with parameters $n = 80$ and $p = 0.4$. Use a suitable approximation to calculate the following probabilities.

(a) $P(X \leqslant 34)$ (b) $P(X \geqslant 26)$ (c) $P(X = 33)$ (d) $P(30 < X \leqslant 40)$.

The values of np and nq are given by $np = 80 \times 0.4 = 32$ and $nq = 80 \times (1 - 0.4) = 48$. Since these are both greater than 5 the normal distribution is a good approximation to the binomial distribution, so you can approximate to $X \sim B(80,0.4)$ by $V \sim N(np, npq) = N(32,19.2)$.

Now that you are working with a normal distribution, V, standardise by letting $Z = \dfrac{V - 32}{\sqrt{19.2}}$. Then $Z \sim N(0,1)$.

(a) $P(X \leqslant 34) \approx P(V \leqslant 34.5) = P\left(Z \leqslant \dfrac{34.5 - 32}{\sqrt{19.2}}\right) = P(Z \leqslant 0.570\ldots)$

$\qquad\qquad = \Phi(0.571) = 0.7160$

$\qquad\qquad = 0.716$, correct to 3 decimal places.

(b) $P(X \geqslant 26) \approx P(V \geqslant 25.5) = P\left(Z \geqslant \dfrac{25.5 - 32}{\sqrt{19.2}}\right) = P(Z \geqslant -1.483)$

$\qquad\qquad = 1 - \Phi(-1.483) = 1 - (1 - \Phi(1.483)) = \Phi(1.483)$

$\qquad\qquad = 0.9310 = 0.931$, correct to 3 decimal places.

(c) $P(X = 33) \approx P(32.5 \leqslant V \leqslant 33.5) = P\left(\dfrac{32.5 - 32}{\sqrt{19.2}} \leqslant Z \leqslant \dfrac{33.5 - 32}{\sqrt{19.2}}\right)$

$\qquad\qquad = P(0.114 \leqslant Z \leqslant 0.342) = \Phi(0.342) - \Phi(0.114)$

$\qquad\qquad = 0.6338 - 0.5454 = 0.0884$

$\qquad\qquad = 0.088$, correct to 3 decimal places.

(d) $P(30 < X \leqslant 40) \approx P(30.5 \leqslant V \leqslant 40.5) = P\left(\dfrac{30.5 - 32}{\sqrt{19.2}} \leqslant Z \leqslant \dfrac{40.5 - 32}{\sqrt{19.2}}\right)$

$\qquad\qquad = P(-0.342 \leqslant Z \leqslant 1.940) = \Phi(1.940) - \Phi(-0.342)$

$\qquad\qquad = \Phi(1.940) - (1 - \Phi(0.342))$

$\qquad\qquad = 0.9738 - (1 - 0.6338) = 0.6076$

$\qquad\qquad = 0.608$, correct to 3 decimal places.

Example 9.7.3

A manufacturer of spice jars knows that 8% of the jars produced are defective. He supplies jars in cartons containing 12 jars. He supplies cartons of jars in crates of 60 cartons. In each case making clear the distribution that you are using, calculate the probability that
(a) a carton contains exactly two defective jars,
(b) a carton contains at least one defective jar,
(c) a crate contains between 39 and 44 (inclusive) cartons with at least one defective jar.

Let D be the number of defective jars in a randomly chosen carton of 12 jars. Then $D \sim B(12, 0.08)$.

Since $np = 12 \times 0.08 = 0.96 < 5$ you cannot use the normal approximation. You must therefore use the binomial distribution.

(a) $P(D = 2) = \dbinom{12}{2} \times 0.08^2 \times 0.92^{10} = 0.1834\ldots$.

The probability that a carton contains exactly two defective jars is 0.183, correct to 3 decimal places.

(b) $P(D \geqslant 1) = 1 - P(D = 0) = 1 - 0.92^{12} = 0.6323\ldots$.

The probability that a carton contains at least one defective jar is 0.632, correct to 3 decimal places.

(c) Let C be the number of cartons containing at least one defective jar in a randomly chosen crate of 60 cartons.

Then C has a binomial distribution with $n = 60$. The probability of success, p, is the value found in part (b). So $p = 0.6323\ldots$.

For this binomial distribution, $np = 60 \times 0.6323\ldots = 37.94\ldots$ and $nq = 60 \times (1 - 0.6323\ldots) = 22.06\ldots$. Since they are both greater than 5, the normal approximation is valid.

The distribution of C is approximately the same as the distribution of V where $V \sim N(60 \times 0.6323\ldots, 60 \times 0.6323\ldots \times (1 - 0.6323\ldots))$. That is, the distribution of C is approximately the same as $V \sim N(37.94, 13.95)$.

So $\quad P(39 \leqslant C \leqslant 44) \approx P(38.5 \leqslant V \leqslant 44.5)$.

Let $Z = \dfrac{V - 37.94}{\sqrt{13.95}}$. Then $Z \sim N(0,1)$.

$$P(39 \leqslant C \leqslant 44) \approx P(38.5 \leqslant V \leqslant 44.5) = P\left(\frac{38.5 - 37.94}{\sqrt{13.95}} \leqslant Z \leqslant \frac{44.5 - 37.94}{\sqrt{13.95}}\right)$$
$$= P(0.150 \leqslant Z \leqslant 1.756) = \Phi(1.756) - \Phi(0.150)$$
$$= 0.9604 - 0.5596 = 0.4008.$$

The probability that a crate contains between 39 and 44 (inclusive) cartons with at least one defective jar is 0.401, correct to 3 decimal places.

Returning to the problem posed at the beginning of this section, you can now use what you have learned to calculate an approximation to the probability of there being more than 150 left-handed students in a school of 1000 students.

Recall that the random variable L was defined as the number of left-handed people in a randomly chosen sample of 1000 people. The distribution of L was modelled by a $B(1000, 0.16)$ distribution.

Now $np = 160$ and $nq = 840$ and both are much greater than 5, so it is valid to use the normal approximation. The distribution of L can be approximated by the random variable $V \sim N(160, 134.4)$ and therefore $P(L > 150) \approx P(V > 150.5)$.

Standardising, let $Z = \dfrac{V - 160}{\sqrt{134.4}}$. Then

$$P(V > 150.5) = P\left(Z > \frac{150.5 - 160}{\sqrt{134.4}}\right) = P(Z > -0.819\ldots) = P(Z < 0.819\ldots)$$
$$= \Phi(0.819\ldots) = 0.7935$$
$$= 0.794, \text{ correct to 3 decimal places.}$$

Exercise 9D

1   State whether the following binomial distributions can or cannot reasonably be approximated by a normal distribution. Write down a brief calculation to justify your conclusion in each case.

(a) $B(50, 0.2)$ (b) $B(60, 0.1)$ (c) $B(70, 0.01)$ (d) $B(30, 0.7)$

(e) $B(40, 0.9)$

2   A random variable, X, has a binomial distribution with parameters $n = 40$ and $p = 0.3$. Use a suitable approximation, which you should show is valid, to calculate the following probabilities.

(a) $P(X \geqslant 18)$ (b) $P(X < 9)$ (c) $P(X = 15)$ (d) $P(11 < X < 15)$

3   The mass production of a cheap pen results in there being one defective pen in 20 on average. Use an approximation, which you should show is valid, to find, in a batch of 300 of these pens, the probability of there being

(a) 24 or more defective pens,   (b) 10 or fewer defective pens.

4   A fair coin is tossed 18 times.

(a) Use the binomial distribution to find the probability of obtaining 14 heads.

(b) Use a normal approximation to find the probability of obtaining 14 heads, and to find the probability of obtaining 14 or more heads. Show that the approximation is valid.

5   In a certain country 12% of people have green eyes. If 50 people from this country are inspected, find the probability that

(a) 12 or more of them have green eyes,

(b) between 3 and 10 (inclusive) of them have green eyes.

Show that your approximation is valid.

6   Pierre attempts to dial a connection to the internet for his email each day. He is successful on his first attempt eight times out of ten. Use a normal approximation, showing first that it is valid, to find the probability that Pierre is successful on his first attempt at dialling a connection on 36 days or more over a period of 40 days.

7   (a) An unbiased dice is thrown 60 times. Find the probability that a 5 is obtained on 12 to 18 (inclusive) of these throws.

(b) In a game two unbiased dice are thrown. A winning score on each throw is a total of 5, 6, 7 or 8. Find the probability of a win on 70 or more throws out of 120 throws.

8   At an election there are two parties, X and Y. On past experience twice as many people vote for party X as for party Y.

An opinion poll researcher samples 90 voters. Find the probability that 70 or more say they will vote for party X at the next election.

If 2000 researchers each question 90 voters, how many of these researchers would be expected to record '70 or more for party X' results?

9 A manufacturer states that 'three out of four people prefer our product (Acme) to a competitor's product'. To test this claim a researcher asks 80 people about their liking for Acme. Assuming that the manufacturer is correct, find the probability that fewer than 53 prefer Acme. If 1000 researchers each question 80 people, how many of these researchers would be expected to record 'fewer than 53 prefer Acme' results?

10 Videos are packed in a box which contains 20 videos. 5% of the videos are faulty. The boxes are packed in crates which contain 50 boxes. Find the probabilities of the following events, clearly stating which distribution you are using and why.

(a) A box contains two faulty videos.

(b) A box contains at least one faulty video.

(c) A crate contains between 35 and 39 (inclusive) boxes with at least one faulty video.

Miscellaneous exercise 9

1 Given that $X \sim N(10, 2.25)$, find $P(X > 12)$. (OCR)

2 The random variable X has the distribution $X \sim N(10, 8)$. Find $P(X > 6)$. (OCR)

3 W is a normally distributed random variable with mean 0.58 and standard deviation 0.12. Find $P(W < 0.79)$. (OCR)

4 X is a random variable with the distribution $X \sim N(140, 56.25)$. Find the probability that X is greater than 128.75. (OCR)

5 The manufacturers of a new model of car state that, when travelling at 56 miles per hour, the petrol consumption has a mean value of 32.4 miles per gallon with standard deviation 1.4 miles per gallon. Assuming a normal distribution, calculate the probability that a randomly chosen car of that model will have a petrol consumption greater than 30 miles per gallon when travelling at 56 miles per hour. (OCR)

6 A normally distributed random variable, X, has mean 20.0 and variance 4.15. Find the probability that $18.0 < X < 21.0$. (OCR)

7 The lifetime of a Fotobrite light bulb is normally distributed with mean 1020 hours and standard deviation 85 hours. Find the probability that a Fotobrite bulb chosen at random has a lifetime between 1003 and 1088 hours. (OCR)

8 The area that can be painted using one litre of Luxibrite paint is normally distributed with mean 13.2 m^2 and standard deviation 0.197 m^2. The corresponding figures for one litre of Maxigloss paint are 13.4 m^2 and 0.343 m^2. It is required to paint an area of 12.9 m^2. Find which paint gives the greater probability that one litre will be sufficient, and obtain this probability. (OCR)

9 The random variable X is normally distributed with mean and standard deviation both equal to a.

Given that $P(X < 3) = 0.2$, find the value of a. (OCR)

10 The time required to complete a certain car journey has been found from experience to have mean 2 hours 20 minutes and standard deviation 15 minutes.

   (a) Use a normal model to calculate the probability that, on one day chosen at random, the journey requires between 1 hour 50 minutes and 2 hours 40 minutes.

   (b) It is known that delays occur rarely on this journey, but that when they do occur they are lengthy. Give a reason why this information suggests that a normal distribution might not be a good model. (OCR)

11 The weights of eggs, measured in grams, can be modelled by a $X \sim N(85.0,36)$ distribution. Eggs are classified as large, medium or small, where a large egg weighs 90.0 grams or more, and 25% of eggs are classified as small. Calculate

   (a) the percentage of eggs which are classified as large,

   (b) the maximum weight of a small egg. (OCR)

12 The random variable X is normally distributed with standard deviation 3.2. The probability that X is less than 74 is 0.8944.

   (a) Find the mean of X.

   (b) Fifty independent observations of X are made. Find the expected number of observations that are less than 74. (OCR)

13 A random variable X has a $N(m,4)$ distribution. Its associated normal curve is shown in the diagram. Find the value of m such that the shaded area is 0.800, giving your answer correct to 3 significant figures. (OCR)

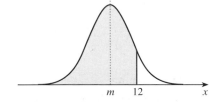

14 A machine cuts a very long plastic tube into short tubes. The length of the short tubes is modelled by a normal distribution with mean m cm and standard deviation 0.25 cm. The value of m can be set by adjusting the machine. Find the value of m for which the probability is 0.1 that the length of a short tube, picked at random, is less than 6.50 cm.

The machine is adjusted so that $m = 6.40$, the standard deviation remaining unchanged. Find the probability that a tube picked at random is between 6.30 and 6.60 cm long. (OCR)

15 A university classifies its degrees as Class 1, Class 2.1, Class 2.2, Class 3, Pass and Fail. Degrees are awarded on the basis of marks which may be taken as continuous and modelled by a normal distribution with mean 57.0 and standard deviation 10.0. In a particular year, the lowest mark for a Class 1 degree was 70.0, the lowest mark for a Class 2.1 degree was 60.0, and 4.5% of students failed. Calculate

   (a) the percentage of students who obtained a Class 1 degree,

   (b) the percentage of students who obtained a Class 2.1 degree,

   (c) the lowest possible mark for a student who obtained a Pass degree. (OCR)

16 The number of hours of sunshine at a resort has been recorded for each month for many
    years. One year is selected at random and H is the number of hours of sunshine in August
    of that year. H can be modelled by a normal variable with mean 130.

    (a) Given that $P(H < 179) = 0.975$, calculate the standard deviation of H.

    (b) Calculate $P(100 < H < 150)$.   (OCR)

17 The mass of grapes sold per day in a supermarket can be modelled by a normal distribution.
    It is found that, over a long period, the mean mass sold per day is 35.0 kg, and that, on
    average, less than 15.0 kg are sold on one day in twenty.

    (a) Show that the standard deviation of the mass of grapes sold per day is 12.2 kg, correct
         to 3 significant figures.

    (b) Calculate the probability that, on a day chosen at random, more than 53.0 kg are sold.
                                                                         (OCR)

18 An ordinary unbiased dice is thrown 900 times. Using a suitable approximation, find the
    probability of obtaining at least 160 sixes.   (OCR)

19 The random variable X is normally distributed with mean μ and variance σ^2. It is given
    that $P(X > 81.89) = 0.010$ and $P(X < 27.77) = 0.100$. Calculate the values of μ and σ.
                                                                         (OCR)

20 It is given that 40% of the population support the Gamboge Party. One hundred and fifty
    members of the population are selected at random. Use a suitable approximation to find the
    probability that more than 55 out of the 150 support the Gamboge Party.   (OCR)

21 Two firms, Goodline and Megadelay, produce delay lines for use in communications. The
    delay time for a delay line is measured in nanoseconds (ns).

    (a) The delay times for the output of Goodline may be modelled by a normal distribution
         with mean 283 ns and standard deviation 8 ns. What is the probability that the delay
         time of one line selected at random from Goodline's output is between 275 and
         286 ns?

    (b) It is found that, in the output of Megadelay, 10% of the delay times are less than
         274.6 ns and 7.5% are more than 288.2 ns. Again assuming a normal distribution,
         calculate the mean and standard deviation of the delay times for Megadelay. Give your
         answers correct to 3 significant figures.   (OCR)

22 State conditions under which a binomial probability model can be well approximated by a
    normal model.

    X is a random variable with the distribution $X \sim B(12, 0.42)$.

    (a) Anne uses the binomial distribution to calculate the probability that $X < 4$ and gives 4
         significant figures in her answer. What answer should she get?

    (b) Ben uses a normal distribution to calculate an approximation for the probability that
         $X < 4$ and gives 4 significant figures in his answer. What answer should he get?

    (c) Given that Ben's working is correct, calculate the percentage error in his answer.
                                                                         (OCR)

23 A large box contains many plastic syringes, but previous experience indicates that 10% of the syringes in the box are defective. 5 syringes are taken at random from the box. Use a binomial model to calculate, giving your answers correct to three decimal places, the probability that

   (a) none of the 5 syringes is defective,

   (b) at least 2 syringes out of the 5 are defective.

   Discuss the validity of the binomial model in this context.

   Instead of removing 5 syringes, 100 syringes are picked at random and removed. A normal distribution may be used to estimate the probability that at least 15 out of the 100 syringes are defective. Give a reason why it may be convenient to use a normal distribution to do this, and calculate the required estimate.   (OCR)

24 On average my train is late on 45 journeys out of 100. Next week I shall be making 5 train journeys. Let X denote the number of times my train will be late.

   (a) State one assumption which must be made for X to be modelled by a binomial distribution.

   (b) Find the probability that my train will be late on all of the 5 journeys.

   (c) Find the probability that my train will be late on 2 or more out of the 5 journeys.

   Approximate your binomial model by a suitable normal model to estimate the probability that my train is late on 20 or more out of 50 journeys.   (OCR)

25 The random variable Y has the distribution $N(\mu,16)$. Given that $P(Y > 57.50) = 0.1401$, find the value of μ giving your answer correct to 2 decimal places.   (OCR)

26 The playing time, T minutes, of classical compact discs is modelled by a normal variable with mean 61.3 minutes. Calculate the standard deviation of T if 5% of discs have playing times greater than 78 minutes.   (OCR)

27* The random variable Y is such that $Y \sim N(8,25)$. Show that, correct to 3 decimal places, $P(|Y - 8| < 6.2) = 0.785$.

   Three random observations of Y are made. Find the probability that exactly two observations will lie in the interval defined by $|Y - 8| < 6.2$.   (OCR)

28 It is estimated that, on average, one match in five in the Football League is drawn, and that one match in two is a home win.

   (a) Twelve matches are selected at random. Calculate the probability that the number of drawn matches is

      (i) exactly three,

      (ii) at least four.

   (b) Ninety matches are selected at random. Use a suitable approximation to calculate the probability that between 13 and 20 (inclusive) of the matches are drawn.

   (c) Twenty matches are selected at random. The random variables D and H are the numbers of drawn matches and home wins, respectively, in these matches. State, with a reason, which of D and H can be better approximated by a normal variable. (OCR)

29 Squash balls, dropped onto a concrete floor from a given point, rebound to heights which can be modelled by a normal distribution with mean 0.8 m and standard deviation 0.2 m. The balls are classified by height of rebound, in order of decreasing height, into these categories: Fast, Medium, Slow, Super-Slow and Rejected.

(a) Balls which rebound to heights between 0.65 m and 0.9 m are classified as Slow. Calculate the percentage of balls classified as Slow.

(b) Given that 9% of balls are classified as Rejected, calculate the maximum height of rebound of these balls.

(c) The percentages of balls classified as Fast and as Medium are equal. Calculate the minimum height of rebound of a ball classified as Fast, giving your answer correct to 2 decimal places.   (OCR)

Revision exercise

1 The table shows the length distribution of pebbles from the bed of a river.

Length, x (mm)	$0 \leqslant x < 5$	$5 \leqslant x < 10$	$10 \leqslant x < 20$	$20 \leqslant x < 50$	$50 \leqslant x < 100$
Frequency	10	8	12	25	30

  (a) You are given that the frequency density for the class $0 \leqslant x < 5$ is 2. Write down the frequency densities for the other classes.

  (b) Represent the data in a histogram.

  (c) Calculate an estimate of the mean length of the pebbles in the sample, and of the standard deviation of the length of the pebbles in the sample.

2 The six faces of an ordinary dice are numbered 1 to 6 in the usual fashion, where the total on opposite faces adds up to 7.

  (a) State, with justification, the assumption that leads to the probability of a given number appearing on the uppermost face being $\frac{1}{6}$ when the dice is rolled.

  (b) Let X be the random variable representing the outcome when the dice is rolled. Calculate the variance of X.

3 A train is due to arrive at Central Station at 09.30 daily. On ten successive days the number of minutes by which the train was late were as follows.

$$3 \quad 0 \quad 4 \quad -2 \quad -3 \quad 13 \quad 8 \quad -2 \quad 6 \quad 3$$

Show that the mean time of arrival was 09.33 and calculate the standard deviation.

On the assumption that the times of arrival are normally distributed with mean 09.33 and the standard deviation you have calculated, find the probability that the train will arrive

  (a) at or before 09.30,

  (b) more than 8 minutes late.

Comment on the assumption that the arrival times are normally distributed. (OCR)

4 A pupil conducting a coin-tossing experiment was surprised when she dropped 20 coins on to the floor and obtained only 5 heads.

  (a) Calculate, using an appropriate binomial distribution, the probability that 20 fair coins dropped onto the floor at random will show exactly 5 heads.

  (b) Show that the probability of obtaining either 5 heads or less, or 15 or more, when 20 coins are dropped on the floor at random is less than 5%.

  (c) State the expected number of heads when 20 fair coins are dropped onto the floor.

  (d) Comment on the result obtained in part (b).

5 The lengths, in cm, of 19 fern fronds are shown ordered below.

   2.3, 2.6, 2.7, 2.8, 3.0, 3.1, 3.2, 3.5, 3.6, 3.8, 4.3, 4.4, 4.9, 4.9, 5.6, 5.9, 6.4, 6.8, 7.2

   (a) Present these data in a simple stem-and-leaf display.

   (b) Use your display to identify the median length and the interquartile range.

   (c) Construct a box-and-whisker plot of these data.

6 Describe an experiment that you may have conducted to illustrate the normal distribution. Justify, with reference to features of this distribution, its use in the experiment.

   The quantity of juice, in ml, that can be extracted from different sizes of oranges follows a normal distribution as given in the table.

	Mean	Variance
Small	70	49
Medium	90	σ^2

   (a) What is the probability that more than 80 ml of juice can be extracted from one small orange?

   (b) It is known that 5% of medium oranges produce more than 105 ml of juice. Calculate the value of σ.

   (c) I buy 5 small oranges. Find the probability that at least 4 of them produce over 80 ml of juice. (OCR, adapted)

7 An experiment consists of shuffling an ordinary pack of 52 cards. Once shuffled, the top card is examined. The card can be a 'picture card', an 'even card' or an 'odd card'. None of these categories overlap. If it is a 'picture card' (there are 16 in a pack), a score of 5 is awarded. Otherwise, if it is an 'even card' (there are 20), a score of 2 is awarded. A score of zero is given for an 'odd card'. This is summarised in the table.

Card	Odd	Picture	Even
Score	0	5	2

   (a) Write down the probability of a score of 5.

   (b) Write down the probability distribution of the score, and calculate its mean and variance.

8 The probability that a toy balloon coming off a production line is faulty is 0.02. The balloons are put into bags containing 10 balloons.

   (a) Assuming that faulty balloons occur at random, calculate the probability that a bag contains at least one faulty balloon.

   The bags are packaged into boxes, each box containing 100 bags.

   (b) Using a suitable approximation, estimate the probability that a box contains 90 or more bags of fault-free balloons.

9 In training, a high jumper, on average, clears a particular height once in every four attempts. The data obtained in training are to be used to model the jumper's performance in a competition.

    (a) In the competition the bar is at this height. Write down an estimate of the probability that the jumper fails at the first attempt.

In this competition each competitor is allowed three attempts at each height. If a competitor fails on the first attempt at the height he is allowed a second attempt. If he fails a second time he is allowed a third attempt. After a third failure at the same height he is eliminated from the competition. Any competitor who clears a height at either his first, second or third attempt proceeds to the next height.

    (b) Stating clearly any assumptions you make, calculate the probability that the jumper
        (i) succeeds at his second attempt at this height,
        (ii) proceeds to the next height.

    (c) Give a reason, other than any assumption you made in part (b), why you think the probability model used above might be unsatisfactory, and say what modification you might make in an attempt to improve it.

10 Under what circumstances would you reasonably expect to be able to use the binomial distribution to model a probability distribution? When may a binomial distribution be approximated by a normal distribution?

Recent astronomical observations indicate that, of the 16 stars closest to our Sun, about half are accompanied by an orbiting planet at least the size of Jupiter.

    (a) Assume that the proportion of such stars in the Galaxy is 50%. Calculate the probability that, in a group of 16 stars, exactly 8 have such a planetary system.

    (b) The Pleiades are a cluster of some 500 stars. Use an appropriate approximation to determine the probability that there are between 230 and 270 (inclusive) stars in the Pleiades with accompanying planets at least the size of Jupiter.　　　　(OCR, adapted)

11 A certain type of examination consists of a number of questions all of equal difficulty. In a two-hour test the number of questions answered by a random sample of 1099 pupils is shown in the table.

No. of questions	0–4	5–9	10–14	15–19	20–24	25–29	30–34
No. of pupils	12	98	308	411	217	50	3

    (a) Construct a cumulative frequency table and, on graph paper, draw a cumulative frequency graph.

    (b) Use your graph to estimate the median and the interquartile range of these data.

    (c) It should be possible for 3% of candidates to answer all the questions. Find how many questions the candidates should be asked to answer in the two hours.

12 The probability that a certain football club has all their first team players fit is 70%. When the club has a fully fit team it wins 90% of its home games. When the first team is not fully fit it wins 40% of its home games.

   (a) Calculate the probability that it will win its next home game.

   (b) Given that it did not win its last home game, find the probability that the team was fully fit.

13 Seven men and five women have been nominated to serve on a committee. The committee consists of four members who are to be chosen from the seven men and five women.

   (a) In how many different ways can the committee be chosen?

   (b) In how many of these ways will the committee consist of two men and two women?

   (c) Assuming that each choice of four members is equally likely, find the probability that the committee will contain exactly two men.   (OCR)

14 In an examination 30% of the candidates fail and 10% achieve distinction. Last year the pass mark (out of 200) was 84 and the minimum mark required for a distinction was 154. Assuming that the marks of the candidates were normally distributed, estimate the mean mark and the standard deviation.   (OCR)

15 A mother has found that 20% of the children who accept invitations to her children's birthday parties do not come. For a particular party she invites twelve children but only has ten party hats. What is the probability that there is not a hat for every child who comes to the party?

   The mother knows that there is a probability of 0.1 that a child who comes to a party will refuse to wear a hat. If this is taken into account, what is the probability that there will not be a hat for every child who wants one?   (OCR)

Practice examination 1

Time 1 hour 15 minutes

Answer all the questions.
The use of an electronic calculator is expected, where appropriate.

1 An amateur weather forecaster has a theory about the chances of flooding affecting the region where he lives. He believes that if there are floods in one year the probability of floods again the next year is 0.7, and if there are no floods one year the probability of no floods the next year is 0.6. Last year, there were no floods in his region.

   (i) Draw a tree diagram showing probabilities for floods and no floods for this year and next year, according to the weather forecaster's theory. [2]

   (ii) Hence find the probability that there is flooding in exactly one of these two years. [2]

2 Two ordinary fair dice are thrown, and the random variable X denotes the larger of the two scores obtained (or the common score if the two scores are equal). The following table shows the probability distribution of X.

x	1	2	3	4	5	6
$P(X = x)$	$\frac{1}{36}$	$\frac{3}{36}$	$\frac{5}{36}$	$\frac{7}{36}$	$\frac{9}{36}$	$\frac{11}{36}$

   (i)   Show clearly why the entry $P(X = 3) = \frac{5}{36}$ in the table is correct. [2]

   (ii)   Show that $E(X) = \frac{161}{36}$, and find $Var(X)$. [4]

3 The box-and-whisker plots in the diagram illustrate the scores in an aptitude test taken by people applying for a job. The scores are expressed on a scale of 0–50, and the results for men and women are shown separately.

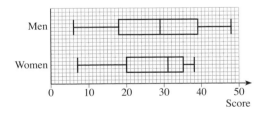

   (i)   For the men taking the aptitude test, state the value of

      (a) the median score, [1]

      (b) the range of the scores, [1]

      (c) the interquartile range of the scores. [1]

   (ii)   Compare briefly the scores obtained by men and women, stating one similarity and one difference. [2]

   (iii) Give a reason why the scores obtained by the women would not be well modelled by a normal distribution. [1]

4 Three married couples, Mr & Mrs Lee, Mr & Mrs Martin, and Mr & Mrs Shah, stand in a line for a photograph to be taken. Find the number of different ways in which these six people can be arranged

    (i)   if there are no restrictions on the order in which they stand,   [1]

    (ii)   if each man stands next to his wife,   [2]

    (iii)   if no man stands next to another man.   [3]

5 A market sells potatoes whose weights are normally distributed with mean 65 grams and standard deviation 15 grams.

    (i)   Find the probability that a randomly chosen potato weighs between 40 grams and 80 grams.   [4]

The market sells potatoes weighing more than 80 grams separately packaged. Potatoes weighing between 80 grams and L grams are labelled as 'large' and potatoes weighing over L grams are labelled as 'extra large'.

    (ii)   Given that a randomly chosen potato is twice as likely to be 'large' as 'extra large', calculate the value of L.   [4]

6 A survey of traffic on a busy road showed that, on average, 75% of the cars using the road carried only the driver, while 25% carried one or more passengers in addition to the driver.

    (i)   Twelve cars using the road are chosen at random. Find the probability that the number of these cars carrying only the driver will be

        (a) exactly 9,   [2]

        (b) more than 9.   [3]

    (ii)   Find the probability that more than 100 out of 120 randomly chosen cars using the road will carry only the driver.   [5]

7 The values, in billions of dollars, of 100 companies registered in a certain country are summarised in the table below.

Value of company, $x billion	$1 \leqslant x < 2$	$2 \leqslant x < 3$	$3 \leqslant x < 5$	$5 \leqslant x < 10$	$10 \leqslant x < 20$
Number of companies	29	23	15	21	12

    (i)   Illustrate the data by means of a histogram, drawn accurately on graph paper.   [4]

    (ii)   Calculate an estimate of the mean value of these companies, and explain briefly why your answer is only an estimate of the true mean value.   [4]

    (iii)   The median value of x for these companies is known to be 2.92. State what feature of the data accounts for the mean being considerably greater than the median.   [1]

    (iv)   Explain briefly why the mean might not be considered as a very good measure of the 'average' value of the companies.   [1]

Practice examination 2

Time 1 hour 15 minutes

Answer all the questions.
The use of an electronic calculator is expected, where appropriate.

1 The weights, X kg, of 10-year-old boys in a certain country may be assumed to be normally distributed. The proportion of boys weighing less than 25 kg and the proportion of boys weighing more than 35 kg are each 35%.

   (i)   Write down the mean of X.   [1]

   (ii) Calculate the standard deviation of X.   [3]

2 In a class of 20 pupils, seven are left-handed and 13 are right-handed. Five pupils are selected at random from the class; the order in which they are chosen is not important.

   (i)   Find the number of possible selections in which two of the five are left-handed and three are right-handed.   [3]

   (ii) Find the probability that the sample of five will include exactly two who are left-handed.   [2]

3 The random variable X takes the values 0, 1, 2, 3 only, and its probability distribution is shown in the following table.

x	0	1	2	3
$P(X = x)$	a	b	0.2	0.05

   (i)   Show that $a + b = 0.75$.   [1]

   (ii) Given that $E(X) = 1$, find the value of b and deduce the value of a.   [3]

   (iii) Does X have a binomial distribution? Give reasons for your answer.   [2]

4 Ali can travel to work either by bus or in his car. The probability that Ali is late for work when he goes by bus is 0.15, and the probability that he is late when he uses his car is 0.1. Ali uses his car for 70% of his journeys to work.

   (i)   Find the probability that Ali will be late for work on a randomly chosen day.   [3]

   (ii) Find the conditional probability that Ali travels by bus, given that he is late for work.   [3]

5   The organisers of a TV game show think that the probability of any contestant winning a
    prize will be 0.7, and that the success or failure of any contestant will be independent of
    the success or failure of other contestants. Six contestants take part on each episode of
    the show.

    (i)   Find the probability that, in one episode of the show, the number of successful
           contestants will be at most 2.   [4]

    (ii)   The show runs for 30 episodes altogether. Find the probability that the total number
           of successful contestants will be more than 120.   [5]

6   A chicken farmer fed 25 new-born chicks with a new variety of corn. The stem-and-leaf
    diagram below shows the weight gains of the chicks after three weeks.

           36   9
           37   6
           38   4 5 6
           39   3 3 7 9 9
           40   2 3 7 8
           41   0 2 6 6
           42   3 5 7
           43   2 4
           44   5
           45   1

    Key: 39|3 means 393 grams

    (i)   Find the median weight gain, and find also the interquartile range.   [3]

    The data may be summarised by $\sum (x-400) = 192$ and $\sum (x-400)^2 = 11\,894$, where
    x grams is the weight gain of a chick.

    (ii)   Calculate the mean and standard deviation of the weight gains of the 25 chicks,
           giving each answer to the nearest gram.   [4]

    (iii) Chicks fed on the standard variety of corn had weight gains after three weeks with
           mean 392 grams and standard deviation 12 grams. State briefly how the new variety
           of corn compares to the standard variety.   [2]

7 Each car owner in a sample of 100 car owners was asked the age of his or her present car. The results are shown in the table below.

Age of car, t years	$0 \leqslant t < 2$	$2 \leqslant t < 4$	$4 \leqslant t < 6$	$6 \leqslant t < 10$	$10 \leqslant t < 15$	$t \geqslant 15$
Number of cars	25	32	20	12	7	4

(i)   Making a suitable assumption about the ages of the oldest cars, draw a cumulative frequency graph on graph paper to illustrate the data.   [4]

(ii) Hence find estimates for

(a) the proportion of cars in the sample that are more than 5 years old,   [2]

(b) the age which is exceeded by the oldest 15% of cars.   [2]

(iii) Would the assumption made in part (i) have any effect on an estimate of

(a) the median age of the cars,

(b) the mean age of the cars?

Give reasons for your answers.   [3]

The Normal Distribution Function

If Z has a normal distribution with mean 0 and variance 1 then, for each value of z, the table gives the value of $\Phi(z)$, where

$$\Phi(z) = P(Z \leq z).$$

For negative values of z use $\Phi(-z) = 1 - \Phi(z)$.

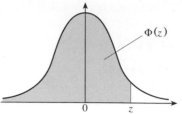

z	0	1	2	3	4	5	6	7	8	9	1	2	3	4	5	6	7	8	9
															ADD				
0.0	0.5000	0.5040	0.5080	0.5120	0.5160	0.5199	0.5239	0.5279	0.5319	0.5359	4	8	12	16	20	24	28	32	36
0.1	0.5398	0.5438	0.5478	0.5517	0.5557	0.5596	0.5636	0.5675	0.5714	0.5753	4	8	12	16	20	24	28	32	36
0.2	0.5793	0.5832	0.5871	0.5910	0.5948	0.5987	0.6026	0.6064	0.6103	0.6141	4	8	12	15	19	23	27	31	35
0.3	0.6179	0.6217	0.6255	0.6293	0.6331	0.6368	0.6406	0.6443	0.6480	0.6517	4	7	11	14	18	22	25	29	32
0.4	0.6554	0.6591	0.6628	0.6664	0.6700	0.6736	0.6772	0.6808	0.6844	0.6879	4	7	11	14	18	22	25	29	32
0.5	0.6915	0.6950	0.6985	0.7019	0.7054	0.7088	0.7123	0.7157	0.7190	0.7224	3	7	10	14	17	20	24	27	31
0.6	0.7257	0.7291	0.7324	0.7357	0.7389	0.7422	0.7454	0.7486	0.7517	0.7549	3	7	10	13	16	19	23	26	29
0.7	0.7580	0.7611	0.7642	0.7673	0.7704	0.7734	0.7764	0.7794	0.7823	0.7852	3	6	9	12	15	18	21	24	27
0.8	0.7881	0.7910	0.7939	0.7967	0.7995	0.8023	0.8051	0.8078	0.8106	0.8133	3	5	8	11	14	16	19	22	25
0.9	0.8159	0.8186	0.8212	0.8238	0.8264	0.8289	0.8315	0.8340	0.8365	0.8389	3	5	8	10	13	15	18	20	23
1.0	0.8413	0.8438	0.8461	0.8485	0.8508	0.8531	0.8554	0.8577	0.8599	0.8621	2	5	7	9	12	14	16	19	21
1.1	0.8643	0.8665	0.8686	0.8708	0.8729	0.8749	0.8770	0.8790	0.8810	0.8830	2	4	6	8	10	12	14	16	18
1.2	0.8849	0.8869	0.8888	0.8907	0.8925	0.8944	0.8962	0.8980	0.8997	0.9015	2	4	6	7	9	11	13	15	17
1.3	0.9032	0.9049	0.9066	0.9082	0.9099	0.9115	0.9131	0.9147	0.9162	0.9177	2	3	5	6	8	10	11	13	14
1.4	0.9192	0.9207	0.9222	0.9236	0.9251	0.9265	0.9279	0.9292	0.9306	0.9319	1	3	4	6	7	8	10	11	13
1.5	0.9332	0.9345	0.9357	0.9370	0.9382	0.9394	0.9406	0.9418	0.9429	0.9441	1	2	4	5	6	7	8	10	11
1.6	0.9452	0.9463	0.9474	0.9484	0.9495	0.9505	0.9515	0.9525	0.9535	0.9545	1	2	3	4	5	6	7	8	9
1.7	0.9554	0.9564	0.9573	0.9582	0.9591	0.9599	0.9608	0.9616	0.9625	0.9633	1	2	3	4	4	5	6	7	8
1.8	0.9641	0.9649	0.9656	0.9664	0.9671	0.9678	0.9686	0.9693	0.9699	0.9706	1	1	2	3	4	4	5	6	6
1.9	0.9713	0.9719	0.9726	0.9732	0.9738	0.9744	0.9750	0.9756	0.9761	0.9767	1	1	2	2	3	4	4	5	5
2.0	0.9772	0.9778	0.9783	0.9788	0.9793	0.9798	0.9803	0.9808	0.9812	0.9817	0	1	1	2	2	3	3	4	4
2.1	0.9821	0.9826	0.9830	0.9834	0.9838	0.9842	0.9846	0.9850	0.9854	0.9857	0	1	1	2	2	2	3	3	4
2.2	0.9861	0.9864	0.9868	0.9871	0.9875	0.9878	0.9881	0.9884	0.9887	0.9890	0	1	1	1	2	2	2	3	3
2.3	0.9893	0.9896	0.9898	0.9901	0.9904	0.9906	0.9909	0.9911	0.9913	0.9916	0	1	1	1	1	2	2	2	2
2.4	0.9918	0.9920	0.9922	0.9925	0.9927	0.9929	0.9931	0.9932	0.9934	0.9936	0	0	1	1	1	1	1	2	2
2.5	0.9938	0.9940	0.9941	0.9943	0.9945	0.9946	0.9948	0.9949	0.9951	0.9952	0	0	0	1	1	1	1	1	1
2.6	0.9953	0.9955	0.9956	0.9957	0.9959	0.9960	0.9961	0.9962	0.9963	0.9964	0	0	0	0	1	1	1	1	1
2.7	0.9965	0.9966	0.9967	0.9968	0.9969	0.9970	0.9971	0.9972	0.9973	0.9974	0	0	0	0	0	1	1	1	1
2.8	0.9974	0.9975	0.9976	0.9977	0.9977	0.9978	0.9979	0.9979	0.9980	0.9981	0	0	0	0	0	0	0	1	1
2.9	0.9981	0.9982	0.9982	0.9983	0.9984	0.9984	0.9985	0.9985	0.9986	0.9986	0	0	0	0	0	0	0	0	0

Critical values for the normal distribution

If Z has a normal distribution with mean 0 and variance 1 then, for each value of p, the table gives the value of z such that $P(Z \leq z) = p$.

p	0.75	0.90	0.95	0.975	0.99	0.995	0.9975	0.999	0.9995
z	0.674	1.282	1.645	1.960	2.326	2.576	2.807	3.090	3.291

Answers

1 Representation of data

Exercise 1A (page 8)

1. (a) 4.3, 5.0, 5.3, 5.4, 5.7, 5.9, 6.1, 6.2, 6.3, 6.4,
      7.1, 7.6, 7.6, 9.2, 9.3
   (b) (i) Quantitative (ii) Continuous

2. (a)
0	4	6						(2)
1	2	5	8					(3)
2	1	5	5	5	7	8	9	(7)
3	0	2	4	6	7			(5)
4	1	3						(2)
5	2							(1)

   Key: 2|7 means 27 k.p.h.

   (b)
0	3	4	7	8	9	9	9	(7)
1	0	1	2	6	8		(5)
2	1	1	3	7			(4)
3							(0)
4	2						(1)

   Key: 2|3 means 2.3 hours

3.
3	0	4	6											(3)
4	8	8												(2)
5	0	0	1	2	3	4	4	6	6	7	8	8	9	(13)
6	0	2	3	4	7	7	8	8	9					(9)
7	0	1	4	4	4	5	5	6	7	9				(10)
8	1	6												(2)
9	1	3	9											(3)

   Key: 7|9 means 79 years

4.
13					(0)
13	7				(1)
14	1	2	3		(3)
14	5				(1)
15	1	1	2	3	4	(5)
15	5	6	6	7	9	9	(6)
16	0	0	0	1	1	1	2	3	4	(9)
16	5	6	7	7	8	8	9	9	(8)
17	0	1	1	1	1	2	3	4	(8)
17	5	6	7	7	8	9	(6)
18	0	0	1	1	1	2	2	3	4	(9)
18	6	6	8	9	(4)

   Key: 17|9 means 179

5.
2996	2	5						(2)
2997	2	4	5	6	9			(5)
2998	0	1	3	4	5	7	8	8	(8)
2999	0	1	3	3	4	6	7	8	(8)
3000	0	7						(2)

   Key: 2997|4 means 299.74 thousand km s^{-1}

6. (a)
132	2	9												(2)
133	2	6	8	9										(4)
134	1	1	2	2	2	4	5	6	7	7	7	8	9	(13)
135	0	1	1	3	3	3	4	4	6					(9)
136	2													(1)
137	0													(1)

   Key: 134|7 means 1.347 kg
   (b) There would be only one stem, which would
       have all the leaves.

Exercise 1B (page 15)

B means 'class boundaries', H means 'bar heights',
F means 'frequency', FD means 'frequency density'.

1. B: 45 60 75 90 105 120 150
   H: 0.8 2.1 3.7 4.8 1.3 0.3

2. B: 4.5 9.5 14.5 19.5 24.5 29.5 34.5 44.5
   H: 0.4 1.0 1.6 2.8 3.4 2.2 0.3

3. B: 129.5 139.5 149.5 159.5 169.5 179.5 189.5
   H: 1 4 11 17 14 13

4. (a) 0, 2.5 and 2.5, 5.5
   (b) B: 0 2.5 5.5 8.5 11.5 15.5
       FD: 6.8 2 1.33 0.67 0.25

5. B: −0.5 9.5 19.5 29.5 34.5 39.5 49.5 59.5
   H: 0.6 2.1 5.1 7.2 9.6 8.2 3.1

6. Assuming data correct to 1 d.p.,
   B: 8.95 9.95 10.95 11.95 12.95 13.95 14.95
   15.95 16.95
   H: 1 4 7 6 9 8 7 3

7. (a) B: 2.875 3.875 4.875 5.875 6.875 7.875
       8.875
       H: 3 4 6 7 10 4
   (b) 2.875, 3.875
   (c) B: 2.875 3.875 4.875 5.875 6.875 7.875
       8.875
       H: 3 4 6 7 10 4

8. (a), (b) B: 16 20 30 40 50 60 80
       FD: 3 4 4.4 4.7 3.2 1.25

Exercise 1C (page 18)

1. Plot at $(45,0)$, $(60,12)$, $(75,44)$, $(90,100)$,
   $(105,172)$, $(120,192)$, $(150,200)$.
   (a) 26%   (b) About 77 k.p.h
2. Plot at $(-0.5,0)$, $(9.5,6)$, $(19.5,27)$, $(29.5,78)$,
   $(34.5,114)$, $(39.5,162)$, $(49.5,244)$, $(59.5,275)$.
   (a) 28% or 29%   (b) 24
3. (a) Plot at $(0,0)$, $(16,14.3)$, $(40,47.4)$,
   $(65,82.7)$, $(80,94.6)$, $(110,100)$.
   (b) 10(.4) million

4 Assuming x is correct to 2 d.p., plot at $(0,0)$, $(2,15)$, $(3,42)$, $(4,106)$, $(5,178)$, $(6,264)$, $(7,334)$, $(8,350)$, $(10,360)$; about 58 poor days and 14 good days.

5 Assuming x is correct to the nearest km, plot at $(0,0)$, $(4.5,12)$, $(9.5,41)$, $(14.5,104)$, $(19.5,117)$, $(24.5,129)$, $(34.5,132)$.
  (a) 8 km   (b) 14 km

6 Plot at $(7,10)$, $(7.05,73)$, $(7.10,150)$, $(7.15,215)$, $(7.20,245)$, $(7.30,250)$; between 7.012 cm and 7.175 cm.

7 Plot at $(2.95,7)$, $(3.95,62)$, $(4.95,134)$, $(5.95,144)$, $(6.95,148)$, $(8.95,150)$; 9%; about 3.07.

Miscellaneous exercise 1 (page 20)

1

0	6 0 8 0	(4)
1	8 9 2 7 4 1 1 6	(8)
2	7 8 5 6 0 1 9	(7)
3	8 1 7 3 6 4	(6)
4	5 3 2 2	(4)
5	7 5	(2)
6	6 3 2	(3)
7	2 5	(2)
8	5 4 6 2	(4)

Key: 4|3 means 43

The diagram indicates how the scores are distributed. But it does not indicate the order in which the scores occurred.

2 B: 0 30 60 120 180 240 300 360 480
FD: 0.07 0.1 0.13 0.27 0.7 0.42 0.3 0.1
About 286 s, obtained from the cumulative frequency graph or by proportion.

3 Plot at $(100,0)$, $(110,2)$, $(120,12)$, $(130,34)$, $(140,63)$, $(150,85)$, $(160,97)$, $(180,100)$; 123 cm.

4 (a) B: 3.95 5.95 7.95 9.95 11.95 13.95 15.95
        F: 3 3 4 11 8 1
  (b) Plot at $(3.95,0)$, $(5.95,3)$, $(7.95,6)$ $(9.95,10)$, $(11.95,21)$, $(13.95,29)$, $(15.95,30)$; 11.4; 3.3%.

5 Groups: 1.0–2.4, 2.5–3.9, 4.0–5.4, 5.5–6.9, 7.0–8.4, 8.5–9.9, 10.0–11.4, 11.5–12.9
F: 13 16 18 15 6 8 2 2
B: 0.95 2.45 3.95 5.45 6.95 8.45 9.95 11.45 12.95
H: 13 16 18 15 6 8 2 2
For example: most times are between 1 and 7 seconds.

6 (a) Plot at $(10,16)$, $(20,47)$, $(30,549)$, $(40,1191)$, $(50,2066)$, $(60,2349)$, $(80,2394)$, $(100,2406)$, $(140,2410)$.
  (b) About 74%
  (c) End boundaries unknown. Use (say) 4–10, 100–140.

7 (a) Using 6 equal classes,
        B: 12.75 14.25 15.75 17.25 18.75 20.25 21.75
        H: 1 2 2 2 7 11
        Although data appear to be correct to 2 d.p., having boundaries 12.745–14.245 would be awkward.
  (b) Plot at $(12.75,0)$, $(14.25,1)$, $(15.75,3)$, $(17.25,5)$, $(18.75,7)$, $(20.25,14)$, $(21.75,25)$.
  (c)

12	76	(1)
13		(0)
14	82	(1)
15	61	(1)
16	53, 97	(2)
17	30, 71	(2)
18		(0)
19	12, 35, 41, 61, 72	(5)
20	02, 21, 27, 34, 40, 52, 57, 69	(8)
21	04, 13, 25, 38, 43	(5)

Key: 16|53 means 16.53

8 (a) F: 17, 11, 10, 9, 3, 4, 2, 4
  (b) B: –0.5 9.5 19.5 29.5 39.5 49.5 59.5 69.5 99.5
        FD: 1.7, 1.1, 1.0, 0.9, 0.3, 0.4, 0.2, 0.13
  (c) Plot at $(-0.5,0)$, $(9.5,17)$, $(19.5,28)$, $(29.5,38)$, $(39.5,47)$, $(49.5,50)$, $(59.5,54)$, $(69.5,56)$, $(99.5,60)$; 42.
  (d) It assumes the data are evenly spread over the class 30–39. There are two each of 31, 33 and 39, and one each of 32, 36, 37, so the assumption is not well founded.

9 (a) Street 1: Plot at $(61,0)$, $(65,4)$, $(67,15)$, $(69,33)$, $(71,56)$, $(73,72)$, $(75,81)$, $(77,86)$, $(79,90)$, $(83,92)$.
        Street 2: Plot at $(61,0)$, $(65,2)$, $(67,5)$, $(69,12)$, $(71,24)$, $(73,51)$, $(75,67)$, $(77,77)$, $(79,85)$, $(83,92)$.
  (b) 69.8 dB on Street 1, 72.3 dB on Street 2.
  (c) Street 1 appears less noisy, in general, than Street 2. For example, there are 56 readings under 71 dB for Street 1, but 24 for Street 2.

10

0	2 2 3 4 5 5 6 8	(8)
1	0 1 2 2 2 3 4 6 6 6 9	(11)
2	0 2 3 4 4 4 5 5 9	(9)
3	4 5 9	(3)
4	0 1 4 8	(4)
5	0 6 8	(3)
6	1 6 7 7	(4)
7	2 6	(2)
8	2 5	(2)
9		(0)
10	4	(1)
11	8 8 9	(3)

Key: 4 | 8 means 48

Assuming data correct to the nearest second,
B: 0 19.5 39.5 59.5 79.5 99.5 119.5
FD: 0.97 0.6 0.35 0.3 0.1 0.2

11 (a) 4 cm (b) 7 (c) 3.0

2 Measures of location

Exercise 2A (page 26)

1 5.4 kg; 5.7 kg

2 40

3 (a) 27.5 k.p.h (b) 1.1 hours

4 13.5

5 $500 approximately

6 4.7 s; 5.0 s, data not evenly spread over class 4.0–5.4.

7 34

8 (a) 78 kg (b) 63 kg
On average men have greater mass than women.

Exercise 2B (page 30)

1 10.5

2 181 cm. Students appear taller, on average than the population. This can be explained by the large values 192, 192, 194 and 196.

3 (a) 11.3 (b) 105.5

4 0.319

5 3.59

6 24.3

7 Assuming the end boundary is 150, 88.8 k.p.h.

8 (a) 0–2.5, 2.5–5.5, 5.5–8.5, 8.5–11.5, 11.5–15.5 (b) 3.56 minutes

9 $12.89; $12.39

10 503.46 ml

Exercise 2C (page 35)

1 (a) 0 (b) No mode (c) 2–3 (d) Brown

2 (a) Mode (b) Mean (c) Median

3 It could be true for mean or mode, not the median.

4 (a) Roughly symmetrical
(b) Skewed
(c) Skewed
(d) Roughly symmetrical

5 (a) Mean 4.875, median 5, mode 6. The data set is too small for the mode to give a reliable estimate of location. The median gives a better idea of a 'typical' mark.
(b) It has a 'tail' of low values.

Miscellaneous exercise 2 (page 36)

1 (a) There would be no entries for stems 12, 13, 14 and 15.

(b)

4	0 0 0 1 2 2 2 6 6 8 8 9 9 9	(14)
5	0 2 2 4 7 9	(6)
6	4 5 6	(3)
7	3 5 6	(3)
8	5	(1)
9	2 4	(2)
10		(0)
11	2	(1)

HI 1.66; Key: 5 | 3 means $0.53

(c) $0.52; $0.617; modes: $0.40, $0.42, $0.49
(d) Median, since it is not affected by extreme values, or mean, since it involves all values.
(e) $0.236

2 (a) 2.56; exact (b) Both 2

3 (a) Both 22.0–23.9
(b) Not supported since modal classes the same. Either $mean_1$ (23.21 °C) is greater than $mean_2$ (22.43 °C) or $median_1$ (≈ 23 °C) is greater than $median_2$ (≈ 22 °C).

4 (a) Histogram
(b) Data inaccurate, grouped data, may not be evenly spread over classes.
(c) About 69 s
(d) No change in median, mean increases.

5 (a) B: −0.5 29.5 39.5 49.5 59.5 69.5 79.5 89.5 100.5
FD: 0.4, 0.7, 1.3, 2.5, 4.6, 7.8, 10.5, 2.9
(b) 72.5 (c) About 77
The marks are higher for mechanics, indicating better performance.

6 Change by $+0.06$ or -0.06 depending on the order of the frequencies.

7 (a) About 20.4 hours
(b) Individual values unknown, data inaccurate, data may not be evenly distributed over the classes.
(c) 21.0 hours
(d) It has a 'tail' of low values.

8 $\bar{x} = 3.6$, me $= 4$, mo $= 3$ and mean is between mode and median.

9 (a) $\overline{m} = 453.9$, $\bar{t} = 462.9$, $\overline{d} = 9.0$; yes
(b) me $m = 294.5$, me $t = 266.5$, me $d = 5$; no

10 (a) There should be no spaces between bars; areas are not proportional to frequencies; incorrect scale on vertical axis.
(b) B: 4.5 9.5 12.5 15.5 18.5 28.5
FD: $2.8, 6.0, 5.0, 1.3, 0.8$
(c) 12.9 m

3 Measures of spread

Exercise 3A (page 47)

1 (a) 17, 9.5 (b) $9.1, 2.8$

2 2.2

3 3

4 $15\,420$, $23\,520$

5 Street 1: $70.1\,\text{dB}$, $4.8\,\text{dB}$
Street 2: $72.6\,\text{dB}$, $4.6\,\text{dB}$
Street 2 is usually noisier, with greater variation.

6 Monday: $Q_1 = 105$, $Q_2 = 170$, $Q_3 = 258$
Wednesday: $Q_1 = 240$, $Q_2 = 305$, $Q_3 = 377$
Wednesday has greater audiences in general, with less variation.

7 Fat content 0: $Q_1 = 41$, $Q_2 = 53$, $Q_3 = 61$;
interquartile range (IQR) $= 20$; range $= 65$
Fat content 1: $Q_1 = 30$, $Q_2 = 37.5$, $Q_3 = 49$;
IQR $= 19$; range $= 46$
Fat content 0 has generally higher rating; has greater spread at extremes.

8 (a) Negative skew (b) Positive skew
(c) Roughly symmetrical

9 Box-and-whisker plots are preferred since they give visual comparison of the shapes of distributions, the quartiles, IQRs and ranges. Histograms will indicate the general shape of the distributions and will give only a rough idea of quartiles and so on. However, means and standard deviations can be estimated from a histogram but not from a boxplot.

10 (a) 38.73, 43.23, 49.24, 54.15, 58.42
(c) Slight negative skew

11 (a) and (b); fences at 14 and 126

12 (a) Fences at 24 and 104
(b) No outliers since all values lie inside fences.
(c) Roughly symmetrical

Exercise 3B (page 53)

1 Mean: (a) 4 (b) 5
SD: (a) 2 (b) 4.899

2 (a) 3.489 (b) 4.278

3 50.728 g, 10.076 g^2

4 ± 1.2

5 149.15 cm, 5.33 cm

6 (a) Anwar is better; his mean of 51.5 is greater than Qasim's 47.42 (Anwar scores more runs than Qasim).
(b) Qasim is more consistent since his standard deviation of 27.16 is less than Anwar's of 34.13.

7 $\bar{f} = 62.3$ kg, SD (female) is 7.34 kg,
$\overline{m} = 75.6$ kg, SD (male) is 8.45 kg
Both distributions have negative skew. Females are lighter than males by about 13 kg on average and less variable than males.

Exercise 3C (page 57)

1 0.740, 1.13

3 797.4 min^2

4 $250.77(5)$ g, 3.51 g
Increase the number of classes; weigh more accurately; use more packets.

5 0.7109

6 -17.2, 247.36

7 135.7 cm, 176.51 cm^2

8 Mid-class values are $18.5, 23.5, 28.5, 33.5, 38.5$, $46, 56, 66$. Mean 37.49 years, SD 11.86 years. In the second company the general age is lower and with smaller spread.

Miscellaneous exercise 3 (page 61)

1 23.16 cm, 1.32 cm; 22.89 cm, 1.13 cm
House sparrows have smaller variability; little difference in means.

2 (a) 18.69 m, 36.20 m^2
(b) 18.92 m, 36.20 m^2

3 (a) Set B (b) Set B (c) 39.5 g, 125 g^2
(d) Individual data values not given.

4 (b) 0.060 cm
(c) 1.34 approx., close to 1.3, so the distribution is roughly symmetrical.

5 (a) The standard deviation is zero, which implies that all data values are equal.
  (b) Ali caught $12.84\,\text{kg}$, Les $12.16\,\text{kg}$ and Sam $2\,\text{kg}$, so Ali won. (c) $3.12\,\text{kg}$

6 (a) $1.854\,\text{cm}$; $1.810\,\text{cm}$, $1.886\,\text{cm}$
  (b) Negative skew (c) $1.850\,\text{cm}$, $0.069\,\text{cm}$
  (d) -0.18, indicating negative skew

7 (a) 8.5 minutes, 9.25 minutes
  (c) 10 minutes
  (d) (i) and (iii) not true, (ii) and (iv) true

8 (a) 26.9 years, 13.0 years (b) 22.4 years
  Median preferred since distribution skewed, more information given by median.

4 Probability

Exercise 4A (page 71)

1 (a) $\frac{1}{2}$ (b) $\frac{2}{3}$ (c) $\frac{1}{2}$ (d) $\frac{1}{2}$ (e) $\frac{1}{6}$
  (f) $\frac{2}{6}$ (g) $\frac{2}{3}$

2 (a) $\frac{1}{2}$ (b) $\frac{3}{13}$ (c) $\frac{5}{13}$ (d) $\frac{5}{26}$ (e) $\frac{9}{13}$

3 (a) $\frac{1}{6}$ (b) $\frac{5}{12}$ (c) $\frac{5}{12}$ (d) $\frac{25}{36}$
  (e) $\frac{11}{36}$ (f) $\frac{5}{18}$ (g) $\frac{1}{6}$ (h) $\frac{1}{2}$

4 (a) $\frac{1}{5}$ (b) $\frac{2}{5}$ (c) $\frac{1}{3}$ (d) $\frac{1}{2}$

5 (a) $\frac{9}{25}$ (b) $\frac{4}{25}$ (c) $\frac{12}{25}$ (d) $\frac{21}{25}$ (e) $\frac{3}{5}$

Exercise 4B (page 78)

1 (a) $\frac{1}{3}$ (b) $\frac{2}{15}$ (c) $\frac{8}{15}$ (d) $\frac{13}{15}$ (e) $\frac{3}{5}$
  No

2 (a) $\frac{11}{221}$ (b) $\frac{10}{17}$ (c) $\frac{7}{17}$ (d) $\frac{77}{102}$

3 (a) 0.27 (b) 0.35 (c) 0.3375

4 (a) $\frac{8}{15}$ (b) $\frac{7}{15}$ (c) $\frac{3}{5}$ (d) $\frac{2}{5}$ (e) $\frac{9}{16}$
  (f) Yes (g) No

5 (a) 0.24 (b) 0.42 (c) 0.706

6 (a) 0.12 (b) 0.44 (c) 0.048 (d) 0.34
  (e) 0.03 (f) 0.07 (g) 0.32

7 (a) $\frac{1}{16}$ (b) $\frac{15}{16}$ (c) $\frac{671}{1296}$

8 0.491

9 0.5073 (Note that this is bigger than 50%.)

10 0.75, 0.8

12 0.0317 . Very small; the test has to be much more reliable for it to give any reliable evidence about a rare disease.
   0.000 998 . The further piece of evidence is not enough to make the prisoner's guilt at all likely; it would have to be much more certain than it is.

Miscellaneous exercise 4 (page 80)

1 (b) $\frac{2}{3}$
2 (a) 0.58 (b) 0.6
3 (a) $\frac{1}{2}$ (b) $\frac{5}{11}$
4 (a) 20% (b) 10%
5 (b) (i) $\frac{23}{189}$ (ii) $\frac{166}{189}$
6 (a) $\frac{3}{20}$ (b) $\frac{9}{35}$ (c) $\frac{7}{12}$
7 (b) $\frac{9}{26}$
8 (a) (i) $\frac{1}{5}$ (ii) $\frac{5}{13}$ (iii) $\frac{17}{25}$ (iv) $\frac{1}{2}$
  (b) $\frac{21}{25}$
9 (a) $\frac{1}{2}$ (b) (i) $5p$ (ii) $4p$ (c) $\frac{1}{40}$
10 $\frac{1}{4}$
   (a) 0.0577 (b) 0.1057 (c) 0.6676
11 (a) $\frac{3}{253}$ (b) $\frac{43}{138}$ (c) $\frac{11}{138}$ (d) $\frac{11}{69}$
12 (a) 0.32 (b) 0.56 ; 8
13 (a) (i) $\frac{3}{8}$ (ii) $\frac{4}{15}$
   (b) (i) $\frac{27}{125}$ (ii) $\frac{8}{125}$ (iii) $\frac{38}{125}$
14 (a) $\frac{1}{8}$ (b) $\frac{3}{8}$ (c) $\frac{8}{9}$
15 0.017 ; $\frac{2}{3}$
16 (a) 0.030 (b) 0.146 (c) 0 (d) 0.712
17 (a) $\dfrac{4n-3}{n(n+1)}$ (b) $\dfrac{9}{4n-3}$

5 Permutations and combinations

Exercise 5A (page 89)

1 5040
2 24
3 120
4 720
6 119 , $\frac{1}{120}$
7 50 400
8 (a) 720 (b) 48
9 64 , $\frac{21}{32}$

Exercise 5B (page 93)

1 22 100
2 215 760
3 (a) 56 (b) 48
4 70 , 63
5 0.25
6 0.0128
7 (a) 0.222 (b) 0.070 (c) 0.112 (d) 0.180

Exercise 5C (page 96)

1 (a) 3 632 428 800 (b) 259 459 200
   (c) 39 916 800 (d) 457 228 800
2 (a) 1024 (b) 210 (c) 0.205
3 (a) 5.346×10^{13} (b) 3.097×10^{12}
   (c) 0.0579
4 (a) 13! (b) 43 545 600
   (c) 609 638 400
5 (a) 1260 (b) 540 (c) 300 (d) 120
6 (a) 39 916 800 (b) 20 736
   (c) 1 814 400
7 (a) 12 (b) 115

Miscellaneous exercise 5 (page 97)

1 3 628 800 , 45
2 (a) 40 320 (b) 1152
3 83 160
4 360
5 (a) 1440 (b) 2880
6 (a) 240 (b) 480
7 210
8 151 200
9 210 , $\frac{2}{7}$
10 (a) 0.112 (b) 0.368
11 (a) 360 (b) 60
12 432
13 (a) 24 (b) 120 ; 2880
14 (a) 70 (b) $\frac{1}{35}$
15 (a) (1,1,8), (1,2,7), (1,3,6), (1,4,5), (2,2,6),
   (2,3,5) (2,4,4), (3,3,4) (b) $\frac{1}{4}$
16 1260
17 (a) 60 (b) 5
18 0.0109 ; the player might conclude that the deals
   were not random.
19 One answer would be $4! \times 23! = 24!$.

6 Probability distributions

Exercise 6A (page 104)

1
x	0	1	2	3	4
$P(X=x)$	$\frac{1}{16}$	$\frac{4}{16}$	$\frac{6}{16}$	$\frac{4}{16}$	$\frac{1}{16}$

2
d	0	1	2	3	4	5
$P(D=d)$	$\frac{6}{36}$	$\frac{10}{36}$	$\frac{8}{36}$	$\frac{6}{36}$	$\frac{4}{36}$	$\frac{2}{36}$

3
x	1	2	3	6	10
$P(X=x)$	$\frac{1}{6}$	$\frac{2}{6}$	$\frac{1}{6}$	$\frac{1}{6}$	$\frac{1}{6}$

4
h	1	2	3	4	5	6
$P(H=h)$	$\frac{23}{36}$	$\frac{7}{36}$	$\frac{3}{36}$	$\frac{1}{36}$	$\frac{1}{36}$	$\frac{1}{36}$

5
m	1	2	3	4	6
$P(M=m)$	$\frac{1}{16}$	$\frac{2}{16}$	$\frac{2}{16}$	$\frac{3}{16}$	$\frac{2}{16}$

	8	9	12	16
	$\frac{2}{16}$	$\frac{1}{16}$	$\frac{2}{16}$	$\frac{1}{16}$

6
Number	0	1	2
Probability	$\frac{5}{12}$	$\frac{1}{2}$	$\frac{1}{12}$

7
c	1	2	3	4
$P(C=c)$	$\frac{1}{13}$	$\frac{16}{221}$	$\frac{376}{5525}$	$\frac{4324}{5525}$

8
Score	3	4	5	6	7	8
Probability	$\frac{1}{216}$	$\frac{3}{216}$	$\frac{6}{216}$	$\frac{10}{216}$	$\frac{15}{216}$	$\frac{21}{216}$

	9	10	11	12	13	14
	$\frac{25}{216}$	$\frac{27}{216}$	$\frac{27}{216}$	$\frac{25}{216}$	$\frac{21}{216}$	$\frac{15}{216}$

	15	16	17	18
	$\frac{10}{216}$	$\frac{6}{216}$	$\frac{3}{216}$	$\frac{1}{216}$

Exercise 6B (page 106)

1 $\frac{1}{20}$
2 0.3
3 0.15
4 $\frac{1}{8}$
5
x	1	2	3	4	5	6
$P(X=x)$	$\frac{1}{4}$	$\frac{1}{12}$	$\frac{1}{4}$	$\frac{1}{12}$	$\frac{1}{4}$	$\frac{1}{12}$

6 $\frac{1}{21}$
7 $\frac{20}{49}$
8 0.2

Exercise 6C (page 107)

1 (a) 130 (b) 40 (c) 120
   (d) 160 (e) 360
2 (a) 105 (b) 105 (c) 245
3 12, 31, 34, 18, 5, 0 (0 is better than 1 because it
   makes the total 100)
4 0.468, 103

Miscellaneous exercise 6 (page 108)

1
Number	0	1	2	3
Probability	$\frac{248}{1105}$	$\frac{496}{1105}$	$\frac{304}{1105}$	$\frac{57}{1105}$

2 (a)

x	0	1	2	3	4	6
$P(X = x)$	$\frac{1}{4}$	$\frac{1}{3}$	$\frac{1}{9}$	$\frac{1}{6}$	$\frac{1}{9}$	$\frac{1}{36}$

(b) 120

3 (a) $\frac{1}{18}$ (b) $\frac{17}{36}$ (c) $\frac{11}{17}$

4 (b) 8.3

5 $\frac{1}{8}$

7 The binomial distribution

Exercise 7A (page 114)

1 (a) 0.0819   (b) 0.0154   (c) 0.0001

2 (a) 0.2561   (b) 0.2048   (c) 0.0005

3 (a) 0.2119   (b) 0.4728   (c) 0.0498

4 (a) 0.0017   (b) 5

5 (a) 0.2461   (b) 0.4102   (c) 0.0195
    (d) 0.9102

6 (a) 0.0781   (b) 0.0176

7 It avoids the calculation of $n!$ or $\binom{n}{r}$ for large values of n.

8 Equality occurs when $(n+1)p$ is an integer.

Exercise 7B (page 117)

1 (a) 0.650
    (b) The students are not chosen independently.

2 0.055; no (the outcomes are still green and not-green).

3 0.114; 0.223; breakages are not independent of each other (if one egg in a box is broken, it is more likely that others will be).

4 0.065; for example: P(hurricane) is constant for each month; hurricanes occur independently of each other; P(hurricane) may not be constant for each month but dependent on the time of year.

5 0.204. The adults must be independent of each other as to whether they are wearing jeans; the probability that each adult is wearing jeans must be the same. (Do not say there must be only two outcomes; this is automatically implied by the question.)

6 More than one relevant outcome on each trial.

7 (a) The boys are not chosen independently of each other.
    (b) The probability that a day is warm is not the same for each month.

8 A, B, C and D are not independent events.

Miscellaneous exercise 7 (page 119)

1 0.580

2 (a) B$(20, 0.1)$ (b) 0.677

3 (a) B$(8, 0.2)$ (b) 0.0563

4 (a) 0.337   (b) 0.135

5 (a) 0.286   (b) 0.754

6 (a) 0.0625, 0.25, 0.375, 0.25, 0.0625
    (b) 0.273   (c) 0.313

7 Trials in which the only possible outcomes are 'succeed' and 'fail' are repeated, with the probability of a 'succeed' being the same for all trials, and all trials being independent of one another.
    (a) 0.035 (b) 0.138; 83

8 (a) 0.116 (b) 0.386 (c) 0.068

9 For example, probability that each hen lays an egg is the same each day for each hen; or hens lay eggs independently of each other, or independently of whether they laid an egg the previous day.
    $\frac{5}{6}$; 1.07, 4.02, 8.04, 6.70

10 (a) 0.9   (b) 0.08   (c) 0.14   (d) 0.3;
    0.747

8 Expectation and variance of a random variable

Exercise 8A (page 126)

1 (a) $1\frac{7}{8}$ (b) 0.05

2 4, 3.6

3 $5\frac{1}{9}, 1\frac{35}{81}$

4 (a) $\frac{7}{3}$, 0.745

(b)

y	2	3	4	5	6
$P(Y = y)$	$\frac{1}{36}$	$\frac{1}{9}$	$\frac{5}{18}$	$\frac{1}{3}$	$\frac{1}{4}$

    $\frac{14}{3}, \frac{10}{9}$

5 E$(A) = \$95\,000$, E$(B) = \$115\,000$; choose B.

6 (a) 0.3, 0.51   (b) 5.7, 0.51
    (c) E$(Y) = 6 - E(X)$, Var$(Y) = Var(X)$. The distribution of Y (the number of unbroken eggs) is the reflection of the distribution of X in the line $x = 3$.

7 $1\frac{25}{36}$, 1.434

8 0.2, 2.8, 1.4

9 $a = b = 0.15$, $\sigma = 1.7$

10 (a)

x	1	2	3	4
$P(X = x)$	$\frac{1}{6}$	$\frac{5}{36}$	$\frac{25}{216}$	$\frac{125}{216}$

(b) 1.172;
0.5177; -20.56

11 (b)

h	0	1	2	3
$P(H = h)$	$\frac{11}{48}$	$\frac{7}{16}$	$\frac{13}{48}$	$\frac{1}{16}$

(c) $E(X) = \frac{7}{3}$, $E(H) = \frac{7}{6}$ (d) $\frac{13}{18}$

Exercise 8B (page 130)

1 (a) $2.8, 2.408$ (b) 0.4550

2 $0.84, 0.9073$

3 $10.5, 6.825$

4 0.2581

5 1.6

6 0.1407

Miscellaneous exercise 8 (page 131)

1 (a) $2.56, 1.499$ (b) 122.9

2 47.90

3 $3, 1.2, 0.3456$

4 $1.3, 1.01, 3.8, 0.76$

(a)

z	3	4	5	6	7	8
$P(Z = z)$	0.15	0.16	0.33	0.19	0.14	0.03

5 Fences at $3.62, 12.38$
(a) Yes (b) No (c) No (d) Yes
$0.0160, 0.0210$

6 (a) 0.8704

(b)

x	1	2	3	4
$P(X = x)$	0.4	0.24	0.144	0.216

(c) $2.176, 1.377$

7

w	0	1	2
$P(W = w)$	$\frac{1}{3}$	$\frac{8}{15}$	$\frac{2}{15}$

0.8

8 (a) 0.06 (b) 1.6644

9 (a)

y	0	1	2
$P(Y = y)$	0.006 72	0.069 12	0.248 32

3	4
0.389 12	0.286 72

(b) $2.88, 0.8576$

9 The normal distribution

Exercise 9A (page 145)

1 (a) 0.8907 (b) 0.9933 (c) 0.5624 (d) 0.1082
(e) 0.0087 (f) 0.2783 (g) 0.9664 (h) 0.9801
(i) 0.5267 (j) 0.0336 (k) 0.0030 (l) 0.4184
(m) 0.95 (n) 0.05 (o) 0.95 (p) 0.05

2 (a) 0.0366 (b) 0.1202 (c) 0.3417 (d) 0.4394
(e) 0.9555 (f) 0.7804

3 (a) 0.8559 (b) 0.2088 (c) 0.0320 (d) 0.1187
(e) 0.4459 (f) 0.95 (g) 0.98 (h) 0.8064
(i) 0.0164

4 (a) 0.44 (b) 1.165 (c) 2.15 (d) 1.017
(e) 0.24 (f) 1.178 (g) 2.452 (h) 0.758
(i) -2.834 (j) -1.955 (k) -1.035 (l) 0
(m) -2.74 (n) -2.192 (o) -1.677 (p) -0.056
(q) 1.645 (r) 1.282 (s) 2.576 (t) 0.674

Exercise 9B (page 145)

1 (a) 0.9332 (b) 0.0062 (c) 0.7734 (d) 0.0401

2 (a) 0.9522 (b) 0.0098 (c) 0.7475 (d) 0.0038

3 (a) 0.1359 (b) 0.0606 (c) 0.7333 (d) 0.7704
(e) 0.8664

4 0.0668

5 (a) 0.1587 (b) 0.0228

6 (a) 54.35 (b) 40.30 (c) 52.25 (d) 41.85

7 (a) 17.73 (b) 14.62 (c) 17.51 (d) 14.45
(e) 3.29

8 (a) 41.6 (b) 29.9 (c) 37.3 (d) 31.7

9 10.03

10 65

11 42.0, 8.47

12 9.51, 0.303

Exercise 9C (page 148)

1 (a) 0.0370 (b) 0.0062 (c) 0.8209

2 (a) 0.2094 (b) 0.0086 (c) 0.1788 (d) 0.6405
105, 4, 89, 320

3 (a) 13 (b) 84 (c) 121

4 (a) 0.0048 (b) 0.1944 (c) 80, 100

5 1970 hours

6 (a) 0.614 (b) 20.9, 16.3 (c) 17

7 336 ml

8 0.041 kg

9 47 hours^2

10 49.1, 13.4

Exercise 9D (page 157)

1 (a) $np = 10$, $nq = 40$, yes
   (b) $np = 6$, $nq = 54$, yes
   (c) $np = 0.7$, no
   (d) $np = 21$, $nq = 9$, yes
   (e) $np = 36$, $nq = 4$, no

2 (a) 0.0288 (b) 0.114 (c) 0.0808 (d) 0.375
   $np = 12$, $nq = 28$, valid normal approximation

3 (a) 0.0121 (b) 0.117
   $np = 15$, $nq = 285$, valid normal approximation

4 (a) 0.0117 (b) 0.0122, 0.0169
   $np = 9$, $nq = 9$, valid normal approximation

5 (a) 0.0083 (b) 0.9110
   $np = 6$, $nq = 44$, valid normal approximation

6 0.083
   $np = 32$, $np = 8$, valid normal approximation

7 (a) 0.300 (b) 0.301

8 0.0168, 34

9 0.0264, 26

10 (a) 0.189, binomial, $np = 1$
    (b) 0.642, binomial, $np = 1$
    (c) 0.223, normal, $np = 32.1$, $nq = 17.9$

Miscellaneous exercise 9 (page 158)

1 0.0913
2 0.9213
3 0.960
4 0.933
5 0.957
6 0.525
7 0.367
8 0.936 for Luxibrite, 0.928 for Maxigloss, Luxibrite
9 18.9
10 (a) 0.886 (b) Probably not symmetric
11 (a) 20.2% (b) 81.0 g
12 (a) 70 (b) 45
13 10.3
14 6.82, 0.443
15 (a) 9.68% (b) 28.5% (c) 40
16 (a) 25 (b) 0.6730
17 (b) 0.069
18 0.1977
19 47, 15
20 0.7734

21 (a) 0.488 (b) 281, 5.00
22 $np > 5$ and $n(1-p) > 5$
    (a) 0.1853 (b) 0.1838 (c) 0.816%
23 (a) 0.590 (b) 0.081
    The model assumes that defective syringes occur independently of each other, but this may not be realistic in a manufacturing process.
    It is convenient to use the normal approximation because less calculation is involved; 0.0668.
24 (a) Late trains occur independently of each other. The probability that a train is late is constant.
    (b) 0.0184 (c) 0.744
    0.803 using the model $N(22.5, 12.375)$
25 53.18
26 10.2
27 0.397
28 (a) (i) 0.236 (ii) 0.206 (b) 0.672
    (c) H, p is closer to $\frac{1}{2}$
29 (a) 46.49% (b) 0.532 m (c) 1.00 m

Revision exercise
(page 163)

1 (a) Frequency densities: 1.6, 1.2, 0.833, 0.6
   (c) 39.88 mm, 28.2 mm
2 (a) Dice is fair, all six faces are equally likely to turn up.
   (b) $2\frac{11}{12}$
3 4.80 minutes
   (a) 0.266 (b) 0.149
   The distribution is unlikely to be symmetrical because some trains will be very late but no trains will be very early.
4 (a) 0.0148 (c) 10
   (d) Slightly surprising; it would happen less than 1 in 20 times.
5 (b) 3.8, 2.6
6 (a) 0.0765 (b) 9.12 (c) 0.000 161
7 (a) $\frac{16}{52}$ or $\frac{4}{13}$
   (b) $P(S = 0) = \frac{4}{13}$, $P(S = 2) = \frac{5}{13}$, $P(S = 5) = \frac{4}{13}$
        $2\frac{4}{13}$, $3\frac{153}{169}$
8 (a) 0.183 (b) 0.013
9 (a) $\frac{3}{4}$
   (b) Assume constant probability of success, independence of outcomes. (i) $\frac{3}{16}$ (ii) $\frac{37}{64}$
   (c) The probability of success may vary.

10 The binomial distribution is appropriate when counting the number of successes in a fixed number of trials which are independent of one another, and have a constant probability of success.

$np > 5$, $nq > 5$.

  (a) 0.196

  (b) 0.933; N(250,125) is the approximation.

11 (b) 16, 7.2

  (c) 26 or 27

12 (a) 0.75   (b) 0.28

13 (a) 495   (b) 210   (c) $\frac{14}{33}$

14 104, 38.8

15 0.275; 0.110

Practice examinations

Practice examination 1 (page 167)

1 (i)

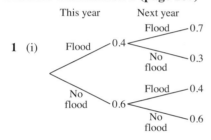

  (ii) 0.36

2 (ii) $\frac{2555}{1296} \approx 1.97$

3 (i) (a) 29   (b) 42   (c) 21

  (ii) Medians are quite similar; men's scores are more spread out.

  (iii) The distribution is not symmetrical.

4 (i) 720   (ii) 48   (iii) 144

5 (i) 0.7935 (ii) 89.3

6 (i) (a) 0.258   (b) 0.391   (ii) 0.0135

7 (i) (Frequency densities are 29, 23, 7.5, 4.2, 1.2.)

  (ii) $4.985 billion; use of class centres is an approximation.

  (iii) Distribution is positively skewed.

  (iv) Approximately two-thirds of the companies are worth less than the mean.

Practice examination 2 (page 169)

1 (i) 30 (ii) 13.0

2 (i) 6006   (ii) $\frac{1001}{2584} \approx 0.387$

3 (ii) 0.45, 0.3

  (iii) No; e.g. $n = 3$ and $np = 1$ give $p = \frac{1}{3}$, but $P(X = 3) \neq \frac{1}{27}$.

4 (i) 0.115 (ii) 0.391

5 (i) 0.0705 (ii) 0.815

6 (i) 407 grams, 31 grams

  (ii) 408 grams, 20 grams

  (iii) With the new variety, weight gains are increased on average, but are more variable.

7 (ii) (a) 33%   (b) 8.7 years

  (iii) (a) No; the position of the final point doesn't affect the part of the graph where the median is found.

  (b) Yes; the centre of the final class interval is affected.

Index

The page numbers given refer to the first mention of each term, or the box if there is one.